Henry Seebohm

Siberia in Asia

A Visit to the Valley of the Genesay in East Siberia

Henry Seebohm

Siberia in Asia
A Visit to the Valley of the Genesay in East Siberia

ISBN/EAN: 9783744759403

Printed in Europe, USA, Canada, Australia, Japan

Cover: Foto ©Andreas Hilbeck / pixelio.de

More available books at **www.hansebooks.com**

SIBERIA IN ASIA.

SIBERIA IN ASIA:

A VISIT TO THE VALLEY OF THE YENESAY IN EAST SIBERIA.

WITH DESCRIPTION OF THE NATURAL HISTORY, MIGRATION OF BIRDS, ETC.

By HENRY SEEBOHM,

AUTHOR OF 'SIBERIA IN EUROPE.'

WITH MAP AND ILLUSTRATIONS.

LONDON:

JOHN MURRAY, ALBEMARLE STREET.

1882.

LONDON :

PRINTED BY WILLIAM CLOWES AND SONS, LIMITED,

STAMFORD STREET AND CHARING CROSS.

PREFACE.

'SIBERIA IN ASIA' is a *pendant* to 'Siberia in Europe.' It is a narrative of a longer and more adventurous journey on the other side of the Urals, undertaken two years afterwards, but with the same objects in view. In 1875 I had the advantage of enjoying the companionship of an ornithologist as enthusiastic as myself, but in 1877 I was obliged to do my bird work alone. It is possible, however, that the general reader may not regret the change, and may find the dash of commercial enterprise and Arctic exploration reflected from Captain Wiggins a pleasant relief from the monotony of the *toujours oiseaux* of my former volume. To some extent, however, 'Siberia in Asia' must be a repetition of 'Siberia in Europe.' Though the meridian of the Caspian is altered to the meridian of the Gulf of Bengal, the latitude remains the same, but I venture to hope that a previous glimpse of the forests and the tundra of the Petchora will have added to rather than have detracted from the interest of the reader in the forests and the tundra of the Yenesay. The more one knows of any subject the more one wants to know. Siberia is no longer the *terra incognita* that it once was. The narrative of the expedition of Drs. Finch and Brehm to the valley of the Obb has not yet appeared in an English dress, but every one interested in Arctic exploration has read Baron Nordenskiöld's account of the wonderful voyage of the *Vega* from Lapland to Behring's Straits, and the overland route from Moscow to Vladivostok forms the *pièce de résistance* in the bill of fare which the Rev. Henry Lansdell offers us in the description of his journey round the world. Siberia is no longer a synonym of dreary barrenness, and the reader is not surprised to learn that it is a magnificent country of superb forests, and cornfields capable of rivalling those of Minnesota, whilst its mineral wealth includes iron equal in quality to that of Sweden, and gold almost as abundant as that of California, to say nothing of copper, salt and coal. Siberia is in fact a second Canada in reserve, and the political geographer, looking into the far future and wondering what is to become of the surplus population and capital of the English and Teutonic races when North America shall be as thickly populated as Europe, may postpone his anxieties for many centuries, to allow time for the civilisation of Siberia to reopen the problem.

I have endeavoured to make the ornithological

part of my book as interesting to the general reader
as possible. As before, I have added particulars of
the geographical distribution of the birds mentioned
in the form of notes, but I have confined these to the
birds which we did not find on the first journey, not
deeming it necessary to repeat the notes of my former
volume.

' Siberia in Asia ' has been written in the intervals
of leisure from other literary work and appears somewhat late, but I trust that the delay in its publication
has not impaired in any way the interest of the
subject, and as most of it is copied from a journal
written on the spot, I hope that it may read as fresh
as if it had appeared at once. I am indebted to my
friend Mr. Charles Whymper for many of the illustrations in this as well as in the former volume, and do
not doubt that the reader will be as much pleased
with them as myself.

The names of places in Siberia which are to be
found in our maps are not reproductions in English
letters of the Russian names. They are, for the most
part, attempts to render the Russian pronunciation
phonetically. The spelling is, however, only phonetic
when it is pronounced by a German. The consequence
is that Englishmen almost invariably pronounce these
names wrongly. To obviate this source of error I have
attempted to spell all the Siberian names phonetically
in English. The irregularities in the pronunciation

of our language have made this somewhat difficult, but by dividing the words into syllables, and by the use of accents, I trust that no doubt can exist as to the correct pronunciation of any word, though possibly in some cases familiar names of places may be scarcely recognisable in their new dress. For instance Irkutsk, Irbit, and Irtish appear as they are pronounced—Eer-kutsk', Eer-beet', and Eer'-tish; whilst Lake Baical and the river Lena are spelt phonetically Lake By-kal' and the river Lay'-na. This does not look very satisfactory, but I have been obliged of two evils to choose the lesser.

CONTENTS.

CHAPTER I.

CHAPTER II.

FROM LONDON TO ODESSA.

CHAPTER III.

CHAPTER IV.

CHAPTER V.

CHAPTER VI.

CHAPTER VII.

CHAPTER VIII.

CHAPTER IX.

CHAPTER X.

CHAPTER XI.

CHAPTER XII.

CHAPTER XIII.

CHAPTER XIV.

CHAPTER XV.

CHAPTER XVI.

CHAPTER XVII.

CHAPTER XVIII.

CHAPTER XIX.

CHAPTER XX.

CHAPTER XXI.

CHAPTER XXII.

CHAPTER XXIII.

CONTENTS.

CHAPTER XXIV.

CHAPTER XXV.

LIST OF ILLUSTRATIONS.

PAGE

       *

SIBERIA IN ASIA.

CHAPTER I.

Sir Hugh Willoughby's voyage to Nova Zembla—Ancient voyages across the Kara Sea—Modern voyages across the Kara Sea—Captain Wiggins's voyage in 1876—Ornithological Arctic expeditions—Letters of introduction from Count Schouvaloff—Recent expeditions to Siberia—Professor Nordenskiöld's extraordinary success—Rare birds obtained by him.

THREE hundred years ago, when Ivan the Terrible reigned over Russia, and the Slave and Tartar races were struggling in mortal combat, a peaceful expedition left the shores of Britain, under the command of Sir Hugh Willoughby.

B

Three ships were **sent** to the **Arctic** region on a wild-goose chase after the semi-fabulous land of Cathay: a country where it was popularly supposed **that** the richest furs might be bought for an old song, where the rarest spices might be had for the plucking, and where the rivers rippled over sands of gold. Like so many other Arctic expeditions, this proved a failure. Poor Sir Hugh Willoughby, **it is** supposed, **dis**covered one of the islands **of** Nova Zembla, but was afraid to winter there, and landed **on** the Kola peninsula, where he and all his crew were starved to death.

Another ship belonging **to** the same expedition, commanded by Richard Chancellor, was **more** fortunate. **It** was separated from the others by a heavy storm, and driven **by** contrary winds into the White Sea. Chancellor not only saved his ship and the **lives of** his crew, but discovered Archangel, which subsequently became a little English colony. **At** that time the inhabitants **of** Archangel were actually carrying **on** a trade **with** this wonderful **land** of Cathay. In their flat-bottomed *loikas*, sewn together with willow twigs, they skirted the east coast **of** the White Sea, and dragged their boats across the Kanin peninsula. They coasted the southern shores of the Arctic Ocean, and passing through the Kara gates, entered the Kara Sea. On the Yalmal peninsula they found a river, the head of which brought them to a narrow watershed, across which they again pushed their boats, coming to another river, which brought them into the gulf of the Obb. Crossing this gulf they entered the gulf of the Taz, at the head of which was the once famous town of Mangasee, where a great annual fair was held.   This fair was frequented by merchants who brought tea, silks, and spices down the Obb and the Yen-e-say' to barter with the Russian merchants, who returned to Archangel the same season.

In the " struggle for existence," which commenced on the opening out of the port of Archangel to British commerce, according to the inevitable law of the " survival of the fittest," this Russian maritime enterprise languished and finally died, and thenceforth the inhabitants of the banks of Dvina received their silks and their tea viâ the Thames instead of the Obb and the Yen-e-say'; and ever since the commercial world seems to have taken it for granted that the Kara Sea was unnavigable, and that the Kara gates were closed by impenetrable bars of ice.

During the last few years considerable efforts have been made, principally by Professor Nordenskiöld of Stockholm and Captain Wiggins of Sunderland to reopen this ancient route, and to re-establish a trade with Siberia viâ the Kara Sea.   In 1874 Captain Wiggins chartered the well-known Arctic steam yacht the *Diana*, and passing through the Kara gates, explored the entrance to the Obb and the Yen-e-say', and returned to England in safety.   In 1875 Professor Nordenskiöld chartered a walrus sloop at Hammerfest, and entering the Kara Sea through the Matoshkin scar, landed in the gulf of the Yen-e-say'.   The walrus sloop returned to Europe in safety, leaving the Professor to make his way up the river in a boat as far as Yen-e-saisk', whence he returned to Stockholm by the overland route.

In 1876 both these gentlemen attempted to take a cargo

to Siberia viâ the Kara Sea. Professor Nordenskiöld was the first to arrive, and fortunately failing to find a channel up the Yen-e-say' deep enough for his steamer, he landed his goods at a little village called Kor'-e-o-poff'-sky, about a hundred miles up the Yen-e-say', and returned to Europe without any mishap. As will hereafter appear, Captain Wiggins was less fortunate. He left Sunderland on the 8th of July in the *Thames*, Arctic steam yacht (120 tons), and entered the Kara Sea on the 3rd of August. The ice prevented him from sailing direct to the mouths of the great rivers, so he spent some time in surveying the coast and the By'-der-at'-skerry Gulf, and did not reach the mouth of the Obb until the 7th of September. Here he lay at anchor some time in the hope that a favourable wind might enable him to ascend the Obb against the strong current; but the weather proving tempestuous and the wind contrary, he abandoned the attempt, and ran for the Yen-e-say'. He commenced the ascent of that river on the 23rd of September, and after a tedious voyage, struggling against contrary winds and shallow water, he finally laid his vessel up on the Arctic Circle, half a mile up the Koo-ray'-i-ka, on the 17th of October, 1200 miles from the mouth of the Yen-e-say'. The following morning the ship was frozen up in winter quarters. A room in a peasant's house on the banks of the river, looking down on to the ship, was rigged up for the crew, and as soon as the ice on the river was thick enough to make sledging safe, Captain Wiggins returned to England by the overland route.

In 1875 Harvie-Brown and I visited the delta of the

Petchora in North-East Russia, and brought home an unusually interesting collection of birds, eggs, and ethnological
curiosities from the *tundras* of Siberia-in-Europe.   In 1876
Drs. Finsch and Brehm made an expedition to the Obb,
extending still further east our recent zoological and ethnological knowledge of these interesting regions.   Hearing
that Captain Wiggins was in England, and likely to rejoin
his ship, with the intention of returning in her to Europe
through the Kara Sea, I lost no time in putting myself in
communication with him.   I was anxious to carry our
ornithological and ethnological researches a step further to
the eastward, so as to join on with those of Middendorf,
Schrenck, and Radde in East Siberia.   I made the acquaintance of Captain Wiggins on the 23rd of February, and
came to the conclusion that an opportunity of travelling
with a gentleman who had already made the journey, and
consequently 'knew the ropes,' might never occur again.
Captain Wiggins told me that it was his intention to start
from London on the return journey in three days.   I finally
arranged with him to give me five days to make the necessary preparations for accompanying him.   I wrote to Count
Schouvaloff, who had given my companion and myself
excellent letters of introduction on our Petchora journey,
asking him to be kind enough to send to my rooms in
London similar letters for my proposed Yen-e-say' expedition,
and I am happy in now having an opportunity of publicly
expressing my warmest thanks to his Excellency for his
kindness in furnishing me, at a moment's notice, with letters
of introduction to General Timarscheff, the Minister of the

Interior at St. Petersburg, which proved of the greatest
service to me on my long and adventurous journey.

OSTYAKS OF THE OBI.

The details of this journey, how we travelled nearly six
thousand miles to the ship, and how we lost her, and had to
travel home again by land, form the subject of the present
volume. The reader may, however, feel some interest in

following the narrative of the attempts to explore the North-East Passage, beyond the loss of the ill-starred *Thames*.

The success of Captain Wiggins in reaching the Yen-e-say' in 1876 encouraged two steamers to make the attempt in the following year, the year of our disasters. The *Louise* succeeded in ascending the Obb and the Ir'-tish as far as Tobolsk, where she wintered, returning with a cargo in safety the following autumn. The *Frazer* reached Gol-cheek'-a on the Yen-e-say', where a cargo of wheat ought to have met her, but in consequence of the cowardice or the blunders—not to say the dishonesty—of the persons in charge, the cargo never arrived, and the steamer was forced to return empty.

Notwithstanding his misfortunes, Captain Wiggins stuck bravely to his enterprise, and 1878 saw him again in the Obb with a steamer, the *Warkworth*, drawing 12 feet of water. The navigation of the lagoon of the Obb is attended with considerable difficulty. Sand banks are very numerous. The regular tide is very unimportant, and the normal condition of the river in autumn is a slow but steady fall from the high level of the summer flood to the low level of winter. Abnormal conditions of great importance to navigation, however, continually occur. A strong south wind accelerates the fall of the river, whilst a violent north wind backs up the water and causes the river to rise many feet. When the *Warkworth* arrived at the last great sand-bank, called the bar, she was stopped for want of water. A large praam laden with wheat awaited her at Sin-cheek'-a, a small port on the south-east of the gulf, 40 miles beyond Na-deem', the most northerly fishing station of the Obb. Captain Wiggins lost some time in searching for a channel among the mosquitoes, but fortunately before it was too late a cold north wind set in, banished the mosquitoes, backed up the waters of the Obb, and enabled the *Warkworth* to cross the bar and anchor within sight of the praam. There was no time to be lost. The ship dare not venture on shallower water, so the poor praam had to leave her haven of shelter and trust herself to the swelling waves. She was probably three or four hundred feet long, only pegged together, with ribs fearfully wide asunder, and commanded by a captain chicken-hearted as Russian sailors alone can be; but, though she writhed like a sea serpent by the side of the steamer, the operation proved successful, and Captain Wiggins turned his face homewards with the wheat on board. The cream of the success was, however, skimmed at the bar. Two hundred tons had to be thrown overboard before the deep channel could be reached, but the bulk of the cargo was brought safe into London.

The seasons of 1879 and 1880 were unfavourable. Long-continued east winds drove the remnants of the Kara Sea ice against the shores of Nova Zembla, and a narrow belt of pack ice blocked the Kara gates. Late in the season of 1879 a Bremen steamer succeeded in finding a passage, and in bringing a cargo of wheat from Na-deem'. It was very fortunate that the English steamers were unable to enter the Kara Sea. Drawing 14 to 17 feet of water, they had literally no chance at all where Wiggins only saved himself by the skin of his teeth, not drawing more than 12 feet.

The crowning feat of this north-east Arctic enterprise was performed by Nordenskiöld in 1878–79, a voyage which may not, perhaps, have any great commercial value, but in a scientific point of view must rank as the most successful Arctic expedition ever made.

Captain Palander left Gothenburg on July 4th, 1878, was joined by Nordenskiöld at Tromsö on the 21st, and entered the Kara Sea on the 1st of August. On the 5th they passed the mouth of the Yen-e-say', and held a clear course until the 12th, when they encountered drift ice and fogs, but succeeded in reaching the North-east Cape in lat. $77\frac{1}{2}°$ on the 19th. On the 27th they passed the mouth of the Lay'-na, but with September their troubles began. On the 3rd the thermometer for the first time fell below zero, and they were compelled to " hug the coast." On the 6th the nights became too dark to permit of safe navigation, and the ice thickened so rapidly that on the 12th, at Cape Severni, they had to lay to for six days. On the 19th they made 50 miles, but during the next six days their progress was very slow, the ship having continually to battle with thick ice, and on the 28th they were finally frozen in in winter quarters in lat. $67°\ 70'$, having failed to accomplish the 4000 miles from Tromsö to Behring's Straits by only 120 miles. The greatest cold they had during the winter was in January, when the thermometer fell to $74°$ below zero. On May 15th the ice was $5\frac{1}{2}$ feet thick. The *Vega* got away on July 18th, having been frozen up nine months and twenty days, and on the 20th she sailed through Behring's Straits, returning to Gothenburg viâ the Suez Canal, after having circumnavigated

Europe and Asia for the first time in the history of the human race.

The enforced delay of the *Vega* on the shores of the Tchuski-Land proved very interesting in an ethnological and ornithological point of view. When Professor Nordenskiöld and Captain Palander were in this country on their return voyage, I had an opportunity of having half-an-hour's chat with them, and learned that they brought home a large collection of skins of birds. The Pacific Eider Duck and the Grey Phalarope appeared in great numbers. The Arctic willow warbler appeared on migration, not by thousands, but by millions. The Emperor Goose formed an important addition to their diet, and they brought home one skin of Ross's Gull. The most interesting bird which they obtained was the spoon-billed Sandpiper, a bird so rare that a few years ago only twenty-four skins were known to exist. After the arrival of the spring migrants, this eccentric bird occasionally formed one of the Professor's dishes for breakfast. It is about the size of a Jack Snipe, and the shape of the bill is so extraordinary that it looks like a freak of nature.

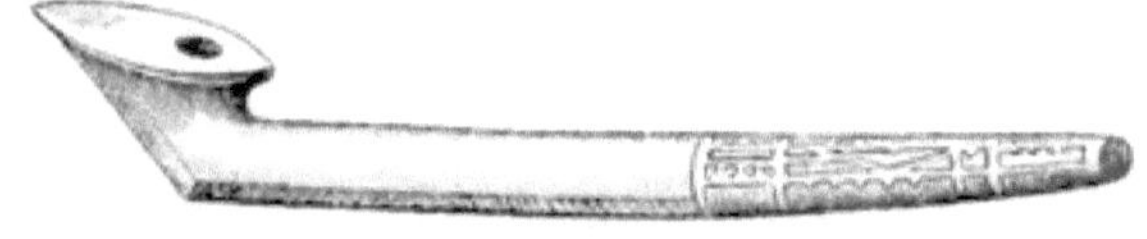

SAMOYADE PIPE.

CHAPTER II.

FROM LONDON TO ODESSA.

At St. Petersburg—Political feeling in Russia—Feeling against England—
Russian arguments against the policy of England—At Moscow—Irkutsk and
the Siberiaks—At Nishni Novgorod—The journey before us—Our sledge—
Birds—At Kazan—Roads between Kazan and Perm—At Perm—At Kongoor—
The Urals—Birds—We enter Asia—Ekatereenburg—Tyumain—The Steppes—
Villages of the Crescent and the Cross—Russian and Mahomedan clergy—
Cheap provisions—Birds.

WE left London on Thursday the 1st of March, at 8.25 P.M.,
and reached Nishni Novgorod on Saturday the 9th inst., at
10 A.M., having travelled by rail a distance of 2400 miles.
We stopped three days in St. Petersburg to present our

letters of introduction, and to pay some other visits. We had audiences with the Minister of the Interior and with the Minister of Finance, both of whom showed great interest in Captain Wiggins's attempt to re-open a trade with Siberia by sea.

At a dinner-party given in our honour at Sideroff's, the well-known concessionnaire of the Petchora, and on various occasions in our hotel and in the cafés, we had abundant opportunity of informing ourselves of the state of political feeling in St. Petersburg. Russia was by no means on the best of terms with England. The Panslavistic party was in the ascendency. As a stepping-stone to its wild scheme of reversing the policy of Peter the Great, and making Russia a great southern power, embracing all the Slavonic nations, it continually urged the government to lay violent hands on Turkey and wrest from her her Slavonic provinces. The military party, always on the *qui vive* for a chance of obtaining promotion and loot, had joined the hue and cry. The wily diplomatists of St. Petersburg, partly under the influence of the old tradition of Russian aggrandisement, and possibly far-seeing enough to perceive that the logical outcome of Panslavism would be a United Slavonia, in which Poland would eventually play the part of Prussia, encouraged the agitators. They shrewdly calculated that whatever might become of Turkey in Europe, some share of the spoil of Turkey in Asia must fall into Russian hands; and that if they only gave the Panslavistic party rope enough it would be sure to hang itself. On the peasantry, absolutely ignorant of European politics and anxious for peace to develop their rising commerce and agriculture, religious fanaticism was brought to bear in favour of war. The moment seemed ripe for action, but England, under the vigorous policy of Lord Beaconsfield, stopped the way. We found the feeling against England amongst the merchants very sore. Even the better educated Russian is remarkably ignorant of European politics. He has a smattering of knowledge and a rudimentary appreciation of logic just sufficient to enable him to express his opinions in syllogistic form. The line of argument which we had to meet and combat was ingenious and plausible; we never once were able to convince an opponent that it contained a single fallacy. The greatest astonishment was expressed that England should want to prop up such a rotten government as that of Turkey. We were assured that a Christian country like England could not possibly love the Turks any more than the Russian could, and that England, that had always been the champion of freedom, could never permanently uphold the slavery of the Slavonic races in Turkey. The explanation of these anomalies was an amusing mixture of truth and error, but so firmly had it taken possession of the popular mind of the day, that nothing that we could say in answer made the slightest impression. The arguments used against us ran pretty much in one strain. Lord Beaconsfield was a Jew. The Jewish party was in power. England had, politically, entirely succumbed to Jewish influences. The Jewish party was the money-lending party. The money-lending party was the creditor of Turkey. England, therefore, under the malign influence of her Jewish prime minister, upheld the integrity of Turkey solely that the Jewish creditors of that anti-Christian and despotic state might obtain as many shillings in the pound as possible from their bankrupt debtor. We could only shrug our shoulders and reflect that a little logic, as well as a little knowledge, is a dangerous thing.

When we left St. Petersburg the weather showed signs of breaking, and we reached Moscow in a complete thaw. As we had a sledge journey before us of between three and four thousand miles, which we hoped to accomplish before the roads became impassable, we made as short a delay in Moscow as possible. A few hours' rest gave us an opportunity of visiting the British Consul, and of enjoying the hospitality of a wealthy Russian merchant of the name of Trapeznikoff. The latter gentleman entertained us in his splendid mansion, and we had a very interesting conversation with him. We had now fairly turned our backs upon Europe and European politics, and discussed Siberian topics only. Mr. Trapeznikoff is a Siberiak, born in Irkutsk, and takes a prominent part in the efforts which the Moscow Geographical Society are making to rival the attempts of Captain Wiggins to open up sea communication between Europe and Siberia. Mr. Trapeznikoff was one of the comparatively few Russian merchants with whom we came in contact who was able to converse in German. The more we heard of Irkutsk the more disappointed we were that we had not time to make a détour to this interesting town. It is not a large place, but we were told that the population was upwards of 30,000. Though situated in the heart of Siberia, it is said to be the most European town of all the Russias. In Irkutsk we were informed that we should find the freest thought, the highest education, the most refined civilisation, the least barbarous luxury of any Russian town.

We reached Nishni Novgorod on Saturday the 10th of March, and were officially received at the railway station by the chief of the police, who was kind enough to conduct us across the Volga to a hotel. We devoted the morning to the purchase of a sledge, and spent some time in buying a stock of provisions for the road, but evening saw us fairly under weigh. We had a long and adventurous journey before us, a sledge journey of more than 3000 miles. We hoped to cross the meridian of Calcutta, 2300 miles north of that city, before the roads broke up, and then to sledge nearly a thousand miles due north, before entering the Arctic Circle. Our sledge was something like a cab on runners, with an empty space under the driver's seat to enable us to stretch our legs at night. We sledged away, day and night, with three horses abreast, stopping to change them every fifteen to twenty miles, with bells tinkling to drive away the wolves. At first our road was down the Volga, and we travelled smoothly along with no greater misfortune than an occasional run through a snow swamp where the thaw had been greatest; but on some of the banks we were knocked about unmercifully, the motion of the sledge resembling that of a boat on a short chopping sea. It was late in the year, and the roads were worn out.

On Sunday we dined at Vassilla. There had been some frost during the night, but it was thawing rapidly at noon. Birds were plentiful for the time of the year. Hooded

Crows,* Jackdaws, and House-Sparrows were very common, and I saw one flock of Snow Buntings. Vassilla is a large town about half-way to Kazan, the distance from Nishni to Kazan being 427 versts (about 280 miles).

We continued to sledge down the bed of the Volga, travelling day and night, with occasional snowstorms and a persistent thaw. The left bank of the river as we travelled down was comparatively flat, but the other bank was hilly. This is the case with the Petchora, and also with the Obb and the Yen-e-say'. There was very little change in the birds on the roadside. House-Sparrows, Jackdaws, and Hooded Crows were the commonest. Once I saw a pair of Ravens, and once a solitary Great Tit, and at a station 61 versts before we reached Kazan Tree-Sparrows were feeding with the House-Sparrows. On the banks of the Volga were numerous holes, evidently the nests of colonies of Sand-Martins, and occasionally Magpies were seen. We did not make any stay in Kazan, but without delay on the evening of our arrival we took a *padarozhna* for Ekatereenburg, 942 versts, or 628 miles, paying, as before, 4 kopeks per verst per horse.

The first night's journey from Kazan was a fearful pull and jolt. The weather was mild, with snow, but the state of the roads was inconceivably bad. We were dashed about to such an extent that in the morning every bone in our bodies ached. No constitution in the world could stand a week of such ill-usage. Before sunrise the thermometer had fallen to zero. This was followed by a magnificent sunshiny morning, and very fair roads. I saw a pair of Bullfinches for the first time since leaving Nishni.

* See ' Siberia in Europe,' page 49.

The next morning the weather still continued fine, but the roads were never good for long at a time. We had got into a hilly country, which was very picturesque, but not at all conducive to the maintenance of good roads, especially so late in the season.

We passed through Perm late in the evening of Thursday the 15th of March, and were glad of an excuse to rest a few hours on Friday at Kongoor. At this town we were most hospitably entertained by Mr. Hawkes, who showed us over his iron steamship building yard. The father of Mr. Hawkes was an enterprising Scotchman, who established a flourishing business in this remote corner of Europe. Shortly after bidding our host a reluctant adieu, we commenced the ascent of the Ural mountains. In this part the range scarcely deserves to be considered more than a succession of hills, the loftiest hardly high enough to be dignified with the name of mountain. The country reminded me very much of the Peak of Derbyshire. For several hundred versts we sledged up one hill and down another, occasionally following the valleys between. In the low lands we frequently passed villages, and a considerable part of the country was culti-vated. For miles together the road passed between two avenues of birches. The hills were covered with forests, principally Scotch and spruce fir, with a few birches and larches. During this part of our journey we had magnifi-cent weather: hard frost but warm sunshine. Birds were more abundant, one of the commonest being the large Bull-finch * with a brick-red breast. Hooded Crows were, perhaps,

---

* See ' Siberia in Europe,' page 37.

C

less frequent, but, on the other hand, Ravens and Magpies were much commoner, and Jackdaws remained as numerous as ever. I noticed several small birds which I had not seen before—Greenfinches, Yellow-Hammers, Marsh Tits, and one or two Jays.

A few stages before reaching Ekatereenburg we left the last hill of the Urals behind us, and an easy slope brought us out of the forests to a more cultivated and level country, in which the villages were more plentiful. As we passed the granite pillar which marks the boundary line between the two continents, we hoped that we had left the mists and fogs of Europe behind us to enter the pure dry climate of Asia. We reached Ekatereenburg on the morning of Sunday the 18th inst., having been 123 hours sledging 628 miles, about five miles an hour, including stoppages. We changed horses sixty-five times. Ekatereenburg has about 30,000 inhabitants. We were most hospitably entertained by M. George Onésime Clerc, the head of the Observatory at Ekatereenburg, to whom I had a letter of introduction from M. Bogdanoff, of St. Petersburg; we also visited M. Vinebourg, an official of the telegraph office and an excellent amateur ornithologist, who went with us to the museum.

Time did not, however, admit of our making much delay. We were anxious to cover as much ground as possible whilst the frost lasted, and we bade a hasty adieu to our friends. The same afternoon we took a *padarozhna* for Tyu-main', and made the 306 versts, or 204 miles, in twelve stages, which we accomplished in thirty-nine hours. The country was gently undulating, well wooded, with numerous villages.

We spent a couple of days at Tyu-main' enjoying the hospitality of Mr. Wardroper, a Scotch engineer; with him we visited M. Ignatieff, and lunched at his house with some of the merchants of this thriving place. The river was full of steamers, all frozen up in their winter quarters, and everything told of commerce and wealth. The house of Ivan Ivanovich Ignatieff was a handsome mansion elegantly furnished in the German style, just such a house as a North German family with an income of 600*l.* or 700*l.* a year would inhabit. We had a quiet but substantial luncheon, roast beef and claret, roast grouse and sherry, ice cream and champagne. One of the guests was a magnificent specimen of a Russian, standing 6. ft. 8 in., and weighing, we were told, twenty-two stone.

From Tyu-main' to Omsk is 637 versts, which we accomplished in sixty-two hours, changing horses twenty-seven times. It was quite holiday travelling; we had good horses and excellent roads. The scene was entirely changed. We were now crossing the great steppes of western Siberia. We had left the Peak of Derbyshire behind us, and were traversing an almost boundless Salisbury Plain. For nearly a thousand miles hardly anything was to be seen but an illimitable level expanse of pure white snow. Above us was a canopy of brilliantly blue sky, and alongside of us a line of telegraph poles crossing from one horizon to the other. Occasionally we came upon a small plantation of stunted birches, and every fifteen to twenty miles we changed horses at some village built on the banks of a frozen river whose waters find their way into the Obb beneath their thick armour of ice. These villages were almost entirely built of wood, floated down in rafts from the forests on the distant hills. Most of them were Russian, with a large stone or brick church in the centre, and a gilt cross on the steeple. Others were Tartar villages, where the crescent occupied the place of the cross; and it was somewhat humiliating to us as Christians to find that the cross was too often the symbol of drunkenness, disorder, dilapidation, and comparative poverty, whereas the crescent was almost invariably the sign of sobriety, order, enterprise, and prosperity. The general opinion amongst the better educated Russians with whom I was able to converse, was, that the chief fault lay with the priests, who encouraged idleness and drunkenness, whilst the Mohamedan clergy threw the whole of their influence into the opposite scale. Living is so extravagantly cheap in this part of the world, that the ordinary incentives to industry scarcely exist. We were able to buy beef at twopence per pound, and grouse at sevenpence a brace. We had a very practical demonstration that we were in a land flowing with hay and corn, in the price we paid for our horses. Our sledge was what is called a "tro'-i-ka," and required three horses. Up to Tyu-main' these horses had cost us sixpence a mile. On the steppes the price suddenly fell to three-halfpence, i.e. a halfpenny a horse a mile. At one of the villages where we stopped to change horses it was market-day, and we found on inquiry that a ton of wheat might be purchased for the same amount as a hundred-weight cost in England.

Whilst we were crossing the steppes we saw very few

birds. The almost total absence of trees and the depth of the snow upon the ground is, of course, a sufficient explanation why birds cannot live there in winter. Occasionally we saw small flocks of Snow-Buntings, whose only means of subsistence appeared to be what they could pick up from the droppings of the horses on the road. These charming little birds often enlivened the tedium of the journey as we watched them flitting before the sledge, as we disturbed them at their meals. They were rapidly losing their winter dress. They only moult once in the year: in autumn. In winter the general colour of the Snow-Bunting is a buffish brown. After the autumn moult each feather has a more or less broad fringe of buffish brown, which almost obscures the colour of the feather lying below it. The nuptial plumage is assumed in spring by the casting of these fringes, which appear to dry up and drop off, whilst at the same time the feathers appear to acquire new life and the colour to intensify, as if in spring there was a fresh flow of blood into the feathers, somewhat analogous to the rising of the sap in trees, which causes a fresh deposit of colouring matter. The Snow-Buntings we saw on the snow-track across the steppes had nearly lost all the brown from their plumage, their backs were nearly black, as were also the primary quills of their wings, whilst the head and under-parts were nearly as white as the snow itself, and at a distance one might often fancy that a flock of black butterflies were dancing before us. The Snow-Bunting had an additional charm for us from the fact that it is a winter visitor to England, whose arrival is always looked for with interest, and a few pairs even

remain to breed in the north of Scotland.   Otherwise, the
Snow-Bunting is remarkable as being the most northerly of
all passerine birds in its breeding range, having been found
throughout the Arctic Circle wherever land is known to exist.
The only other birds we saw on the steppes were a few
Sparrows, Jackdaws, and Hooded Crows in the villages. The
Bullfinches and the Tits disappeared with the trees, and the
summer birds had not yet arrived, though Mr. Wardroper at
Tyu-main' told us that Starlings, Rooks, Geese, and Ducks
were all overdue.   It was, perhaps, fortunate for us that the
season was an unusually late one, otherwise the roads might
have been in many places impassable.

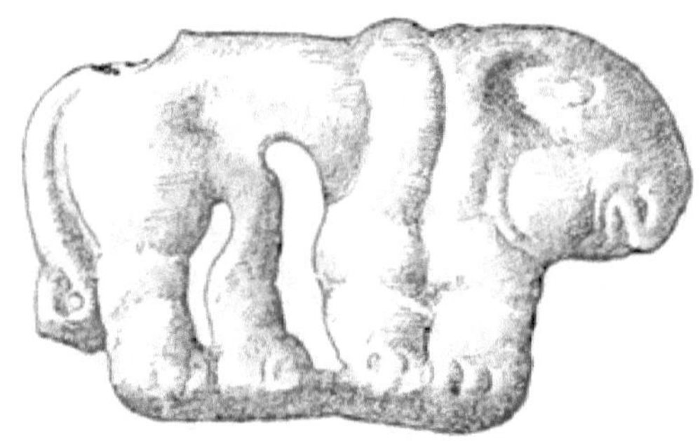

BRONZE ORNAMENT FROM ANCIENT GRAVE NEAR KRASNOYARSK.

SLEDGING IN A SNOW-STORM.

CHAPTER III.

I HAD a letter of introduction from General Timarscheff, the
Minister of the Interior, to the Governor-General of West
Siberia in Omsk. Unfortunately the Governor was from
home, but his lady received us very kindly. Her excellency
spoke good French and German, and had an English

governess for her children.   M. Bogdanoff, in St. Petersburg, had given me a letter of introduction to Professor Slofftzoff, who found for us a friend of his, M. Hanson, a Dane, as an interpreter.   Professor Slofftzoff is an enthusiastic naturalist.   He showed us a small collection of birds in the museum.   Among these were several which have not hitherto been recorded east of the Ural Mountains, for example, the Blackcap, the Garden-Warbler, and the Icterine Tree-Warbler; but as there are no special labels with these examples to authenticate the localities, the fact of their really having been shot in the neighbourhood of Omsk must be accepted with hesitation.   In museums, which profess to be local museums only, birds from distant localities continually creep in by accident, and many errors in geographical distribution are thus propagated.

I gave the Professor some Sheffield cutlery in exchange for a curiously inlaid pipe of mammoth ivory, and a flint and steel, the latter inlaid with silver and precious stones.   He told me that both were made by the Burryats in the Transbaical country, but the pipe is not to be distinguished from those made on the tundras of the north, and I suspect it to be of Samoyade origin.

Twenty years ago Omsk was only a village, now it is much larger than Tyu-main', and has thirty to forty thousand inhabitants.   This increase is very largely accounted for by the fact that the seat of government has in the meantime been removed from Tobolsk to Omsk.   From Omsk to Tomsk is 877 versts, or 585 miles, which we accomplished in eighty-five hours, including stoppages, an average of 10¼ versts an hour. We changed horses thirty-seven times. We had now got into the full swing of sledge travelling; snow, wind, rain, sunshine, day, night, good roads, bad roads, nothing stopped us; on we went like the wandering Jew, only with this difference, that we had a fixed goal. However rough the road might be, I could now sleep soundly as in a bed. My sledge fever was entirely gone. I began actually to enjoy sledge travelling. I found a pleasant lullaby in the never-ceasing music of the " wrangling and the jangling of the bells." After having sledged 2762 versts, or 1841 miles, one begins to feel that the process might go on *ad infinitum* without serious results.

The weather was mild, with no absolute thaw, but now and then we had snow-storms, generally very slight. Our way lay across flat steppes with scarcely a tree visible, until we came within 150 miles of Tomsk, when we again passed through a hilly well-wooded country like an English park. We saw the same birds as heretofore, with an occasional Hazel Grouse* and Great Tit. On the steppes Snow-Buntings were, as before, very common. On the whole the roads were good, in the flat district very good.

In Omsk I had seen some very curious Kirghis' arms, at Professor Slofftzoff's, and I had vainly tried to purchase some. In Tomsk I learned that Barnaul was the place to obtain them. There is a museum in that town. I was told that M. Bogdanoff, a mining engineer, and M. Funck, a shot-maker, spoke German, and further, that there is an anti-quary of the name of Goulaieff. Tomsk is a very business-

---

* See ' Siberia in Europe,' page 89.

like place, apparently about the same size as Omsk. From Tomsk to Kras-no-yarsk' is 554 versts, or 369 miles, which we accomplished in sixty-four hours and in twenty-seven stages. The weather was very mild, and we had several slight falls of snow. The country was generally hilly, and well-wooded, and the roads on the whole good, but occasionally we had them extremely bad. After the 27th of May (15th Russian style) we had to pay for an extra horse, and upon entering the Yen-e-saisk' Government, the cost of each horse was doubled. Magpies were as common as ever. Jackdaws much less so. Hooded Crows disappeared soon after leaving Tomsk. Ravens were rather more numerous than before. Bullfinches were plentiful in the woods, and Snow-Buntings on the plains. The Great Tit was only occasionally seen. House-sparrows were very common, but we saw no Tree-Sparrows. We reached Kras-no-yarsk' on Monday the 2nd of April, and paid a visit, first to M. Dorset, the government "Vet." of the district. He was a German, and kindly placed himself at our disposal as interpreter. He introduced me to a M. Kibort, a Polish exile, who engaged to procure me skins of birds, and send them to England. We visited the governor, who gave me a Crown *padarozhna,* and an open letter of introduction to all the officials. In Kras-no-yarsk' prices were as follows :—

Wheat	40 kop. per pood.
Flour	60 " "
Swan's-down	12 to 15 rbl. "
Goose-down	8 rbl. " "
Feathers	3 rbl. " "
Pitch	3 to 3½ rbl. "
Hemp seed	20 kop. " "

We spent the evening at the house of Sideroff's agent, M. Glayboff. We also bought some fine photographs of the gold mines, &c.

A warm south-west wind blew all Sunday, and continued during the night. In Kras-no-yarsk' we found the streets flooded, and everybody travelling upon wheels. In the evening the post refused us horses, on the plea that sledging was impossible. There was nothing for it but to go to bed. In the morning the south-west wind was as warm as ever. The red hills of Kras-no-yarsk' were almost bare. We were obliged to take to wheels, and organise a little caravan. Equipage No. 1 was a "Rosposki," on which our empty "pavoska" was mounted, a yems'-chik standing on the box at the back, and driving his three horses over the top. Equipage No. 2 was a "Tarantass," with two horses, drawing our luggage. Equipage No. 3 was another tarantass, containing our two selves. We got away about 11 A.M., and trundled along over snow, mud, grass, or gravel up the hill, through a series of extempore rivers, and across the steppes, a wild bleak country, like a Yorkshire moor, for 35 versts, at an expense of fifteen roubles. The next stage was 28 versts. The road was a little better. We dismissed the rosposki, and travelled in the otherwise empty sledge, but retained one tarantass for our luggage. This stage cost us six roubles. Night came on, and after a squall of wind, snow, and sleet, it grew a little colder. The next stage was 23 versts. We travelled as on the last, but transferred our luggage from the tarantass to a sledge. We had reached the forest, the roads soon became better, the wind got more northerly, the night was cooler, and we got off for four roubles. At the end of this stage we repacked our sledge, got horses at the regular price of three kopeks per verst per horse, and matters began steadily to improve. Our five horses were soon knocked down to four, and finally to three. What little wind there was blew cold, the sky was clear, the sun shone brightly, and all our troubles were over for the present. The road became excellent. The country was hilly, and the scenery grew once more like an English park with fine timber. We might easily have fancied ourselves in the Dukeries in Nottinghamshire. Hooded Crows had entirely disappeared, but the Carrion Crow was several times seen. In the evening we dined at the roadside station, kept by a Jew. We had potato soup and fish, two spoons, but *only one plate.* We reached Yen-e-saisk' at 9 A.M. on Thursday the 5th of April, having been nearly forty-eight hours in travelling 330 versts, in consequence of the thaw in the earlier part of the journey. There were thirteen stages in all.

Arrived at Yen-e-saisk' we took rooms at the house of a M. Panikoroffsky, and enjoyed a few days' rest. We had brilliant sunshine, with the thermometer at or near zero, and we were told that there was no great hurry, that we might expect to have a month's frost in which to travel to Toor-o-kansk.

By this time we had sledged 3646 versts, or 2431 miles, and had fairly earned a rest. We had plenty of visitors. First, there was Mr. Boiling, a Heligolander, who left his native island thirty-five years ago. He was a boat builder, and spoke German very well, and knew enough English to make his way. Then there was M. Marks, a Pole, an elderly man, a political exile. He was a photographer, a dealer in mathematical instruments, an astronomer, a botanist, and had had a university education, and spoke French, though somewhat rustily. A most active, useful little man was the head of the police, who offered to do anything for us, but unfortunately he only spoke Russian. Then there was Schwanenberg, the captain of Sideroff's schooner, who was on his way down the river. He spoke English and German. The telegraph master also spoke German, so that altogether we had no difficulty in finding society.

Marks told me that Middendorf made no stay at Yen-e-saisk'. He gave me the following as a complete list of the scientific expeditions which have visited the Yen-e-say' during the term of his exile :—

1829. Hansten, an astronomer.

1843. Middendorf, the celebrated ornithologist.

1873. Tchekanoff-ky, a zoologist and geologist, who collected a large number of birds, now in the museum at St. Petersburg.

1874. Fritsche, an astronomer.

1875. Tunstién, a botanist, who accompanied Nordenskiöld.

1876. A Swedish expedition, amongst whom Dr. Theel was the ornithologist.

There were very few birds at Yen-e-saisk' during our stay. Magpies were plentiful. There were no Jackdaws. House- and Tree-Sparrows were very abundant, and in equal numbers. The Carrion Crow was very common. Boiling told me that about three years ago a pair or two of Hooded

Crows paid a visit to Yen-e-saisk', and were most hospitably received by their black cousins, so much so that they allowed them to intermarry in their families. The consequence now is, that perhaps seventy-five per cent. of the Yen-e-saisk' Crows are thorough bred Carrion Crows, five per cent. Hooded Crows, and twenty per cent. hybrids of every stage between the two. Middendorf, however, mentions the interbreeding of these birds as long ago as 1843, so Boiling's story must be taken for what it is worth. Now and then we saw a Great Tit, and flocks of Redpoles and Snow-Buntings frequented the banks of the river, the latter bird having, we were told, only just arrived.

Our lodgings were very comfortable. The sitting-room was large, with eight windows in it, of course double. The furniture was light and elegant. A few pictures, mostly coloured lithographs, and two or three mirrors ornamented the walls; and a quantity of shrubs in pots, materially assisted the general effect: they were roses, figs, geraniums, &c.

Whilst we were resting at Yen-e-saisk' the great festival of Easter took place. Every Russian family keeps open house on that day to all their acquaintances. The ladies sit in state to receive company, and the gentlemen sledge from house to house making calls. A most elaborate display of wines, spirits, and every dish that is comprised in a Russian "zakuska," or foretaste of dinner, fills the side-board, and every guest is pressed to partake of the sumptuous provisions. Captain Wiggins had made a good many acquaintances during his previous visit to Yen-e-saisk', so that we had an opportunity of seeing the houses of nearly

all the principal merchants and official personages in the
town.   Some of the reception-rooms were luxuriously
furnished.

FISHING STATION ON THE OBB.

The most important business which claimed my attention
in Yen-e-saisk' was the selection of a servant.   On the whole
I was most fortunate.   All to whom I mentioned my require-
ments shook their heads, and told me it was a hopeless case.
Of course I wanted as good a servant as I could get, honest,
industrious, and so forth.   Two qualifications were a *sine quâ
non*.   He must be able to skin birds, and speak either
French or German.   I soon learned that there was not a

single person in Yen-e-saisk' who had ever seen a bird skinned for scientific purposes. After many fruitless inquiries, I at last succeeded in finding a young Jew of the name of Glinski, about four-and-twenty years of age, who three months before had married the daughter of the Israelitish butcher in Yen-e-saisk'. Glinski spoke bad German and bad Russian, and had an inconvenient habit of mixing up Hebrew with both these languages, but on the whole I might have had a worse interpreter, as he did his best to translate faithfully what my companion for the time being said, instead of telling me what, in his (the interpreter's) opinion, my companion ought to have said, as too many interpreters are in the habit of doing. Nevertheless, Glinski was, without exception, one of the greatest thickheads that I have ever met with. He was an exile from the south of Russia. At fourteen years of age he had committed some crime, stolen and destroyed some bills or securities, for which his father was liable, and had spent some years in prison. He was afterwards exiled, and his term of exile had just expired. He had scarcely any notion of arithmetic, and his other acquirements were so scanty that he was continually chaffed even by the simple-minded Russian peasants. He was very short-sighted, but clever with his fingers. I asked him if he thought he could learn to skin birds. He said he thought he could, but should like to see how it was done. I skinned a couple of Redpoles in his presence, and gave him a Bullfinch to try his hand on. With a little help and instruction he made a tolerable skin of it. We afterwards skinned a few birds together at various stations on the journey, and when we arrived at our winter quarters I turned over this part of my work entirely to Glinski. At the end of a week he could skin better and quicker than I could, and on one occasion, as will be hereafter recorded, he skinned forty-seven birds for me in one day. I always found him industrious, honest, and anxious to do his best. He asked me twenty roubles a month wages, I of course paying his board and lodging and travelling expenses. I agreed to those terms, and promised also an additional bonus of ten kopeks per skin. During the time that Glinski was with me he skinned for me more than a thousand birds, for which I paid him more than a hundred roubles, besides his wages, but for all that I am told that since I left Yen-e-saisk' he has abused me roundly to my friends there because I refused to lend him fifty roubles more when I parted from him. No one must expect gratitude from a Russian Jew.

Another important business which I transacted in Yen-e-saisk' was the purchase of a ship. Boiling had a schooner on the stocks which had been originally intended to bring to Yen-e-saisk' the cargo which Professor Nordenskiöld left at Kor'-e-o-poff'-sky. Other arrangements were made by which Kitmanoff was to bring these goods up in his steamer, and the schooner was sold to me. Captain Wiggins undertook to rig it at the Koo-ray'-i-ka, where it was to be delivered by Boiling as soon as the ice broke up. Boiling and I were to sail in her a thousand miles down the Yen-e-say' to Doo-din'-ka ornithologising as we went along, whilst Captain Wiggins went up the Koo-ray'-i-ka to take on board a cargo of graphite, which Sideroff's plenipotentiary, Captain Schwanenberg, was to have ready for him. In Doo-din'-ka the schooner was to be disposed of on joint account, or kept as a second string to our bow across the Kara Sea, as circumstances might render desirable.

The addition of Glinski to our party also made fresh arrangements for travelling necessary. Now that there were three of us, we required two sledges. We were told that the roads were bad, and that the sledge we had bought in Nishni Novgorod was too heavy for the roads north of Yen-e-saisk'. We accordingly bought a couple of light sledges, mere skeletons of wood covered with open matting. One of them, which Captain Wiggins and I reserved for ourselves, had an apology for a hood.

We had arrived at Yen-e-saisk' in a hard frost, but before we had been there three days the south wind overtook us. The snow began to melt, and taking right at once, we left at 11 o'clock on the evening of Monday the 9th of April. For the first few stations the road was through the forests or along the sloping banks of the river, and we thought ourselves fortunate if we did not capsize more than half-a-dozen times between two stations. Afterwards the road was down the river, a splendid road as long as we kept on it, perfectly level, except on arriving at a station. where we had to ascend from the winter level of the ice to the villages, which are built on the bank above the level of the summer floods. The villagers generally came out to meet us, and help us up the steep ascent. The assistance they gave us in descending was still more important.

It sometimes almost made our hearts jump into our mouths to look down the precipice which led to the road. We commenced the descent with three or four peasants holding on to each side of the sledge. As the pace became fast and furious, one or two of our assistants would come to grief, and have a roll in the snow, but the help they rendered was so efficient that we ourselves always escaped without an accident.

In spite of the thaw, and the consequent bad roads, we made seventy-eight versts the first night, and were entertained by an official whom we had met at the house of the Ispravnik in Yen-e-saisk'. As is always the case in Russia, we were very hospitably received, and on taking leave of the Sessedatel, we were provided with a courier. The Easter holidays were not yet over, and we might have difficulty or delay in obtaining horses. This courier accompanied us to the " grenitza," or boundary of the province of Yen-e-saisk', a distance of about 300 versts. About 200 versts before reaching Toor-o-kansk' we were met by a cossack, who brought us a letter from the Sessedatel of that town, informing us that he had sent us an escort to assist us on our way.

The thaw had cut up the roads a good deal. We had generally three, rarely only two, frequently four and sometimes five horses in our sledge, but in all cases they were driven tandem. The smaller sledge was driven with two, and occasionally three, horses. Although to all appearances the road was a dead level from one to two miles wide, it was in reality very narrow, in fact too narrow for a pair of horses to run abreast with safety. We were really travelling on a wall of hard trodden snow from five to seven feet wide, and about as high, levelled up on each side with soft snow. Whenever we met a peasant's sledge, the peasant's poor horse had to step off the road, and stand on one side up to the traces in snow. After our cavalcade had gone by, it had to struggle on to the road again as best it could. Our horses were generally good and docile, and they kept the road wonderfully, though it sometimes wound about like a snake. A stranger might naturally wonder for what inscrutable reason such a tortuous road should be made along a level river. It was carefully staked out with little bushes of spruce fir, from two to five feet high, stuck in the snow every few yards. The explanation is very simple. When Captain Wiggins travelled up the river in December, little or no snow had fallen. At the beginning of the winter the ice breaks up several times before it finally freezes for the season. When the roads were first staked out by the " starrester " of the village, the little bushes that now reared their heads above the snow were trees eight to twelve feet high, and the road had to be carefully picked out between shoals and hills of ice slabs lying scattered about in every direction. After the winter snow had fallen we could see nothing of all this, except the tops of the trees. Everything was buried to a depth of six feet. Our horses got well over the ground, and for two-thirds of the way we averaged a hundred and fifty versts in the twenty-four hours; but on the sixth, seventh, and eighth days of our journey from Yen-e-saisk' to 'Toor-o-kansk' we passed through a district where an epidemic had prevailed amongst the horses. Here we were obliged to travel slowly, and frequently had to wait for horses at the stations, and consequently only scored about half our previous average. These epidemics amongst the cattle occur with some regularity every spring, or, to speak more correctly, during the last month or two of winter, for in these latitudes there is no spring. The cause is not very far to seek. It is unquestionably insufficient food. The corn has been finished long ago, and the hot sun and occasional thaws have caused the hay to foul.

On this journey we had the same variable weather as heretofore. Since leaving Kras-no-yarsk' we had been racing the south wind. A couple of days after leaving that town we thought we had fairly beaten it, but we had not been two days in Yen-e-saisk' before it overtook us again. We had no absolute rain, however, until we reached the entrance to the Kah'-min Pass, not far from the point where the Kah'-min-a Tun-goosk' joins the Yen-e-say'. This pass is twenty versts in length, and is extremely picturesque. The river here flows through a comparatively narrow defile, between perpendicular walls of what looked like mountain limestone rock. This is considered the only dangerous part of the journey. The channel is deep and tortuous, and the current so rapid that open water is visible in places even in the hardest winters. We reached the station at the entrance of this pass in the evening. A heavy gale from the south-west was blowing, and the rain was beating loudly against the windows of the station-house. We were told that it was impossible to proceed, and that we must remain in our present quarters until a frost should set in. We were not sorry to be compelled to take a night's rest, but the prospect of having to stop a week or two until the weather changed was not pleasant. The south wind seemed to have completely beaten us, and we went to bed somewhat disheartened. When we woke the next morning we heard the wind still howling. We were making an effort to be resigned to our fate, and as a preliminary step we turned out to inspect our sledges, and see if our baggage had escaped a complete soaking. We were, however, soon driven in again. Although the wind was still blowing hard, it had shifted a point or two, and cut like a knife. The rain was all gone, the snow was drifting in white clouds down the pass, and a thermometer placed outside the window fell down to 3° above zero. As the mercury fell our spirits rose; with the thermometer 29° below freezing point the worst roads must be safe, so we ordered our horses, breakfasted, and were soon in the Kah'-min Pass.

When Captain Wiggins came through this pass in the previous December it was on a brilliantly sunshiny day. The blue ice was then piled in fantastic confusion on each side. The snow had not yet fallen and buried the signs of the skirmishes which had taken place between the river and winter before the latter finally conquered. The thermometer was below zero, and the sunshine glistened on the frozen waterfalls that hung down the cliffs like young glaciers, and clouds of dense white steam were rising from the open water in the centre of the river. We saw it under very different circumstances. The strong wind was driving the fine drifted

snow in clouds down the pass, and everything was wrapped in
haze.   A thin band of open water rippled black as we
passed by.   The scene was fine and constantly changing,
and reminded me very much of the " Iron Gates " on the
Danube.

During the rest of the journey we had no more anxiety on
the score of weather.   Once or twice the south wind overtook us again, but we had at length reached a latitude in
which we could afford to laugh at our old enemy.   Whatever attempts he made to stop us with rain only ended in
snow, and we found that a thin sprinkling of snow on the
hard crust of the road was rather advantageous to rapid
travelling than otherwise.   It was like oil to the runners of
our sledge.

SAMOYADE SNOW SPECTACLES.

SIBERIAN DOG SLEDGE.

CHAPTER IV.

Stations—Hospitality of the peasants—Furs and their prices—Dogs drawing sledges—Birds—Visit to a monastery—Graphite—Captain Wiggins's former travelling companion—An honest Russian official!—Installed as guests in the house of the Sessedatel—Toorokansk—We turn shop-keepers—The Scopsee—Scarcity of birds—Old Gazenkampf—Our host's tricks—The Blagachina—The second priest—The priest's accomplishments—The postmaster—The Secretary of the Sessedatel—Schwanenberg's troubles.

THE distance from Yen-e-saisk' to Toor-o-kansk' is 1084 versts, or 723 miles. The road is divided into forty-four stages, which we accomplished in nine days and ten nights. The stations where we changed horses were frequently in villages containing not more than half-a-dozen houses.

Those we visited were always scrupulously clean and everywhere we were most hospitably received. The best the peasants had was placed before us—tea, sugar, cream, bread, and occasionally soup, fish, beef, or game. Frequently we were treated as guests, and our offers of payment refused. The drivers, or "yems'-chiks," were always very civil, and some of the younger ones were fine-looking fellows. However numerous our horses were, we only paid for three, at the rate of three kopeks per verst per horse, to which we added vodka money—ten kopeks to each yems'-chik. At most of the houses furs were to be bought. I picked up a fine bear-skin, for which I paid six roubles: ermine* was to be had in almost any quantity at from ten to fifteen kopeks a skin. Squirrel† was even more abundant at about the same price. Skins of a light-coloured Stone-Marten,‡ which the peasants called Kor-lor-nok', were occasionally offered to us at fifty kopeks to a rouble each. I bought two Gluttons' skins, one for four and the other for five

---

* The Common Stoat (*Mustela erminea*) is a circumpolar quadruped. In cold climates in winter it becomes white, except the tip of its tail, and is then called the Ermine. In cold winters it regularly assumes its white dress in Scotland, and in England as far south as the Derbyshire moors.

† The Grey Squirrel (*Sciurus vulgaris*) is a Palæarctic quadruped, being represented on the American continent by a closely allied form (*Sciurus hudsonius*). In the British Islands only the red variety occurs, but in Siberia every intermediate form is found between Red and Grey Squirrels.

‡ The Beech-Marten (*Martes foina*) has been recorded as a British quadruped, but recent investigations seem to have proved that the Pine-Marten (*Martes abietum*) is the only species found in our islands. Both species are strictly Palæarctic, and neither of them are found on the American continent; indeed, it is doubtful if their range extends into Asia. In Siberia they are represented by the allied species *Martes sibirica*) mentioned above.

roubles. Otter and **Blue Fox** * were offered us at ten to twelve roubles, and **White Fox** at three to five roubles. We made many inquiries for Sable and **Black Fox**,† but did not succeed in ever seeing any. They are all carefully reserved for the Yen-e-saisk' merchants, who no doubt would be very angry if they heard of any of these valuable skins

---

* The Blue Fox, as it is called in its summer dress, when it is of a bluish-grey colour, or the Arctic Fox, as it is called in its snow-white winter dress (*Vulpes lagopus*), is a circumpolar quadruped. The Siberian merchants in Yen-e-saisk', as well as the Hudson Bay merchants in London, maintain the distinctness of the two forms, and attempt to prove their statements by producing both summer and winter skins of each. A possible explanation is, that like the Stoat, the Arctic Fox changes the colour of its fur with the seasons throughout the greater part of its range ; but towards the northern limit of its distribution the summers are so short that it is not worth while for it to turn dark, whilst towards the southern limit of its range snow does not lie long enough on the ground to make the whiteness of the fur protective. My impression is, however, that the Blue Fox is a variety of the Arctic Fox, bearing somewhat the same relation to the latter form as the Black Fox does to the Red Fox. It is difficult to explain otherwise the facts that skins of Blue Fox are obtained very far north, and those obtained in winter have very glossy, long, and thick fur.

† The Sable (*Martes zibellina*) is only found in Siberia, being represented in America by a nearly allied species (*Martes americana*), which is said to differ from its Siberian cousin both in the form of the skull and the shape of the teeth. There is little or no difference in the general appearance of the two species, and they are subject to much the same variation in the colour and quality of the fur, though I have never seen skins from Hudson Bay in which the hairs were as long or as thick as in Siberian skins, nor are the American skins ever quite so dark as the finest Asiatic ones, though when dyed it is sometimes difficult to detect the difference at a glance. The price of sables in St. Petersburg, at the best shops, varies from 2*l.* to 25*l.* each, according to quality. The quality at 6*l.* (60 roubles) is, however, rich enough and dark enough for ordinary use.

The Red Fox (*Vulpes vulgaris*) is a circumpolar quadruped. The Arctic form is of a richer, deeper red than that found in more temperate regions, and has longer hair and a much more bushy tail. On both continents a melanistic form, called the Black or Silver Fox, occasionally occurs, the Silver Fox having white tips to the black hairs. In St. Petersburg, fine skins of the Silver Fox fetch 25*l.*, but the best skins of Black Fox are sold as high as 50*l.*

"going past" them. We were told that the price of Black Sable was twenty-five roubles and Black Fox double that price or more. The Beaver has been extinct on the Yen-e-say' for many years. We bought a few skins of Red Fox with wonderfully large brushes, and the general colour a richer and intenser red than ours, the price varying from two to four roubles.

As we got further north we found fine dogs at the stations, and occasionally we met a sledge drawn by dogs. These animals are most sagacious. A Russian traveller will hire a sledge with a team of six dogs, travel in it ten or fifteen miles to the next station, where he gives the dogs a feed, and sends them home again alone with the empty sledge. On several occasions we met empty sledges returning alone with the team of dogs. They are fine fellows, a little like a Scotch shepherd's dog, but with very bushy hair. They have sharp noses, short straight ears, and a bushy tail curled over the back. Some are black, others white, but the handsomest variety is a grey-fawn colour. Another sign of having entered northern latitudes met us in the appearance of snow-shoes, and occasionally our "yems'-chiks" would run on them at the sides of the sledge for a mile or more together.

We had very little opportunity of seeing the birds of the district, as our road was almost always on the river. Sparrows and Magpies disappeared before we reached the Kah'-min Pass. At most stations Carrion Crows and Snow-Buntings were seen, and now and then a Raven flew over our heads. We were often offered Willow Grouse, Capercailzie and Hazel Grouse, but we very seldom saw these birds alive. Seven hundred versts north of Yen-e-saisk' the Nutcracker appeared. At most stations one or two of these birds were silently flitting round the houses, feeding under the windows amongst the Crows, perching on the roof or on the top of a pole, and if disturbed, silently flying, almost like an owl, to the nearest spruce, where they sat conspicuously perched on a flat branch, and allowed themselves to be approached within easy shot. I secured eight of them without difficulty. In the summer this river must be a paradise for House-Martins. At every station the eves of the houses were crowded with their nests, sometimes in rows of three or four deep. Two hundred versts south of Toor-o-kansk' I bought the skin of a Bittern* which had been shot during the previous summer. The only four-footed wild animal we saw was a red fox.

Thirty versts from Toor-o-kansk' we stopped to inspect a monastery. Two hundred and fifty years ago the ancient town of Man-ga-zay', at the head of the gulf of the Taz, was

---

* The Bittern (*Botaurus stellaris*) was formerly a common bird in the fen districts of the British Islands, where it was a resident. It is still occasionally found, but only as a rare straggler, in most counties of the three kingdoms, including the Hebrides. It has not been recorded from Norway, but in Sweden, Finland, and North Russia, it is a summer visitor. In Central and Southern Europe, throughout Africa down to the Cape, and in the Azores and the Canary Islands, it still breeds in suitable localities, migrating southwards in winter from districts where the cold is excessive. It is found throughout Asia as far south as Scinde, Central India, China, and Japan. In the Ural Mountains, it is said to have been found as far north as lat. 57°, and I found it in the valley of the Yen-e-say' as far north as lat. 64°. On the American continent it is represented by a nearly allied species, *B. lentiginosus*.

destroyed by the cossacks. An attempt was made to remove the annual fair which used to be held at Man-ga-zay' a degree or two to the east. The village now known as Toor-o-kansk' was founded under the name of No-vah'-ya Man-ga-zay'. The relics of the patron saint of the monastery at Man-ga-zay' were mostly destroyed by fire. The monastery was rebuilt a little to the south of the New Man-ga-zay' opposite the junction of the Nizh'-ni Tun-goosk' with the Yen-e-say'. Here such of the relics of St. Vas-seel'-ye as survived the fire were removed, and in due time inspected by us. They consist of an iron belt with iron shoulder-straps called a Ti'-kon, and a heavy iron cross, which it is said he wore as a penance. In a small building outside the church is a cast-iron slab covered with Slavonic inscriptions, which is said to be the saint's tombstone. Such is the story, at least, which the Bishop told us through the medium of my thick-headed interpreter. At the station where we changed horses, close by the monastery, we were shown some samples of graphite, which was said to come from the Nizhni Tun-goosk' river, and appeared to be of excellent quality.

When Captain Wiggins came through Toor-o-kansk' the previous autumn, he had the misfortune to pick up as a travelling companion an adventurer of the name of Schwanenberg, a Courlander who spoke German and English. This man was in the service of Sideroff, a merchant of considerable notoriety in St. Petersburg, and well known throughout the length and breadth of Siberia as more unprincipled than Russian merchants usually are. Schwanenberg's great object was to secure a monopoly of the trade by sea between Europe and Siberia to Sideroff, and so to twist every little success of Captain Wiggins that it might redound to the honour and glory of Sideroff. The consequence was that he caused Captain Wiggins to commit a grave indiscretion. The cargo of odds and ends and rubbish which Captain Wiggins had picked up in Sunderland was landed from the *Thames* packed on sledges, and the caravan, headed by Schwanenberg, commenced a triumphal march up country. Unfortunately, Captain Wiggins fell into the trap, and made matters ten times worse by hoisting the Union-Jack. The Sessedatel of Toor-o-kansk' was naturally astounded at such extraordinary proceedings, and from excess of zeal impounded the goods and refused horses to the travellers. After a desperate quarrel, nearly ending in bloodshed, in which the Blagachina and the Postmaster conspired against the Sessedatel, the travellers proceeded to Yen-e-saisk', leaving the goods behind them. The Sessedatel had other enemies. Two of the principal merchants of the Lower Yen-e-say', who shall be nameless—I call them the arch-robbers of the Yen-e-say'—joined the conspiracy. The Sessedatel was too honest; he would not accept the bribes which these worthies pressed upon him in order to blind his eyes to their nefarious and illegal practices. The upshot of it all was, that when Captain Wiggins and Schwanenberg passed through Kras-no-yarsk' they were able to bring so much pressure to bear upon the good-natured Governor that the Sessedatel of Toor-o-kansk' was removed from his office, and when we arrived at this Ultima Thule we found that a new Sessedatel reigned in his place. This gentleman had received orders from head-quarters to assist Captain Wiggins to the utmost of his power, and had also been advised of my intended visit. The cossack who escorted us for the last two hundred versts had strict orders to bring us to the Sessedatel's house, and we were immediately installed as his guests. He placed his dining-room at our disposal, and we occupied the two sofas in it at night. We tried hard to avoid trespassing upon his hospitality, but he would take no refusal.

Toor-o-kansk' is a very poor place, built on an island. It may possibly consist of forty to fifty houses. Most of these are old, and the whole place bears an aspect of poverty. We met no one who could speak English, French, or German, and we probably saw most of the inhabitants. The Sessedatel gave back to Captain Wiggins possession of his goods, and placed at his disposal an empty house, where the Captain displayed them, and kept open shop for a couple of days. Glinski and I helped him, to the best of our ability, to measure ribbons, printed calicoes, and silks ; and though more people came to see the goods than to buy, we nevertheless all had to work hard. Captain Wiggins was, I am sure, heartily sick of his job, and many times, I have no doubt, devoutly wished his wares were in Kamtchatka. They were mostly consignments from Sunderland shopkeepers, which the Captain, in a rash moment, induced these tradesmen to intrust to his care. Most of the goods were utterly unsuited to the market, and many of them seemed to me to be prized at more than double their value in England. In spite of that, we sold some hundred roubles worth at prices leaving a profit of 10 to 50 per cent.

Among the people who came to inspect the goods was a smooth-chinned, pale-faced man, who, we found on inquiry, was one of the Scopsee, a strange sect of fanatics, who have made themselves impotent " for the kingdom of heaven's sake." They live in a village sixteen versts from Toor-o-kansk', in four houses, and are now reduced to ten men and five women. They were exiled to this remote district as a punishment for having performed their criminal religious rite. Most of them come from the Perm government. They occupy themselves in agriculture, and in curing a small species of fish like a herring, which they export in casks of their own manufacture.

We saw very few birds in Toor-o-kansk'; two or three pairs of Carrion Crows seemed to be the only winter residents. I saw no other birds except a flock of Snow-Buntings, which, we were informed, had not long arrived. House-Martins come in summer, as their nests bore ample evidence. We were told that these birds arrive in Toor-o-kansk' during the last week in May, old style; that is, the first week in June of our style.

We left Toor-o-kansk' at five o'clock on the afternoon of Sunday the 22nd of April. We were not sorry to escape from the clutches of our host. A man with such a faculty for annexing adjacent property I never met with before. He was interesting as a type of the old-fashioned Russian official, ill-paid, and sent by the Government to an out-of-the-way place to pay himself; a wretched system, said to be now abolished in all civilised communities except in the British Post-Office. We must, however, do the latter institution the justice to observe that its ill-paid officials are not allowed to plunder, but are only permitted to beg. This seemed also to be the system adopted by the Sessedatel of Toor-o-kansk', and a more shameless beggar never asked alms. Old von Gazenkampf—for this was his name—might have been sixty-five years of age. He had imposed himself and his cossack servant on a well-to-do widow, who boarded and lodged the pair gratis, but sorely against her will. She dared not refuse them anything, and was afraid to ask for payment. I asked our host to choose a knife or two out of the stock I brought with me for presents; he immediately took six of the best I had, and the day following asked me for a couple more to send to a friend of his in Omsk. He offered me a pair of embroidered boots for six roubles. I accepted the offer. He then said that he had made a mistake, and that he could not sell them because he had promised to send them to his friend in Omsk. Half-an-hour afterwards he offered me the same pair for twelve roubles; I gave him the money, and packed them up, for fear his friend in Omsk should turn up again, and I might have to buy them the next day for twenty roubles. From Captain Wiggins he begged all sorts of things, annexed many more without asking, and finally begged again and again for his friend in Omsk. It was very amusing, and—very expensive; otherwise the old buffer was as jolly as possible, talked and laughed and made himself and us at home, gave us the best he (or rather the poor widow) had, and kissed us most affectionately at parting.

The Blagachina was a tall, comparatively young man, with long flowing hair parted in the middle. He was a widower. So far as we could see, he appeared to be a true man, anxious to do all the good that lay in his power, and to give us every information possible. He was very kind and generous to us, and invited us several times to his house; he had, however, the too common Russian failing of being fonder of vodka than was consistent with due sobriety.

The second priest was a teetotaler, a small, keen-eyed man, with an excellent wife and a row of charming children. He had a turning-lathe in his house, and was skilful in making cups, boxes, &c., out of cedar and mammoth ivory. He had been amongst the Ost'-yaks of the Tazz, and had visited the ruins of the ancient town of Mangazay. He was something of an ethnologist and archæologist, and made very fair pencil sketches. I rather liked him; but Captain Wiggins thought him something of a Jesuit, poking his nose into everything, ubiquitous, and taking upon himself to answer every question, no matter to whom addressed. He had taken the side of the deposed Sessedatel in the quarrel between that gentleman and the two captains in the previous year, and so had incurred the anger of the Postmaster and the Blagachina, who nicknamed him the "Thirteenth Apostle." From what I afterwards learned, I am, however, disposed to think he was in the right. The Postmaster appeared to be a good-natured fellow, something of a sportsman, but of the heavy-brained type of Russian. The secretary of the Sessedatel was a Pole, a very intelligent man; he dined with us every day, and appeared to be hand-and-glove with Von Gazenkampf, but we heard later that he was very anxious to escape from his bondage. No wonder.

To be compelled to live in such a miserable place is exile indeed. After we had left I had a peep behind the scenes of Russian official life in Toor-o-kansk'. Captain Schwanenberg told me all the troubles he had to endure in this place the week before we arrived. As Sideroff's agent, it was part of his duty to obtain a certificate from the Sessedatel of Toor-o-kansk', testifying that this worthy official had visited the graphite mines of Sideroff on the Koo-ray'-i-ka, and satisfied himself that a definite amount of graphite had been dug from them. Without such a certificate Sideroff's monopoly to procure graphite from these mines would lapse. The Russian Government, in order to encourage the development of the mineral resources of the country, very liberally grants to the discoverer of a mine a right of private property in it; but, very justly, it requires the mine to be worked in order to maintain this right. The difficulties that Schwanenberg had to contend with were threefold. First, the mine had, in fact, been standing idle a sufficient length of time to vitiate Sideroff's claim to it. Second, it had never been visited by the Sessedatel. And third, Schwanenberg had contracted with Sideroff to take all the necessary steps to secure his rights. Old Von Gazenkampf was quite prepared to sign everything that Schwanenberg required, and a sum had been agreed upon as the price of the Sessedatel's conscience; but at the last moment the mysterious friend in Omsk had turned up, and poor Schwanenberg had to part with his watch-chain and the rings off his fingers, at which he was secretly very angry, as he assured me that Sideroff would never recoup him for these losses. The

Nihilists blame the Emperor for all this sort of plundering, but most unjustly. No Government can command honesty in its servants, unless it is supported by public opinion, and hitherto public opinion in Russia remains on the side of the successful thief. I need only point out the fate of old Gazenkampf's predecessor to show how impossible it is for an honest official to live in the present atmosphere of commercial morality in Russia. Let us hope that the valley of the Yen-e-say' is exceptionally bad in this respect. It is not at all improbable that the demoralization which usually emanates from gold-mines may be an important factor in the case. Peculation has undoubtedly been overdone in this district. The officials are gradually killing the geese that lay the golden eggs. The villages are dwindling away. Toor-o-kansk' is only the wreck of what it once was; and when one looks at the tumble-down church, and the few miserable straggling houses that nowhere else would be called a town, one wonders how Toor-o-kansk' ever came to be printed in capital letters in any map.

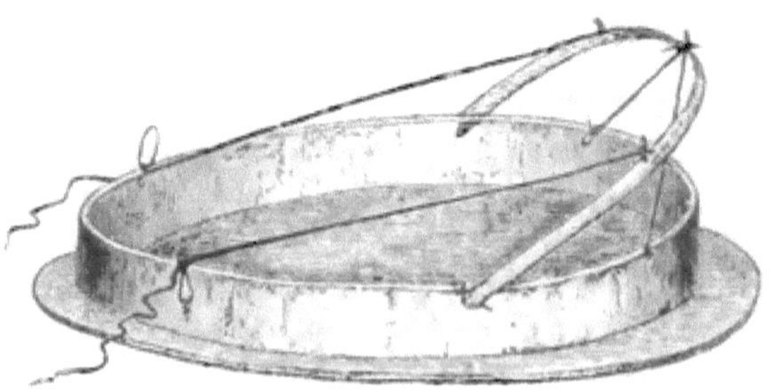

OSTYAK CRADLE.

INSIDE AN OSTYAK CHOOM.

CHAPTER V.

THE road from Toor-o-kansk' to the Koo-ray'-i-ka is very little frequented. So far to the north the traffic has dwindled down to almost nothing. Consequently the snow never gets trodden down hard, and sledging in heavy *sankas* is impossible. We were therefore obliged once more to abandon our sledges, and to have still lighter ones. As there were only four stages we decided to hire them from stage to stage, and repack our baggage into fresh sledges at each station. We had the remains of the Captain's merchandise to take with us, so we required six sledges, each drawn by one horse. The first stage was on land, wearisomely long, with bad roads and worse horses. The second stage was on the river, a much better road, but in consequence of bad horses very slow. The baggage was packed as before, on three one-horse sledges. To each of our three sledges, containing also a fair share of baggage, were harnessed six dogs. They went splendidly, never seemed tired, and never shirked their work. The pace was not rapid, but at the next stage we had to wait an hour for the horses with the baggage. The harness was simple in the extreme; consisting merely of a padded belt across the small of the back, and passing underneath between the hind legs.

The two last stages were travelled with reindeer. We had six sledges, as before, for ourselves and the baggage, and four sledges for our drivers. Each sledge was drawn by a pair of reindeer, so that we required twenty reindeer to horse our caravan. This was by far our fastest mode of travelling. Sometimes the animals seemed to fly over the snow. During the last stage the reindeer that drew my sledge galloped the whole way without a pause. The journey from Toor-o-kansk' to the Koo-ray'-i-ka is 130 versts, and occupied about twenty-two hours.

We reached the winter quarters of the *Thames* on Monday the 23rd of April at three o'clock in the afternoon—delighted once more to be amongst English voices and English cooking. We had sledged from Nishni Novgorod to the

Koo-ray'-i-ka, a distance of 4860 versts; or 3240 English miles. Including stoppages we had been forty-six days on the road, during which we had made use of about a thousand horses, eighteen dogs, and forty reindeer. The total number of stages was 229. My share of the expenses from London was 87*l.*, exclusive of skins, photographs, &c.; purchased—an average of about $3\frac{3}{4}d$. per mile, including everything.

The Yen-e-say' is said to be the third largest river in the world. In Yen-e-saisk' the inhabitants claim that the waters of their river have flowed at least two thousand miles (through Lake By-kal') to their town. In Yen-e-saisk' the river must be more than a mile wide. From Yen-e-saisk' to the Koo-ray'-i-ka is about eight hundred miles. During this distance it has gradually increased to a little more than three miles wide. From the Koo-ray'-i-ka to the limit of forest growth; where the delta may be said to begin, is generally reckoned another eight hundred miles, for which distance the river will average at least four miles in width. To this we must add a couple of hundred miles of delta and another couple of hundred miles of lagoon, each of which will average twenty miles in width, if not more.

On reaching the ship we found the crew well and hearty. The men had been amply provided with limejuice, had always some dried vegetables given them to put into their soup, and the captain had left strict orders with the mate that exercise should be taken every day, and that during the winter trees should be felled and cut into firewood ready for use on board the steamer on her voyage home. The consequence of these sanitary precautions was, that no symptoms

of scurvy had presented themselves. On the other hand,
we afterwards learned that the crew of Sideroff's schooner,
which had wintered four degrees further north, not having
been supplied by Captain Schwanenberg with these well-
known preventives, had suffered so severely from scurvy
that the mate alone survived the winter.

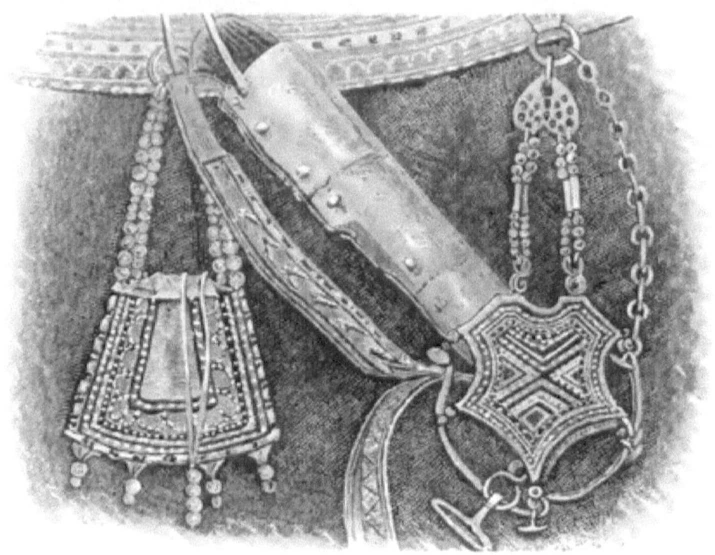

DOLGAHN BELT AND TRAPPINGS.

Our winter quarters were very picturesque. The *Thames*
was moored close to the north shore of the Koo-ray'-i-ka, at
the entrance of a small gully, into which it was the captain's
intention to take his ship as soon as the water rose high
enough to admit of his doing so, and where he hoped to
wait in safety the passing away of the ice. On one side of
the ship was the steep bank of the river, about a hundred
feet in height, covered with snow, except here and there

where it was too perpendicular for the snow to lie. On the top of the bank was the house of a Russian peasant-merchant, with stores and farm buildings adjacent, and a bath house occupied by an old man who earned a living by making casks. One of the rooms in the house was occupied by the crew of the *Thames* during the winter. As we stood at the door of this house on the brow of the hill, we looked down on to the "crow's nest" of the *Thames*. To the left the Koo-ray'-i-ka, a mile wide, stretched away some four or five miles, until a sudden bend concealed it from view, whilst to the right the eye wandered across the snow-fields of the Yen-e-say', and by the help of a binocular the little village of Koo-ray'-i-ka might be discerned about four miles off on the opposite bank of the great river. The land was undulating rather than hilly, and everywhere covered with forests, the trees reaching frequently two, and in some rare instances three, feet in diameter.

Not long after our arrival I purchased a pair of snow-shoes, unpacked my gun, and had a round in the forest. The sun was hot, but the wind was cold. On the river the depth of the snow was six feet, but in the forest I found it rather less. The trees were principally pine, fir, larch and birch. I found more birds than I expected. A pair of what I took to be Ravens were generally in sight, and now and then a small flock of Snow-Buntings flitted by. Outside the door of the sailors' room, picking amongst the refuse thrown out by the cook, were half-a-dozen almost tame Nutcrackers* hopping about. They allowed us to go within

* The range of the Nutcracker (*Nucifraga caryocatactes*) extends from

three feet of them, and sometimes they even permitted us to touch them with a stick. They seemed to be quite silent, never uttering a sound, and their feathers were so fluffy that their flight was almost as noiseless as that of an owl. I saw one or two of these birds as I entered the wood, but none afterwards. The Lapp-Tit was very common and very tame. I saw one black-and-white Woodpecker, but did not get a shot at him. Some Willow-Grouse flew over my head out of shot, and I saw many Pine Grosbeaks. I thought I heard a Jay scream, but could not get a sight of the bird.

The following day I had a long round on snow shoes through the forest in the morning, and another nearly as long in the afternoon. The sun was burning hot, but a cold north wind was still blowing, and it was freezing hard in the shade. I then discovered that the Nutcracker was by no means the silent bird he appeared to be when close to the houses. I got amongst

the Atlantic to the Pacific. In Norway it has not been recorded north of lat. 64°. Harvie Brown and I did not find it in the Petchora, but Hoffmansegg found it in lat. 62°, near the sonrces of that river. In the valley of the Yenesay I found it between lat. 64° and lat. 67°. In Europe it breeds in the pine forests of South Norway and Sweden, and is said to breed in the mountains of Southern Spain and Sardinia. It certainly breeds in the Alps and the Carpathians, and in winter is a more or less irregular and accidental visitor to the rest of Europe (with the exception of Turkey and South Russia), including the British Islands, occasionally appearing in some parts of the continent in very large flocks. It probably breeds in all the mountains of Central Asia, from North-eastern Turkestan to the Amoor, occasionally wandering in winter to Japan and North China. In Cashmere it is represented by a very nearly allied species, *N. multipunctata*, differing only in being of considerably larger size, and in having the white on each feather much more largely developed and the brown much darker. To the south-east, in the Himalayas, where the climate is more tropical and the rainfall excessive, it is replaced by *N. hemispila*, as large a bird as the preceding; but the change in the plumage has been exactly in the opposite direction—the brown parts are browner, and the white on the feathers less developed.

quite a colony of them in the forest. At one time there were eight in one tree. At another time they flew from tree to tree, screaming at each other. They have two distinct notes, both harsh enough. One, probably the call note, is a little prolonged and slightly plaintive. The other is louder and more energetic—an alarmed or angry tone. This is probably the alarm note, and is the one which on the previous day I mistook for the scream of a Jay. It is almost as grating to the ear as the note of a Corncrake. I found the Pine Grosbeak as common as they had been the day before, and shot males both in the red and yellow plumage. I was also fortunate enough to get a shot at one of the pair of birds which the sailors called Ravens, and which they assured me had wintered at the Koo-ray'-i-ka. I was surprised to find him so small a bird, and I am now convinced that he was only a large Carrion Crow. His croak was certainly that of a Crow and not that of a Raven.

I continued to make excursions in the forest every day with greater or less success. After all, the forest was nearly denuded of birds. I sometimes trudged along on my snowshoes for an hour or more without seeing one. Then all at once I would come upon quite a small family of them. The few birds there were seemed to be gregarious. Pine Grosbeaks and Lapp-Tits were generally together, perhaps three or four of each. On the 27th I succeeded in securing the Woodpecker, and found him to be, as I expected, the Three-toed Woodpecker. On the banks of the river small flocks of Snow-Buntings occasionally passed, and the Nutcrackers continued as common as ever. The latter birds were remarkably sociable, three or four usually congregating together about different parts of the ship, and apparently watching with interest the operations of our sailors, who, assisted by some Russian peasants, were busy cutting away the ice all round the vessel. The river was frozen solid to the bottom where the *Thames* was moored, and the captain was afraid that when the water rose she would remain attached to the bed, and be swamped instead of rising with the water. This was no imaginary danger, for I remember a case in point which happened in the Petchora. The ship I refer to did certainly float when the water rose, but she left her keel ice-bound to the bottom of the river. The *Thames* was frozen very fast indeed. The last couple of feet was frozen mud, as solid as a rock, and the men found it hard and tedious work chipping away this icy mass with their pickaxes.

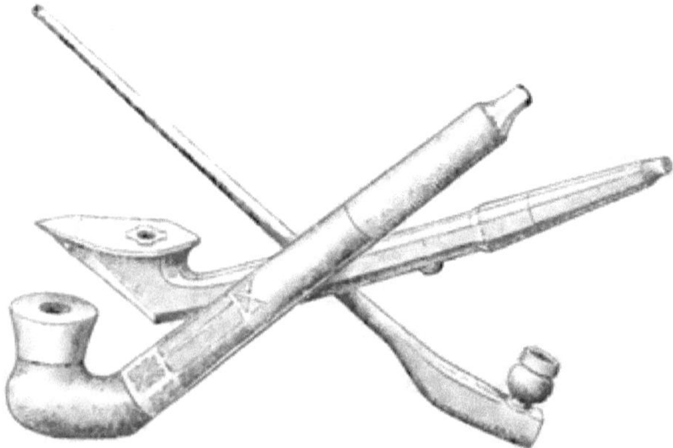

SAMOYADE PIPE OF MAMMOTH IVORY.—OSTYAK PIPE OF WOOD INLAID WITH
LEAD.—TUNGOOSK PIPE OF WROUGHT IRON.

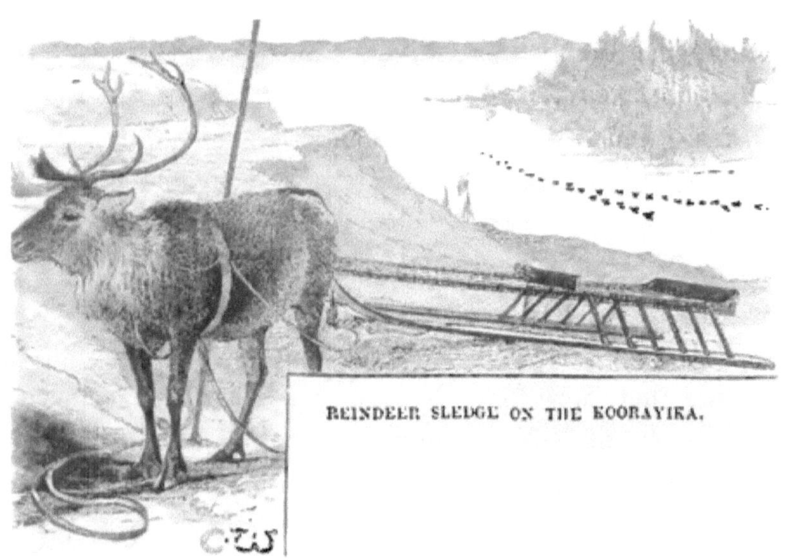

REINDEER SLEDGE ON THE KOORAYIKA.

CHAPTER VI.

The Ostyaks of the Yenesay—An Ostyak baby—A new bird—Visit from the
Blagachina and the Postmaster—Black-Cocks in the forest—The Capercailzie—
Wary crows—Stacks of firewood—Result of a week's shooting.

WHILST we were waiting patiently for summer to return I
was much interested in observing the natives of these
northern climes. Every day our house was visited by Ost'-
yaks who came with Squirrel Ermine and Fox skins, to
barter for meal or black bread from the Russian peasant
merchant. These Ost'-yaks must not be confounded with
the Ost'-yaks of the Obb. The latter are a Finnish race
allied to the Voh-gools' of the Urals, the Zyr-ri-ah'-ni of
the Izhma, and the Kvains of Lappland. The Ost'-yaks of
the Yen-e-say', on the other hand, are allied to the Sam'-o-

yades. At least this was the opinion I formed, as the result of my inquiries into their language. There were several Ost'-yak chooms at a short distance from our winter quarters. These chooms, or tents, were exactly like the summer tents of the Petchora Samoyades, covered with birch bark; their sledges also were of precisely the same construction as those of their North European relations. Judging from their clothes they must have been very poor. Their reindeer were large, and looked healthy. On one occasion one of the women brought a baby, a queer little thing, with black eyes and black hair. The cradle was a wooden box about three inches deep, with rounded ends, almost the shape of the child. The bottom of the box was oval, and projected an inch beyond the box at either side, and three or four inches at each end. A quantity of sawdust lay at the bottom of the box, which was covered with a piece of flannel over the child's legs, and a hare's skin with the fur on over the body. The baby was placed in the box, having on nothing but a short cotton shirt. The flannel was carefully wrapped over its feet and lashed securely, from two places on each side, to a brass ring over its knees. The arms were placed close to the body, and wrapped up with it in the hare's skin, which was secured as before to a brass ring over the breast. Half a hoop of wood, the two ends of which were loosely fastened to the sides of the box, was raised so as to be at an angle of 45° with the bottom of the box; it was kept in that position by lashings from the top and bottom; when a handkerchief was thrown over this it formed a hood over the child's head. The little one cried as the complicated operation of being put to bed was performed, but as soon as it was finished the Ost'-yak woman sat down upon the floor, took the box upon her knee, and quieted the child by giving it the breast.

On the 28th I added a new bird to my list. I had walked an hour in the forest without seeing a feather. I then all at once dropt upon a little party of Tits, in company, as usual, with some Pine Grosbeaks. I shot at what I thought was the handsomest Tit, and had the pleasure of picking up a Nuthatch.* Half-an-hour afterwards I came upon the same or another party. I watched each bird very closely, and soon found there was a Nuthatch among them. The note was different from that of the Tits, a sort of *zt*, something like the note of our Tree-Creeper, and an occasional *whil*, or very liquid *whit*. The two birds proved to be male and female. On the same excursion I heard a Redpole or two, the first trace of these birds I had seen since leaving Yen-e-saisk'. I also saw a flock of Snow-Buntings, and shot a second Three-toed Woodpecker.

The same evening the Blagachina and the Postmaster came to visit Captain Wiggins. They had sledged over from Toor-o-kansk'. I had hoped, with the assistance of Glinski as interpreter, to get some interesting information from

---

* The Siberian Nuthatch, *Sitta uralensis*, is found across Northern Siberia, from the Urals to the Pacific and in the north island of Japan. A Nuthatch nearly allied to the present species, *S. amurensis*, is found in the valley of the Amoor, the island of Askold near Vladivostok, and in the central island of Japan, apparently connecting it with the Chinese species, *S. sinensis*. To the westwards from the Urals, in North Russia, Denmark, and Scandinavia, *S. europæa* occurs, distinguished by its more chestnut flanks.

these gentlemen, but they seemed to have found it necessary to fortify themselves against the cold during the journey, and when the sledge arrived the Blagachina was so fast asleep that we had the greatest difficulty in waking him. He slept most of the following day, apparently waking just to eat and refresh himself with the vodka of the Russian merchant; so we saw little or nothing of our visitors, and got no information from them.

On Sunday the wind shifted from north-east to north-west, but produced no change in the weather. The sun was burning hot all day, and on any steep bank exposed to its rays it made a slight impression, but not a drop of water survived the night's frost, and to all intents and purposes we were still in mid-winter. We used occasionally to see a cloud in the evenings, but generally the sky was brilliantly clear. As I could make nothing out of our guests, I left them to drink and sleep, and turned into the forest. To my surprise, I found quite a covey of Black-Cock on the top of the hill, but I was in very bad shooting order, and missed every shot until I came suddenly upon a bird sitting on the thick branch of a pine. It fell down with a crash on the snow, and I found that I had secured a hen Capercailzie. Her crop was full of the small needle-like leaves of a species of fir, allied to our Scotch Fir, which the Russians call the Cedar.

Early on the following morning our visitors left, and Captain Wiggins and I hired a sledge, and drove across the Yen-e-say' to the village of Koo-ray'-i-ka. Before we started I noticed that a fresh pair of Carrion Crows had arrived, and as soon as we reached the village we saw three or four more feeding on the green **in the centre, which** at that time of the year was a large manure yard, with **here and there** some dirty snow visible. One of **these crows** seemed **to be** nearly, if not quite, a thoroughbred Hoodie. Two of them were about half and half, and one was **black** with a grey ring round its neck. They evidently knew that we were strangers, and retired into the forests **as** soon as we arrived: one of the Russian peasants, of whom they seem to have no fear however, promised to get me some in a day or two. **In** the woods **which** were close to the village the trees **were** small, principally birch. All the large cedars and pines had been cut down to build the village with, **and** to furnish an annual supply of firewood **for** the steamers which during **the** short summer ply between Yen-e-saisk' and Gol-check'-a. Quite a mountain of this firewood was stacked on the edge of the cliff, representing **the** winter's work of the villagers. There were hardly any small birds in the forest, the only ones I saw being a pair of Lapp-Tits. Black game was however abundant. **In one** tree I counted six Black-Cocks, whilst six more were **in** trees close by. **A** good rifle shot might have made a large bag. I got **at** least five shots at 70 to 90 yards, but with a 20-bore gun missed them all. The villagers were very hospitable, inviting us into their houses and offering us tea **and milk. In the afternoon** I had a stroll in the forest, on the other side of the Koo-ray-i-ka. The sun was burning hot, but whenever I exposed myself to the wind, it was icy cold. I bagged a pair **of** Lapp-Tits, a brace of Pine Grosbeaks, and a couple of Nuthatches.

We had now been a week at our winter quarters, and were

hoping that the advent of May would bring us warmer weather and more birds. My tale of skins had only reached 40, and many of these were Snow-Buntings, which I shot merely to keep Glinski in practice. My list of birds identified within the Arctic Circle had only reached 12, and I was beginning to be impatient of the slow progress.

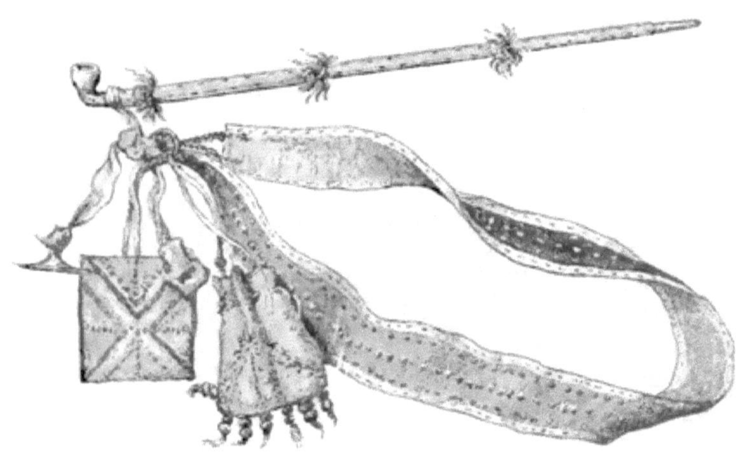

TUNGOOSE PIPE AND BELT.

WINTER QUARTERS OF THE " THAMES."

CHAPTER VII.

ON the 1st of May a long round in the forest, with a cool wind and a burning hot sun, did not result in much more than so many hours' practice on snow-shoes. In one clump of spruce fir I got a couple of Pine Grosbeaks and a pair of Lapp-Tits. In another I shot a Three-toed Woodpecker and Nuthatch, letting the Tits go by. I picked up an odd

Tit afterwards, saw another Pine Grosbeak, and a few Black game, which completes the list of all the birds I saw in six hours. Every excursion I made impressed upon me the two facts, of the scarcity of birds, and the gregariousness of the few there were.

The sun was as brilliant and warm on the following day as ever, but the wind was higher, a nor-wester, cold as ice. I shot a Nuthatch and a Woodpecker in the morning, but stayed at home in the afternoon, finding an excellent excuse in the arrival of a party of Ost'-yaks from a distance, whose reindeer looked very picturesque picketed on the snow round the house. From one of these poor fellows I bought a bow and some arrows, and from another a pair of snow spectacles. The latter are a great curiosity. The frame is made of reindeer skin with the hair left on, and the spectacles are tied on behind the head with thongs of reindeer skin without hair. The eye-pieces are roughly the shape of the eye, sewn into the skin. The poor Ost'-yak who had made these was apparently unable to procure metal enough of one kind to furnish both eye-pieces, so one was made of sheet-iron and the other of copper. A narrow horizontal slit leaves the eye well protected from the glare of the hot sun on the white snow, and yet allows a much wider range of vision than one would expect.

I found it very difficult to get any accurate information about the dress and habits of the various races inhabiting these parts. There are so many races, they are so mixed together, and with the Russians; and my "muddle-headed Hebrew" being such a poor interpreter, I was almost ready to despair of getting at the exact truth. So far as I was able to ascertain, the Ost'-yak dress is a short jacket of reindeer skin, more or less ornamented, long reindeer skin boots coming up to the thighs, a "gore" shaped head-dress tying under the chin at the two points, and edged with foxes' tails, one going over the brow and the other round the neck. In winter the jacket is made of skins with the hair outside, generally lined with skins, the hair of which is next the body; and in severe weather an overcoat is worn, made of similar material, shaped like a dressing-gown. In summer similar dresses are worn made of reindeer leather, stained or dyed in fanciful patterns. I am of opinion that the Ost'-yaks of the Yen-e-say' are a race of Sam'-o-yades, who migrated southwards into the forest region, and adapted the national dress to a more southerly climate, borrowing more or less the costume of the Tun-goosk's. They seem to be very poor. Living, as they do, principally on the banks of the mighty river, fishing in the summer-time and hunting in the winter, they come far too much into contact with the Russians, who, with the aid of their cursed vodka, plunder them to almost any extent.

On the 3rd of May Captain Schwanenberg left us on a wild-goose chase up the Koo-ray'-i-ka in search of graphite. He and eight men went up the river for about a hundred versts. He chartered a party of Ost'-yaks, who engaged to take him, his men, and his baggage, including a pump and a sledge-load of spades, pickaxes, &c., at the rate of 30 kopeks per pood. His destination was a waterfall in a part of the river which is very narrow, and where the banks are perpendicular rocks of graphite. A quantity of this graphite was brought down to the winter quarters of the *Thames* the previous autumn. Capt. Wiggins took a sample with him to London, which was unfavourably reported upon; so Sideroff, who has the concession for these mines, instructed Schwanenberg to dig deep into the ground and try and find graphite of a better quality. Of course the expedition turned out a disastrous failure, as will hereafter appear.

The Ost'-yaks seem to reverse St. Paul's recommendation to women to have the hair covered. In summer the men wear no head-dress out of doors. In the house the women wear nothing on the head, but the men tie a handkerchief round the brow, and when I asked the reason of this custom, I was told that a man must not expose his hair.

In the afternoon I had a long round on snow-shoes, but saw only half-a-dozen birds. Four of them were Pine Grosbeaks; I was chasing the fourth when I saw a large bird stretch its neck out from a well-leaved branch of a pine-tree, and immediately draw it in again. I could not see anything, but I fired at the foliage, and down tumbled a Hazel-Grouse. Shortly afterwards I caught a momentary glimpse of a bird alighting in a distant pine. I carefully stalked it, but although my snow-shoes made noise enough on the frozen crust of the snow, as soon as I doubled in full view of the tree, the bird remained standing on a conspicuous branch within easy shot. The birds turned out to be male and female. These were the first Hazel-Grouse I had seen. I saw a solitary Nutcracker in the forest. These were the only birds I saw during a ramble of four hours.

except close to the house where a flock of Snow-Buntings, half a-dozen Nutcrackers, and a pair of Crows were constantly to be seen. In the evening I bought a coat of a Tun-goosk'. He could not speak Russian, but he tried to make me understand that he was Tun-goosk' and not Ost'-yak by showing me his hair. It was brushed back and tied in a knot in the neck like an incipient pigtail. He gave me to understand that the Ost'-yaks wore their hair loose and tumbling over the forehead.

On the 4th of May the weather still showed no sign of change. A burning hot sun was trying to thaw the snow. An icy cold nor-wester was freezing it again directly. I shirked the cold morning, and got one of the sailors to take me in the dog-sledge a couple of miles up the Koo-ray'-i-ka in the afternoon. We were about three hours in the forest. My bag was one Hazel-Grouse, four Pine Grosbeaks, three Lapp-Tits and one Mealy-Redpole. The latter was the first of this species which I had shot since leaving Yen-e-saisk'. In the evening the man whom I had commissioned to shoot Crows for me came from his village without any. I asked him why he had neglected my orders. He told me that it was unlucky to shoot a Crow, that a gun which had once shot a Crow would never shoot any other bird afterwards; and he assured me that he had once shot a Crow, and had been obliged to throw his gun away. So much for the intelligence of the Russian peasant.

The next morning I walked across the Yen-e-say' to the village where the Crows were, but I could not get a shot at them, they were so wary. I found the peasant had shot me a

couple of Striped Squirrels * and a brace of Black-Grouse, but
no Crows. I had a round in the forest, but came home with
an empty bag. The wind was as cold as ever, but when I
got back to the ship, however, I heard that a Swan had been
seen flying over it, so we began to look forward a little more
hopefully to the possibilities of approaching spring.

One of the peculiarities of this part of the country is
that it is a land of dear glass. You rarely see a window
with square panes. In the houses of some of the poorer
peasants it is not an uncommon thing to find one entirely
composed of broken pieces of glass of all sizes and
shapes, fitted together like a puzzle, and carefully sewn into
a framework of birch bark which has been elaborately cut
to fit each piece. Sometimes glass is dispensed with altogether, and pieces of semi-transparent fish-skin are stitched
together and stretched across the window-frame. In winter
double windows are absolutely necessary to prevent the
inmates of the houses from being frozen to death. The outside windows project about six inches in front of the inside
ones. If the inside window reveals the poverty of the
inhabitants, the outside window seemingly displays his
extravagance. To all appearances it is composed of one solid
pane of plate-glass nearly three inches thick. On closer
examination this extravagant sheet of plate-glass turns out to

---

* The Striped Squirrel (*Tamias
asiaticus*) is common to both continents.
In America it is called the Chipmunk.
A very near ally (*Tamias lysteri*) is
also found on the latter continent, but
this species has a somewhat more
southerly range, being found as far
south as Mexico. The former species
is arctic or subarctic in its range, and
has never been found so far south as
the British Islands.

be a slab of ice carefully frozen into the framework, with a mixture of snow and water in place of putty.

On Sunday, the 6th of May, I had a short stroll, if walking on snow-shoes can be called strolling, in the forest, but I shot nothing except a Black-Cock. In the afternoon I draughted out all the notes I had dotted down about the geographical distribution of the native tribes in these parts. Most of this information I obtained from my most intelligent friend the second priest of 'Toor-o-kansk', whom Captain Wiggins and his friends nicknamed the " Thirteenth Apostle."

The most northerly race are the Sam'-o-yades. They extend from the Kah'-nin peninsula in Europe to the North-East cape in Asia. They occupy a strip of land extending from the coast southwards for about three hundred miles, exceeding that distance at the gulf of the Obb and the Tazz, the whole of the shores of which they frequent.

The Yu-raks are a small race nearly allied to the Sam'-o-yades. They occupy the district between the east shore of the gulf of the Tazz and the Yen-e-say' from the Arctic Circle to about 70° North lat.

The Ost'-yaks are a much larger race, not so nearly allied to the Sam'-o-yades as the Yu-raks are. They are distributed immediately south of the Yu-raks from the Arctic Circle to nearly as far south as the Kah'-min pass.

The Dol-gahn' territory is bounded on the north by the Sam'-o-yade land about 70°-North lat., on the south by the Arctic Circle, on the west by the Yen-e-say', from which river it extends eastwards three or four hundred miles. These people belong to an entirely different race, and are very nearly allied to the Tartars.

The Yah-kuts' occupy the district watered by the Kat'-an-gar' river from 70° to about 73° North lat. They are near allies of the Dol-gahn' and Tartar races.

The Tun-goosk's occupy the districts on the east bank of the Yen-e-say', drained by the two great rivers, the Nish'-ni Tun-goosk' and Kah'-min-a Tun-goosk' as far east as the watershed of the Leh'-na. They are copper-coloured like the Dol-gahns and Yah-kuts, but their language bears no resemblance to any of the races I have mentioned.

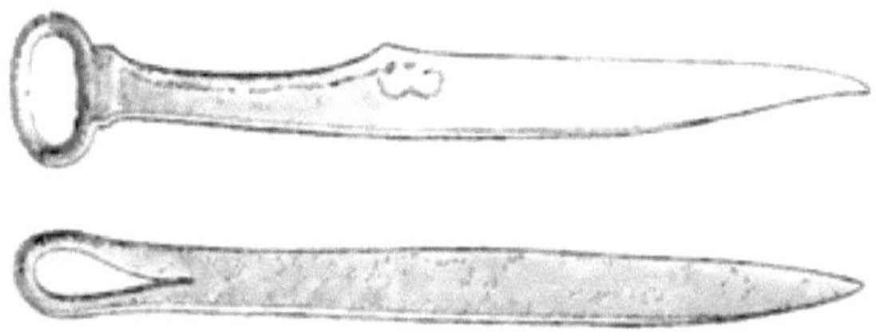

BRONZE KNIVES FROM ANCIENT GRAVE NEAR KRASNOYARSK.

OSTYAK CHOOM.

CHAPTER VIII.

Erection of an Ostyak Choom—Ornithological results of the week—An Ostyak feast—Comparison of Ostyaks and Tungoosks—Snowy Owl—Our first rain in the Arctic Circle—Further signs of approaching summer—Northern Marsh Tit—Ornithological results of the third week—White-tailed Eagle—Snowstorm —A solitary Barn Swallow—A wintry day—A Fox—The river rises—Five roubles for an Eagle—What became of the roubles—Visit from our Ostyak neighbour—A baby Fox—Our two babies—A crow's nest—The Blue-rumped Warbler.

On the 7th of May I recorded in my journal another sign of approaching summer, namely, the arrival of an Ost'-yak family, who in the course of the day erected a tent or choom on the banks of the Koo-ray'-i-ka close by the ship. The migrations of the natives in these parts are facts in natural history almost as much guided by instinct as those of birds. The Ost'-yak is a hunter. In the winter he lives in the forest and hunts birds to eat, and fur-bearing animals to provide the means of obtaining meal and tobacco from the Russian peasant merchant, and to satisfy the claims of the Russian tax-gatherer. In summer he migrates to the banks of the great river to hunt fish, in which operation he is very expert. Our new neighbour seemed very poor. He had no reindeer, and arrived with a couple of dog-sledges. His dogs were a queer mongrel lot, and seemed half-famished. He soon cut down some slender birch-trees and erected his choom, exactly on the pattern of the Petchora Sam'-o-yades. He covered it with rolls of birch bark, carefully sewn together with reindeer sinew into broad sheets, which wound diagonally round the choom. On the day of his arrival the wind was west, and for the first time since our arrival the sky was cloudy. I had a long round through the forest, but only shot a single bird, a Three-toed Woodpecker. We had then been a fortnight in our winter quarters. My second week was not a very successful one ornithologically; I certainly added another fifty skins to my plunder, but only two new species to my list.

The 8th of May was the first day on which there was any sign of thaw in the shade. What little wind there was came from the sou-west, but the air was raw and chilly. I did not go into the forest, but on the banks of the river I fired into a flock of Snow-Buntings, in order to find Glinski something to do, and killed six. Six more ran away wounded over the snow.

They were pursued and caught by the Ost'-yak children, who carried them to their father, who was chopping firewood near the choom. The Snow-Buntings were then divided amongst the party, rapidly plucked, and greedily eaten, warm, raw and bleeding! Before this was accomplished the youngest child, certainly not more than five years old, having either heard or smelt what was going on, came running out of the choom with scarcely a rag of clothes on, and howled and screamed until its share of the spoil was thrown to it.

The Ost'-yaks are a very different looking race from the Tun-goosk's. They might be mistaken for a half-breed between the Russians and Tun-goosk's. The Ost'-yaks are of sallow complexion, have high cheek-bones and flattish noses, but the Tun-goosk's are copper coloured, have still higher cheek-bones, and sometimes scarcely any bridge at all to the nose. One also occasionally sees brown hair amongst the Ost'-yaks, but this may, of course, indicate the presence of Russian blood. Although I did not turn out on my snow-shoes on that day, I nevertheless added a new bird to my list. This was a handsome Snowy Owl, almost white. It was sent me in the flesh by Mr. Numellin, the mate of Schwanenberg's schooner, who had left us a day or two previously, to sledge down to the islands where she lay moored. In a note which accompanied it he told me that he had picked it up a few stations north of our quarters. It had been caught in a fox-trap. I found on dissecting the Black-Grouse and Hazel-Grouse that they had been feeding on the buds of the birch and alder.

On the 9th of May we had the first attempt at rain since

our arrival in the Arctic Circle. The wind continued son-west, and the snow began to thaw fast. The mate also saw a Goose fly over the ship, and our hopes of the arrival of summer began to rise. I also watched a Rough-legged Buzzard majestically sailing in wide circles near us, but it took care never to come within shot. The rain continued all the following day, and became very heavy at night. A flock of six Geese flew over, and we rejoiced at the prospect of an early end to the long winter. The wind continued west during the 11th, but the rain turned to snow with intervals of sunshine. A couple of Peregrine Falcons arrived, to the discomfiture of the Snow-Buntings. In the afternoon the clouds cleared away, and we had a calm bright evening. I tried a round in the forest, but the snow was very treacherous after the rain, and I came to grief on my snow-shoes more than once. In a pine-tree not far from our quarters I found a Crow's nest containing one egg.

On the following day, when I made my usual round in the forest, I found a nor-west wind blowing, and although the sun frequently shone, it was very cold. Travelling was easy enough. There was a frozen crust on the snow, hard enough to bear my weight when distributed over a pair of snow-shoes. I met with only one party of birds, but that was a very interesting one. It consisted of a flock of about a dozen Tits, far more than I had ever before seen together. I shot five of them. To my great surprise, two of them proved to be Northern Marsh Tits. I have always looked upon the Tits generally as non-migratory birds. Some partial migration must have taken place in this instance.

Capt. Wiggins told me that when he left the Koo-ray'-i-ka in the middle of November the forest swarmed with Tits. No doubt many of these birds died during the winter, which probably kills off more birds even in temperate climates than is popularly supposed. Others may have migrated southwards. I do not think it possible that I could have overlooked the Marsh Tit thus far. It must either have then just arrived, or is extremely rare.

A five hours' ramble on Sunday with a nor-west wind, a leaden sky, and a smart frost, produced nothing but a Hazel-Grouse and a passing glimpse of a Rough-legged Buzzard. Monday the 14th of May brought our third week to a close, a perfect wintery day, with bright hot sun and hard frost. It had been a somewhat dreary week. I increased my number of skins by only twenty, but added five fresh species to the list.

On the 15th of May we had a smart breeze from the sou-east, and it was bitterly cold. There was some sunshine in the morning, but the afternoon was cloudy, and in the evening we had snow. I walked across the Yen-e-say' to the village and shot a Crow. It was all but a thoroughbred Hoodie. I bought a Capercailzie and a Willow-Grouse from one of the peasants. The latter bird was beginning to show the summer plumage, having changed the feathers of the upper part of the neck. Another bird which I added to my list was the White-tailed Eagle. It was perched on a pine on the banks of the great river. I tried to stalk it, but snow-shoes are too noisy on a frozen crust of snow for the keen ears of an eagle, and I failed. Finding that the peasant was still resolved not to ruin his own gun by shooting unlucky birds with it, I arranged with him to drive me over to the ship in the evening, and to lend him my muzzle-loader in order that with it he might shoot me some Crows. On my return to the ship I saw a couple of Peregrines and a large Owl, and heard that four Geese had been seen flying over.

During the night a considerable quantity of snow fell, and in the morning the wind was sou-west with sleet. In the afternoon we had an occasional gleam of sunshine, and in the evening the wind fell, but the sky was cloudy. The snow was very soft, but it thawed slowly. We had, nevertheless, many indications of summer. I saw at least a dozen flocks of Geese, each containing from six to twenty birds. The first harbinger of musquitoes also arrived, the first insect-eating bird, a most characteristic one, no less a novelty to us than a Barn-Swallow. Poor little bird! he must have got strangely wrong in his almanack, and curiously out of his latitude. He was the only one of his kind which I saw within five hundred miles of the Arctic Circle, and at the time of his arrival I don't think there was a solitary insect upon the wing, whatever there might have been in sheltered nooks and crannies. I dropped him on the snow as he was industriously hawking in a gleam of sunshine, a much quicker and less painful death than dying of starvation.

Sancho Panza was very right when he said that one swallow does not make a summer. I never saw more complete winter weather than we had on the day following the appearance of our adventurous little pioneer. A cold wind blew from the north, howling round the peasant's house, and in the rigging of the ship, driving the snow into the cook's passage and into the cabin. All day long fine dry snow fell, drifting into every hollow, completely shutting the great river out of view, and casting a thick haze over the nearest objects. I do not think I ever saw a more miserable day. To add to my discomfort I had a heavy cold in my head, the first attack of the kind since leaving England. I expected to have had an absolutely blank day, but late in the evening the weather cleared up with a hard frost, and the peasant across the Yen-e-say' drove up with five Crows which he had shot with the muzzle-loader I had lent him. Two of these Crows were thoroughbred Carrions, and the other three cross-breeds between that bird and the Hoodie.

The next day my cold continued very heavy, and I did not take my gun out at all; the north wind was still blowing a gale, but there was not a cloud in the sky, and it was freezing hard in the shade. In the afternoon I saw a Fox crossing the Koo-ray'-i-ka not far from the ship. The dogs caught sight of it and gave chase, but they had only recently returned from a journey and were tired, and the Fox reached the forest without their gaining upon him. The following day was another dismal one. The wind shifted south, sou-east and sou-west, and snow and sleet fell continually.

On Sunday we had again sunshine, with a north and nor-west wind, with frost in the shade. Another sign of approaching summer became now observable. The river must have risen considerably in consequence of the melting of the snow down south. The channel round the ship, which the sailors had cut out of the ice, filled with water, and we came upon water after digging down into the snow a couple of feet. There was no open water visible, but in the centre of the river we could see large discoloured patches, as if the snow there was saturated with water. On that day I was able to complete the identification of one of my previous week's new birds. After seeing the Eagle on the other side of the river, I offered five roubles to the peasants if they would shoot or trap it for me. At the next village, twenty versts down the river, a White-tailed Eagle was trapped, and a joint expedition from the two villages came over to the ship in a couple of reindeer sledges to bring me the bird and claim the promised reward. This I gladly paid them, as I was in hopes that I might in this or some other way obtain a specimen of Pallas's Sea-Eagle. On receipt of the five roubles the whole party turned into the Russian peasant merchant's store near the ship. The end of it was, that during the night the five roubles filtered out of the pockets of my elated friends, and in the morning they were all penniless and dead drunk. To add to their misfortunes, the reindeer had broken loose from their moorings in the snow, and had wandered off up the Koo-ray'-i-ka in search of food. When the peasants came to their senses during the following afternoon they started off on snow-shoes to follow the tracks, but whether they ever recovered the animals or not I never heard. No wonder that a land like Siberia, full of wealth of all sorts, remains poor for want of labour to realise its resources.

In the evening the Ost'-yak from the choom came with his son down into the cabin, apparently to pay us a visit. They sat down stolidly, and partook of some tea which we happened to have on the table. We were wondering what could be the object of their visit, whether it might not be one of ceremony, to show a neighbourly feeling, when the boy pulled out from under his fur coat a Squirrel and a Hazel-Grouse, which his father had shot during the day. After we had examined these for some time, the old man in his turn pulled out from his sleeve a live Fox, a few days old. It was sooty black, with a white tip at the end of its tail. It was still blind, but we hoped it might turn

OSTYAK COSTUME.

out to be a veritable Black Fox, so we decided to buy it and try and bring it up by hand. We rigged up an excellent bottle with the tube of my pocket filter and part of a kid-glove. We got Glinski to tell the Ost'-yak to search for and find the hole where he got the young Fox, and to lie in wait for the mother. This he did, and on the next day he came again in triumph, bringing the mother and five more young ones, exactly like the one we had. The mother was red enough, but we bought another young one to keep our other baby company. It was only by dint of great perseverance that we succeeded in bringing these two babies up with the bottle, but as soon as they began to feed themselves they grew fast. They were very quarrelsome in their play, and often would spit at each other like cats. They grew up tame and timid, but the red hairs developed themselves in due time, and our hope of being able to rear a couple of Black Foxes soon faded.

On the 21st of May I climbed up to the Crow's nest which I discovered on the 11th, and found that it contained five eggs. I had a good view of the parent birds, and ascertained that they were hybrids between the Carrion Crow and the Hoodie. The wind was sou-west, but there was no sunshine, and it froze hard. Further south, however, the thaw must have been going on apace. The river kept steadily rising. When the water first broke in upon the sailors, who were cutting away the ice from under the *Thames*, it rose to four feet on the ship's bow. On the 21st it stood at eight feet. I had a short round in the forest in the afternoon, and scarcely saw a bird. One was, however, new to me. At first I thought it was a Tit. It was flitting about from tree to tree, apparently seeking insects on the trunks below the level of the surface snow in the hollows round the stems caused by the heat of the sun absorbed by their dark surfaces. It gave me a long chase, flying rapidly, but never rising higher than three or four feet above the ground. At last I got a long shot at it. It was alive when I secured it, and I remarked its brilliant large pale blood-red eye. It was the Blue-rumped Warbler,* and made the third new species added to my list during the fourth week of our residence within the Arctic Circle. My booty was also increased by some forty skins.

---

* The Blue-rumped Warbler (*Tarsiger cyanurus*) is nearest allied to the Redstarts, though Sharpe, in his catalogue of the Birds in the British Museum, has unwisely included it in the Flycatchers. It breeds in Siberia, south of the Arctic Circle, occasionally crossing the Ural mountains into Eastern Russia, and extending westwards as far as China and Japan. In Cashmere and the Himalayas it is replaced by a very nearly-allied species, *T. rufilatus*, differing in having the upper parts of a much richer, deeper blue, and in having a white eye-stripe.

BRONZE BIT FROM ANCIENT GRAVE NEAR KRASNOYARSK.

DRIVING WITH THE ICE ON THE
KOORAYIKA.

CHAPTER IX.

THE fifth week of weary watching and waiting for a
summer, which some of the sailors began to think would
never come, commenced with a cloudy sky and an occasional

attempt at a snowstorm, the wind chopping about from sou-east to sou-west. Many Geese flew over during the day, and Hawks were more frequently seen than before; so far as I could identify them, Peregrine Falcons and Rough-legged Buzzards. Late in the evening a large brown Owl, probably the Ural Owl,* sailed up and down the banks of the Kooray'-i-ka, but it never came within shot.

On the morning of the following day the wind was west, but before evening it turned round to the north, accompanied with hard frost in the shade. My attention was called to a pair of Ravens, who seemed to have excited the jealousy of the Crows who had their nest close by. The efforts of the latter birds to drive away the new-comers were untiring. I shot the female Raven, which was a fresh bird for my list. I also picked up a dead Short-tailed Field-Mouse, nearly as large as a rat. The migration of Geese continued all day, and a further migration of Ost'-yaks took place. Before night we had three Ost'-yak chooms near the ship.

On the 24th of May a great source of anxiety was removed from our minds. When we turned into our berths the previous night the water at the ship's bow stood at eleven feet. At four o'clock in the morning we were suddenly

---

* The Ural Owl (*Syrnium uralense*) is a resident in Northern Europe below the Arctic Circle, as far west as Bohemia, and as far south as Transylvania. In Asia it extends across Siberia to Northern Japan. Like most other Owls, it has two so-called " phases of plumage." In the one the white parts are very white, and the dark parts very dark and grey. In the other both are more or less suffused with rufous. So far as this species is concerned it would seem from the examination of a fine male, which Mr. Kiolert sent me from Krasnoyarsk, that the grey phase belongs to the Arctic climate of Siberia, and the brown phase to the milder climates of Western Europe and Japan.

awoke by a convulsion like an earthquake. We started from our berths, and found that the ship had burst through the bands of ice, risen to her level, and righted herself. Her bow showed eight feet only, so she must have risen three feet. There was, however, no change at the stern, which probably remained aground.

A long round in the forest proved almost a blank; my bag being but one solitary bird, a Willow-Grouse, with traces of summer plumage on the head and neck. The sun was warm, but the wind was north, and to all intents and purposes it was still mid-winter. The succession of partial thaws and frosts had made the crust of the snow so hard that we could walk anywhere without snow-shoes. My afternoon's ramble again produced only one bird, but as this was a new one, a fine male Hen Harrier, I looked upon the day's work as a success. The Harrier had the remains of a Snow-Bunting in its stomach.

The next day was very cold, with a nor-west wind and brilliant sunshine. The river had risen so much that the ship floated both fore and aft. We could perceive that the ice in the centre of the river was gradually lifting its heavy burden of snow, the water in many places having risen to the level of its surface, causing large greyish patches, and making the snow look more or less piebald. As the river rose it gradually widened. Outside the centre snow-covered ice, a narrow belt of ever-widening thin black ice was a feature in the landscape. The migration of Geese was stopped by the cold. It had evidently been premature. Many flocks passed over during the day, but they were all flying south, having overshot their mark and flown faster than the rate at which the ice was breaking up, into a region still frost-bound, and where, consequently, no food could be obtained. Hawks became abundant, a sure sign that their prey were not far off and would very soon become so also. I shot another male Hen Harrier, and missed a shot at the female. I also saw a pair of Sparrow-Hawks and a Rough-legged Buzzard, and in the evening one of the engineers shot a male Peregrine Falcon. The female was sitting on the same tree at the time.

There was no change during the next three days. On the 26th I shot a Bean Goose, which was apparently the species of which all the flocks we had hitherto seen were composed. I found an excellent place on the bank of the main river, where I could lie concealed like a grouse-shooter behind his butts. The Geese came up at a terrific pace in parties of five or six, exactly like Grouse in a drive. They were scarcely in sight before they whizzed over my head, and out of shot again before I had time to turn round. I wasted at least a dozen cartridges before I secured a bird, which fell to the ground with a tremendous crash. I saw another male Hen Harrier and another Rough-legged Buzzard, and a small Hawk which I have little doubt was a Merlin. On the 28th, besides the flocks of Geese, flocks of Swans constantly passed over, and I added to my collection a Raven and a female Hen Harrier. At night, as we went to bed, the thermometer stood at 25° on deck. My week's work was about forty birds skinned and three new species identified. We were all weary of winter. The peasants told us that they never remembered so late a season.

On Tuesday the 29th of May we commenced our sixth week in the Arctic Circle, and a very eventful one it proved. The little wind there was was southerly, and the sun was hot, but still there was scarcely any perceptible thaw, and the river rose but very slowly. I did not see a single Hawk all day. At noon the Snow-Buntings were perched together in a birch-tree, and in the evening they disappeared. I had two long rounds in the forest—not a bird visible. I heard a Mealy-Redpole, but failed to catch a sight of the bird. We seemed to be reduced to the pair of Hybrid Crows nesting near, and the Nutcrackers, which I did not shoot because I wanted their eggs. At that time they did not appear to have the least idea of building. Their tameness was quite absurd; there was generally a pair in the rigging of the ship. About four were usually to be found close to the house, and I occasionally came upon a pair or two in the forest. A few flocks of Geese and Swans passed over during the day, now flying northwards.

On the following day it was the old story again—a clear sky and thaw in the sunshine, with a cold north wind and hard frost in the shade. The river rose three or four inches during the day, but it froze as fast as it rose. Several flocks of Geese passed over, evidently yesterday's rash birds, who had turned back and were now all going south. Half-a-dozen Snow-Buntings put in an appearance, and the Hen Harrier was twice seen.

The last day of May was warm, with a gentle breeze from the nor-west. I had a very long round in the forest, and saw a few Lapp-Tits and a Nuthatch. During the day many

Swans and Geese flew over, all going northwards again. I saw a Hen Harrier and a Sparrow-Hawk, but no Snow-Buntings. I shot a Hazel-Grouse, and saw a couple of Siberian Herring Gulls steadily migrating down the Yen-e-say'.

On the 1st of June a revolution took place in the ice. There had been scarcely any frost during the night. The wind was south, not very warm, but the sun was unusually hot. As we turned out of the cabin after breakfast we were just in time to see a small range of mountains suddenly form at the lower angle of juncture between the Koo-ray'-i-ka and the Yen-e-say'. The river had risen considerably during the night, and the newly-formed strip of thin ice, on each side of the centre ice, was broader than it had ever been. The pressure of the current underneath caused a large field of ice, about a mile long and a third of a mile wide, to break away. About half the mass found a passage down the strip of newly-formed thin ice, leaving open water behind it; the other half rushed headlong on to the steep banks of the river, and driven on irresistibly by the enormous pressure from behind, it piled itself up into a little range of mountains, fifty or sixty feet high, and picturesque in the extreme. Huge blocks of ice, six feet thick and twenty feet long, in many places stood up perpendicularly. Others were crushed up into fragments like broken glass. The real ice on the river did not appear to have been more than three feet thick, clear as glass and blue as an Italian sky. Upon the top of this was about four feet of white ice. This was as hard as a rock, and had no doubt been caused by the flooding of the snow when the water rose, and its subsequent freezing. On the top of the white ice was about eighteen inches of clear snow, which had evidently never been flooded. Everything remained *in statu quo* during the rest of the day. The river was certainly rising, but slowly. Captain Wiggins anticipated no sudden change, and laughed at some of his sailors who, alarmed at the apparition of the ice mountains, began to remove their valuables out of the ship. I did not make any long excursion, but kept near our quarters. I got a flying shot at the Sparrow-Hawk, and dropped him upon the snow. That we were on the eve of summer was everywhere apparent. Great numbers of Geese and large flocks of Swans were continually passing northwards. I had strolled out on the edge of the river bank without my snow-shoes, and just at the moment I had stepped upon a treacherous bank, and was struggling up to the breast in snow, when a flock of Geese passed right over my head. I had my gun in my hand, but was perfectly helpless. These Geese were smaller than the one I had shot, and showed black on the belly. They were no doubt the Lesser White-fronted Goose.* An arrival of Gulls also took place. Besides the large dark-mantled species which I had seen the day before, a smaller pale-mantled species arrived, which I afterwards identified as the Common Gull. Another

---

* The Lesser White-fronted Goose (*Anser erythropus*) breeds above the limit of forest growth in Europe and Asia, from Lapland to Behring's Straits, wintering in Southern Europe, Northern Africa, India, Japan, and China. It has not been observed in Great Britain, but a near ally, the Greater White-fronted Goose (*Anser albifrons*) is a regular though rare winter visitor to our shores.

bird, which heralded the speedy presence of mosquitoes, was the White Wagtail. A small party of these charming birds arrived, one of them not having quite attained its full breeding plumage. There were still many white feathers on the throat. These birds belonged to the Indian form of the White Wagtail.* I also saw a very handsome male Brambling, but did not get a shot at him.

We turned into our berths at half-past nine, having first instituted an anchor watch, in case any further movement of the ice should take place. We had but just fallen asleep when we were suddenly roused by the report that the river was rising rapidly and the ice beginning to break up. We immediately dressed and went on deck. The position of affairs was at once obvious. The melting of the snow down south was evidently going on rapidly, and the river was rising at such speed that it was beginning to flow up all its tributaries in the north. This was a contingency for

---

* The Siberian White Wagtail (*Motacilla dukhunensis*) appears to be confined to Siberia and India. There can, however, be no doubt but that *M. alba*, the White Wagtail of Europe, and *M. dukhunensis*, are the same species, the white on the wing coverts, on which their claims to specific distinction rest, being a character so variable as to possess no scientific value. In the valley of the Yenesay both varieties were equally common. The geographical distribution of this bird is very curious. We may take the watershed of the Yenesay and Lena as its eastern boundary, whence it extends westwards as far as the Atlantic on the continent of Europe, but only appears accidentally in the British Islands, where it is replaced by the Pied Wagtail (*M. yarrelli*). As you ascend the Yenesay from the Arctic Circle, this bird abounds on the banks of the river until you near Yenesaisk (about lat. 59°), when suddenly it disappears, and its place is taken by *M. personata*, which extends westwards as far as the meridian of Calcutta. Still further to the east, between Yenesaisk and Lake By-kal, a colony of *M. dukhunensis* appears. From this colony they migrate in great numbers across Mongolia and the extreme west of China, and, doubtless, find their way thence to India.

which we were utterly unprepared. We were anchored opposite the entrance to a little creek, into which it was the Captain's intention to take his ship when the water rose sufficiently high to admit of his doing so. In this little creek he hoped to wait in safety the passing away of the ice. In a moment his plans were utterly frustrated. The entrance to the creek was perfectly high and dry. A strong current was setting up the Koo-ray'-i-ka. Small floes were detaching themselves from the main mass and were running up the open water. In a short time the whole body of the Koo-ray'-i-ka ice broke up, and began to move up stream. As far as the Yen-e-say' the tributary stream was soon a mass of pack-ice and floes marching up the river at the rate of three miles an hour. Some of these struck the ship some very ugly blows on the stern, doing considerable damage to the rudder, but open water was beyond, and we were soon out of the press of ice with, we hoped, no irretrievable damage. All this time we had been getting up steam as fast as possible, so as to be ready for any emergency. On the opposite side of the river we could see a haven of perfect safety, a long creek already full of water, and having the additional advantage of not being on the scour side of the river. When we had got sufficient steam to turn the engine, we found, to our dismay, that the ice which had already passed us had squeezed us towards the shore, and that there must have been a subsequent fall in the water, for we were at least two feet aground at the stern, and immoveable as a rock. The current was still running up the river, and against it there was no chance of swinging the ship round.

A mile astern of us was the edge of the Yen-e-say' ice. There was nothing to be done but to wait. In a short time the river began to rise again rapidly, and with it our hopes that we might float and steam into safety, when suddenly we discovered, to our terror, that the ice on the Yen-e-say' was breaking up, and that a dread phalanx of ice-floes and pack-ice was coming down on us at quick march. On it came, smashed the rudder, ground against the stern of the ship, sometimes squeezing her against the shore so that she pitched and rolled as if she were in a heavy sea, and sometimes she would get between a couple of small floes which seemed to try and lift her bodily out of the water. Once or twice an ice-floe began to climb up the ship's side like a snake. Some of the sailors got overboard, and scrambled over the pack-ice on to the shore. Others threw their goods and chattels to their comrades ashore. At length an immense ice-floe of irresistible weight struck the ship. There was no alternative but to slip the anchor and allow her to drive with the ice. Away we went up the Koo-ray'-i-ka, the ice rolling and tumbling and squeezing alongside of us, huge lumps climbing one upon the top of another. We were carried along in this way for about a mile, until we were finally jammed into a slight bay, wedged between blocks of pack-ice. Soon afterwards the river fell some five or six feet, the stream slackened, the ice stood still, and the ship and the pack-ice were aground. The ship went through the terrible ordeal bravely. So far she had made no water, and there was no evidence of any injury except to the rudder. This had been broken to pieces, and all trace of it carried away—a loss which it would take some weeks to repair. No one but an Englishman could have committed the inconceivable blunder of fitting out an Arctic yacht with every precaution against ice, and leaving it with a complicated rudder, exceedingly difficult to replace, and without provision for its being unshipped.

The question now demanding immediate consideration was what would take place when the ice began to move again. It seemed most probable that the ship would either be stranded on some sandbank or carried down with the ice to sea. The Captain decided that it was wisest to get as many valuables out of her as possible, and to make preparations for abandoning her if the worst came to the worst. The sailors accordingly occupied themselves in getting the cargo ashore over the lumps of stranded pack-ice and ice-floes.

The pitch of excitement at which we were naturally kept by the alarming character of the events in which we were forced to take such an active part, was by no means allayed by the weather. The brilliantly clear skies to which we had become accustomed changed to stormy clouds, followed by drizzling rain and mist. All nature seemed to share in our excitement. The revolution in the ice took place to the accompaniment of a perfect babel of birds. Above our heads we continually heard the *gag, gag* of Geese and the harsh bark of Swans, as flock after flock hurried past us to the Tundra. Wherever there was a little open water between the ice-floes and pack-ice, crowds of Gulls were fishing as if they had not had a meal for a week, and their derisive laugh, as they quarrelled over their prey, seemed to mock our misfortunes, while ever and anon the wild weird cries of the Black-throated and Red-throated Divers, like the distant scream of tortured children, came from the creek opposite. A few flocks of Wild Ducks also passed us, and along the shore small birds flitted from bush to bush in hitherto unknown profusion. Bramblings and White Wag-tails passed in pairs, Shore Larks in small flocks, and Redpoles in large flocks, and I shot a solitary Wheatear. In the midst of his troubles on board his half-wrecked steamer, Captain Wiggins seized his gun and shot a Goose, which was flying over the ship, and which proved to be the Little White-fronted Goose, the species which I had missed shooting the day before.

The ice remained quiet until about midnight, when an enormous pressure from above came on somewhat suddenly. It had apparently broken up the great field of ice to the north of the Koo-ray'-i-ka, but not to an extent sufficient to relieve the whole of the pressure. The water in the Koo-ray'-i-ka once more rose rapidly. The immense field of pack-ice began to move up-stream at the rate of five or six knots an hour. The *Thames* was soon afloat again, and driven with the ice up the river, she was knocked and bumped along the rocky shore, and her stern-post was twisted to such an extent, that she began to make water rapidly. At nine o'clock on Sunday, the 3rd of June, all hands left her, and stood watching on the steep bank. The stream rose and fell during the day, the current sometimes standing, sometimes becoming very rapid, the unfortunate ship being occasionally afloat, but generally aground. At night the stern-post seemed to have come back to its place, the undaunted Captain, with part of his faint-hearted crew, went on board, and the pumps reduced the water in the hold. The chances were ten to one that she was a hopeless wreck, but still the sailors struggled on to the last. The marvel was, where all the ice that had gone up the Koo-ray'-i-ka could possibly be stowed. I calculated that at least 50,000 acres of ice had passed the ship.

Late on the night of Monday, the 4th of June, the ice on the Koo-ray'-i-ka almost entirely cleared away. Steam was got up, and by the help of ropes ashore, the *Thames* was steered into the little creek below the house, where it had been the original intention of the Captain to have waited in safety the passing away of the ice. The season had been so severe, that the snow, which ought to have melted and swollen the river before the breaking-up of the ice, still remained upon the land. The consequence was, that when the great revolution commenced, the entrance to the creek was high and dry. The *Thames* entered the creek at two o'clock in the morning. By noon the water had sunk five or six feet, and the vessel lay on her side, with her bow at least three feet aground. These sudden falls in the level of the water were no doubt caused by the breaking-up of the ice lower down the river, which dammed it up until the accumulated pressure from behind became irresistible. Some idea of what this pressure must have been may be realised by the fact, that a part of the river a thousand miles long, beginning with a width of two miles, and ending with a width of six miles, covered over with three feet of ice, upon which was lying six feet of snow, was broken up at the rate of a hundred miles a day. Many obstacles would cause a temporary stoppage in the break-up of the ice: a sudden bend in the river, a group of islands or a narrower place where the ice might jam. But the pressure from behind was an ever-increasing one. Although the river frequently fell for a few hours, it was constantly rising on an average, and in ten days the rise, where we were stationed, was seventy feet. Such a display of irresistible power dwarfs Niagara into comparative insignificance. On several occasions we stood on the banks of the river for hours, transfixed with astonishment, staring aghast at icebergs, twenty to thirty feet high, driven down the river at a speed of from ten to twenty miles an hour.

The battle of the Yen-e-say' raged for about a fortnight, during which the Koo-ray'-i-ka alternately rose and fell. Thousands of acres of ice were marched up-stream for some hours, then the tide turned and they were marched back again. This great annual battle between summer and winter is the great event of the year in these regions, like the rising of the Nile in Egypt. Summer, in league with the sun, fights winter and the north wind, and is hopelessly beaten, until she forms an alliance with the south wind, before whose blast the armies of winter vanish into thin water, and retreat to the pole. It was a wonderful sight to watch these armies alternately advancing and retreating. Sometimes the pack-ice and floes were jammed so tightly together that it looked as though one might scramble over them to the opposite shore. At other times there was much open water, and the icebergs "calved" as they went along, with much commotion and splashing that might be heard half a mile off. No doubt it is the grounding of the icebergs which causes this operation to take place. These icebergs are formed of layers of ice, piled one on the top of the other, and imperfectly frozen together. In passing along the bottom layer grounds, but the velocity at which the enormous mass is going will not allow it to stop. It passes on, leaving part of the bottom layer behind. The moment it has passed, the piece left behind rises to the surface like a whale coming up to breathe. Some of the "calves" must have come up from a considerable depth. They rose out of the water with a huge splash, and rocked about for some time, before they settled down to their floating level.

At last the final march past of the beaten winter forces, in their fourteen days' battle, took place, and for seven days more the ragtag-and-bobtail of the great Arctic army came straggling down the Koo-ray'-i-ka—worn and weather-beaten little icebergs, dirty ice-floes, that looked like floating mud banks, and straggling pack-ice in the last stages of consumption. Winter was finally vanquished for the year, and the fragments of his beaten army were compelled to retreat to the triumphant music of thousands of song-birds, and amidst the waving of green leaves, and the illumination of gay flowers of every hue.

This sudden change, in the short space of a fortnight, from midwinter to midsummer can scarcely, by courtesy, be called spring. It is a revolution of nature, and on a scale so imposing, that the most prosaic of observers cannot witness it without feeling its sublimity. Looked at in a purely scientific point of view, the lesson it impresses upon the mind is exactly the opposite of that intended to be conveyed by the old fable of the traveller whose cloak the wind and the sun alternately try to steal from him. In these Arctic regions the sun seems to be almost powerless. The white snow seems to be an invulnerable shield, against which the sun-darts glance harmless, reflected back into the air. On the contrary, the south wind seems all-powerful. In spite of mist and cloud, the snow melts before it like butter upon hot toast, and winter tumbles down like a pack of cards.

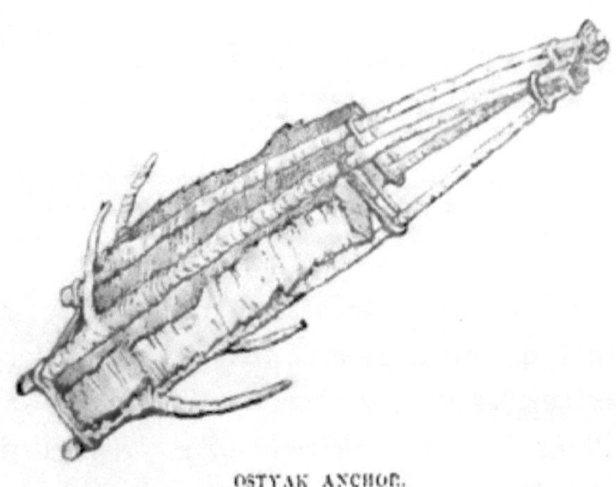

OSTYAK ANCHOR.

GULLS AMONG THE ICEBERGS.

CHAPTER X.

As soon as I was able to resume my shooting, I found
that there had been a general arrival of migratory birds.
It was very difficult to get about in the melting snow, but
in the willows on the steep bank of the river, little birds
were feeding, industriously picking up insects on the naked
branches, and sometimes making little flights in the air to

catch a gnat upon the wing. Presently I heard a plaintive *weest,* which reminded me of Heligoland, and on shooting the bird I picked up a Yellow-browed Willow-Warbler,[*] as I expected. There was quite a little party of these diminutive creatures, and they were so tame after their long journey, that I watched them for a long time, hopping from twig to twig, diligently searching for food. I was often within four feet of one of them, and could distinctly see its white eye-stripe and the two bars across its wing.

My attention was called away from these charming little warblers by hearing a still more plaintive call-note, which proceeded from a very nearly-allied species, almost as small, the Siberian Chiffchaff. During the day I repeatedly heard the song—if song it may be called—of this little Black-legged Willow-Warbler, which I had learned to recognise in a moment, by hearing it so often in the valley of the Petchora. I soon put its identity beyond question by shooting a fine male, and discovered that it had arrived in considerable numbers, as its note was often heard during the day, but generally from some pine-tree which was for the moment inaccessible, being surrounded by snow too soft to bear my weight, even on snow-shoes, and too deep to struggle through with any chance of a successful pursuit.

[*] The Yellow-browed Barred Willow-Warbler (*Phylloscopus superciliosus*) breeds in North Siberia, and at a high elevation in the mountains of South Siberia. It winters in South China, Burmah, and North India. The special interest attaching to this bird is that a few stragglers annually pass into Europe on migration, one or two of which have wandered as far as the British Islands. I did not meet with this species further north than lat. 70°, nor did I observe it on my return voyage.

But, interesting as the arrival of these two rare warblers was to me, having made this group my special study, I was even more delighted to hear the unmistakable song of our common European Willow-Warbler, a bird I had never dreamt of meeting with so far east. I shot a pair, and thus satisfactorily demonstrated that our ornithological books were all wrong in giving the Ural range as the eastern limit of this well-known species, during the breeding season. It seems too bad to shoot these charming little birds, but, as the " Old Bushman " says, what is *hit* is *history*, and what is *missed* is *mystery*. My object was to study natural history, and one of the charms of the pursuit is to correct other ornithologists' blunders and to clear up the mysteries that they have left unsolved.

The next birds that claimed my attention were some small parties of Thrushes, which were very wild, keeping mostly to the forest, where I could not pursue them, but at last I secured one, as he was feeding on the steep bank of the river, where the snow had melted, and had the pleasure of picking up a Dusky Ouzel,* a bird I had never seen in the flesh before. The call-note of these birds reminded me of that of the Redwing.

---

* The Dusky Ouzel (*Merula fuscata*) breeds in Siberia from the valley of the Yenesay eastwards among the willow bushes in the sheltered gorges on the Tundra, above the limit of forest growth, and in a similar climate in the mountain regions near Lake By-kal. On migration it passes through south-east Mongolia and north China, and winters in Japan and south China, occasionally straying westwards as far as Assam and even north-west India. Individuals sometimes wander as far eastwards as Europe, having been found in Belgium and Italy. I afterwards found it breeding in lat. 69°.

Wagtails rapidly became very numerous, and were to be seen running about close to the edge of the water, sometimes perched on a little ice-floe, and coming inland to the pools formed by the melting snow. They were mostly the Indian form of the White Wagtail, but I shot a fine male Yellow-headed Wagtail, a bird whose acquaintance I had first made on the banks of the Petchora. Ducks were flying up the river at intervals, but none came near enough for me to identify the species. I shot a solitary Lapland Bunting, a bird for which I had been on the look-out for some time, as, in the valley of the Petchora, it had been amongst the earliest arrivals. The season was, no doubt, late, and this species breeds on the Tundra above the limit of forest growth, where winter still reigned supreme.

We had brilliant sunshine on the following day, the 5th of June, without a breath of wind. The snow was thawing very fast. Ice came down the river slowly, but the current was still up the Koo'-ray-i-ka. The water rose considerably during the afternoon, and the *Thames* was again afloat· The Captain was busy putting ballast into the fore part of the ship, so as to raise the stern as much as possible out of the water. When this was done she was moored so that the stern might ground as soon as the next fall of the water took place, that we might be able to form some idea of the extent of injury she had sustained. She was at that time making about two inches of water an hour.

Birds continued to be very abundant for some days. Flocks of Green Wagtails arrived. I shot three males; one of them showing rudiments of an eye-stripe. The Blue-throated Warbler also arrived. I shot four, two males and two females. I also shot a Brambling and another little White-fronted Goose. Meanwhile, all day, the Cuckoo was vigorously announcing that he too had reached these regions. I shot a Great Snipe, and Captain Wiggins shot another. I also shot a Plover which turned out to be a species

OSTYAK PIPE.

which I had never seen in the flesh before, the Asiatic Golden Plover.*

In the evening there was an Ost'-yak funeral. The wife of one of the men, living in a choom near the ship, died. The funeral party consisted of half-a-dozen Ost'-yaks. Early in the morning they crossed the creek, where the ship was lying, in a boat, and then mounted the hill to the top of the bank. First came the Ost'-yaks,

---

* The Asiatic Golden Plover (*Charadrius fulvus*) has never been found breeding except on the occasion referred to in the text. Middendorf obtained both this species and the Western Golden Plover (*C. pluvialis*) during the breeding season on the Taimoor peninsula, where it doubtless breeds as far towards the east as Behring's Straits. It passes through Mongolia, Japan, Tibet, and China on migration, and winters in the islands of the Malay archipelago, the Malay peninsula, India, Australia, and occasionally in New Zealand. Swinhoe's statement that it breeds on the island of Formosa, and Layard's account of its having been seen with its young on an island near New Caledonia, no doubt refer to some other species. It occasionally strays as far as Europe, and has been obtained on Heligoland and in Norfolk.

carrying the corpse slung on a pole. Then followed men, with axe, pick, and spade, then women with materials for baking bread and making tea, and finally came the empty coffin. It took nearly all day to dig the grave out of the frozen ground. A fire was made, bread was baked, tea drunk, and we were told the tea cups were buried. Finally a small birch-tree was felled, a rough cross, with the Russian oblique foot-board, was made and placed at the foot of the grave.

In the evening there was hardly any ice left in the river, and the surface was as smooth as glass, so we took the boat and rowed across to the creek on the other side of the Kooray'-i-ka. The Captain and I each shot a Siberian Herring Gull. I also shot a brace of Teal.

Another lovely morning broke upon us, with scarcely a breath of wind. Birds were coming faster than I could keep pace with. In my journal of the 6th of June I find recorded that in a quarter of an hour I shot a brace of Indian Pintail Snipe,* a Red-throated Pipit, and a Green Wagtail. I also identified some Pintail Ducks, some Wood Sandpipers, and Temminck's Stints. I repeatedly heard the loud wild *mĕĕ'-yoo* of the Widgeon, but did not see the bird.

I had a fine view of a male Smew. Wagtails were

---

* The Indian Pin-tailed Snipe (*Scolopax stenura*) breeds on the tundras of Siberia east of the watershed of the Obb and the Yenesay, probably as far as Behring's Straits, and in similar climates on the mountains of Southern Siberia and north-east Mongolia. It winters in India, the Malay peninsula, China, and the islands of the Malay archipelago. It may at once be recognised from the Common Snipe by its very narrow and stiff outer tail feathers.

extremely abundant, principally the White Wagtail. There were many Green Wagtails, and I shot one Grey Wagtail.* I shot one Red-throated Pipit in winter plumage and a couple of female Scarlet Bullfinches.

The forest was utterly impenetrable. In most places the snow was too soft for snow-shoes, but I could hear a multitude of Thrushes and Willow-Warblers singing. Now and then a few late Geese and Swans passed over, and Ducks of various species were constantly on the wing.

The tide in the Koo-ray'-i-ka had turned apparently. All day long the ice came slowly drifting back, and both rivers were once more full of pack-ice.

I saw a couple of Terns, most likely Arctic Terns.

The next day was again lovely and smiling, with scarcely a breath of wind, but the snow thawed more slowly than we wished, for it froze every night for an hour or two. Four-and-twenty hours of warm south wind would have made a wonderful difference. The river had risen again, and during the night and the following day pack-ice and floes floated up the Koo-ray'-i-ka. This we were told was the Tun-goosk' ice coming down. All this time the great migration of birds

---

* The Grey Wagtail (*Motacilla melanope*) breeds throughout Central and Southern Siberia, Turkestan, Cashmere, and North China; wintering in India and the islands of the Malay archipelago. As the specimen referred to is the only one I procured, it is possible that I was in the extreme northern limit of its range (66½°). A very nearly-allied western form, differing only in having a slightly longer tail, occurs in Persia, Asia Minor, the whole of Europe, (with the exception of Scandinavia and North Russia,) and North Africa, including the Canaries and the Azores. In the British Islands it is a partial resident in mountainous districts, appearing only in winter in more low-lying localities.

was going on. My list for that day was forty birds shot,
thirty two skinned. The most interesting were : the Golden
Plover, Wood Sandpiper, Temminck's Stint, Little Bunting, a
couple of male Scarlet Bullfinches, and a couple of Dark
Ouzels.* The latter was a new species for me, which I had
hitherto only known from skins.

The following day was again brilliantly fine. The wind, if
the gentlest zephyr may be called wind, changed continually,

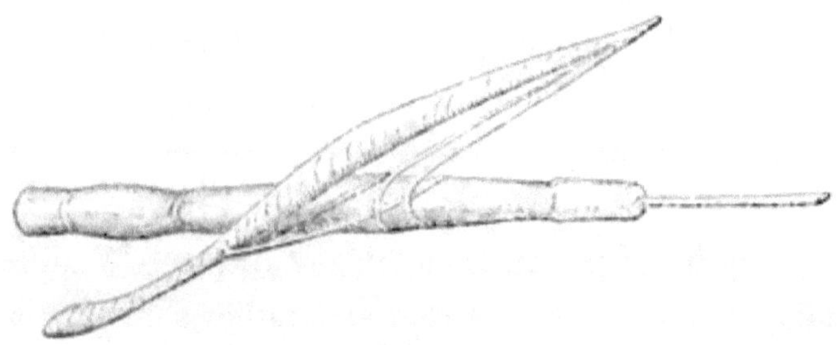

OSTYAK DRILL.

east, south, and west. The stream of ice went on uninter-
ruptedly, but this time it was down the Koo-ray'-i-ka. Birds
were not quite so numerous, nevertheless I added four to my
list. The first was a Fieldfare down by the river side, then
I secured a Terek Sandpiper on the flooded grass behind the
store. In the afternoon a flock of half-a-dozen Ringed Plover
arrived, and I shot a brace of them. The last was a Lesser

* The Dark Ouzel (*Merula obscura*) breeds in East Siberia between lat. 63° and lat. 67° in the valley of the Yene-say, and further east in the pine regions of Lake By-kal and the Amoor. It passes through China and Mongolia on migration, and winters in Assam, Mal-acca, and the islands of the Malay archipelago. Stragglers are occasionally found as far west as Turkestan, Nepal, and Europe. I did not meet with this interesting Ouzel farther north than the Arctic Circle.

Whitethroat* in the trees at the top of the banks of the Koo-ray'-i-ka. In the forest, birds were abundant enough. A Woodpecker made the woods ring again with its loud tapping. Willow-Warblers and Bluethroats were the principal song-sters. I heard the Siberian Chiffchaff repeatedly, and shot a Yellow-browed Warbler while uttering its note most voci-ferously. I also saw several Scarlet Bullfinches.

On the grass around the house, Shore Larks and Lapland Buntings congregated in a large flock. Both species occa-sionally run and occasionally hop, but I think the Shore Larks hop oftener. I noticed also that the Lapland Buntings when disturbed generally sought refuge in a tree. Another very common bird was the Pintail Snipe. I could have shot a score a day had I possessed cartridges to spare. They came wheeling round, uttering a loud and rather shrill cry *pēezh*, then dropped down with a great whirr of wing and with tail outspread, an occupation which seemed so engrossing that they did not discover until upon the ground that they had alighted within twenty yards of a man with a gun. I made two good shots. One, another of the Dusky Ouzels, the other, a second Asiatic Golden Plover. By this time many mosquitoes were on the wing, but as yet their bite was not very virulent.

---

* The Eastern or Siberian form of the Lesser Whitethroat (*Sylvia affinis*) differs from the well-known home species in its wing formula; but ex-amples occasionally occur in Europe agreeing with the Eastern bird in this respect. It breeds throughout Siberia, extending northwards almost to the limit of forest growth, and southwards into North Persia, Turkestan, and North-east China. It winters in Ba-luchistan and the whole of India and Ceylon. I did not observe this species further north than lat. 67°.

Late in the evening clouds began to gather, and rain came on which continued all night. The river soon began to rise, and the tide of ice turned again up the Koo-ray'-i-ka, proving that the mouth of the Yen-e-say' was still blocked with ice.

RUSSIAN PIPE.

DOLGAHN HUNTER WITH OSTYAK BOW AND DRUM OF SAMOYADE SHAMMAN.

CHAPTER XI.

Four species added to my list—Dotterel—Rapid rise of the river—Open water—
Arrival of the Great Snipe—Pallas's Sand-Martin—Common Sandpiper—
Characteristics of the native tribes—Ship repairs—Pine Bunting—Ice lost in
the forest—Glinski's industry—Ruby-throated Warbler—Waxwings—Death
of a Tunguosk—Funeral rites—Disease of the natives—Their improvidence—
Uselessness of the priests.

IT rained off and on the whole of Saturday the 9th of June,
nevertheless birds were plentiful. The first great rush of

migration seems to take place as soon as the ice and snow melt. Indeed many birds, as we have seen, are in too great a hurry to reach their breeding grounds, overshoot the mark, and finding no food are obliged to turn back. Any little oasis of land in the vast desert of snow, like the cleared ground between the house and the ship, is soon full of birds, and I found myself in a favourable situation for noting the new arrivals, some of whom were almost sure to be attracted by the black spot, and to drop down to feed. I was constantly running in and out, and made an excellent bag. Unfortunately our position did not command a good view of the chief stream of migration which appeared to follow the main valley of the Yen-e-say'. There were no bare hills in the neighbourhood from which to watch, and our house stood on a small patch of cleared ground surrounded by forest except on the river side. Very few large flocks of birds passed over, and those which visited us appeared to be stragglers from the great line of migration. They stayed a few hours to feed, hurried on again, and fresh stragglers took their places. The day's bag, however, added four new species to my list: the Yellow-breasted Bunting, the Ruff, the Sand-Martin, and Middendorf's Reed Bunting.* In addition to these novelties, I secured four Asiatic Golden Plovers and a couple of Dusky Ouzels. The latter were singularly tame compared with the Fieldfare and Redwing, both of which were common

---

* Middendorf's Reed Bunting (*Emberiza passerina*) is only known to breed on the Taimoor peninsula. The birds I procured on the Koorayika were probably on migration. It passes through Krasnoyarsk (whence Mr. Kibort has sent me skins), Lake By-kal and the Amoor, on migration, and winters in Turkestan, Mongolia, and China.

but very wild. In the evening I added a fifth bird to my list, viz., the Dotterel.

For three days we had seen no Snow-Buntings, but Shore Larks and Lapland Buntings were still common. A few Swans and Geese passed over, and Ducks were flying about in all directions.

All day the wind was north and nor-west; the river rose more than it had ever done in one day before. The current was still up the Koo-ray'-i-ka, but as far as we could see both rivers were almost clear of ice.

On the morning of Sunday we had a breeze from the west with drizzling rain, and an open river gently rising, with a slight current up the Koo-ray'-i-ka. By noon the wind dropped and the water began to fall. The afternoon was calm but cloudy, with an occasional gleam of sunshine and now and then a shower of rain. The Yen-e·say' southwards seemed to be clear of ice, but in the afternoon the Koo-ray'-i-ka was one crowded mass of pack-ice and floes, drifting down to the sea at the rate of three to four knots an hour. Birds were not very numerous, but I shot more Thrushes than usual. A peasant from the opposite village brought me a couple of Ducks, a Widgeon, and a Red-breasted Merganser. In the afternoon I shot a Pintail Duck and saw a Diver for the first time, but whether Red-throated or Blackthroated I was not near enough to determine. The forest was still impenetrable, though the rain had made havoc with the snow.

We had a warm south wind on the following day, and the march past of ice continued down the river, getting slower and slower, and coming to a final block about noon. In the afternoon the wind shifted round to the west, the river began to rise slightly, the tide in the Koo-ray'-i-ka turned, the ice which had not rounded the corner into the Yen-e-say' was marched back again, and in the afternoon and evening we had open water.

Birds were not quite so numerous as heretofore. A flock of two or three Dotterels came down to feed, and by the river-side I came across a couple of Ruffs, a pair or two of Terek Sandpipers, a Golden Plover, and a few Ringed Plover. I nevertheless succeeded in adding four new species to my list : the Common Skylark, the only example I obtained in the Arctic Circle, the Double Snipe, and the Siberian Stone-chat, of which I shot a female, and what I took to be the House-Martin. Several pairs of the latter arrived, and were soon busily hawking for flies and occasionally examining their old nests. I shot a couple, so that I might have tangible evidence of the existence of this bird in the valley of the Yen-e-say'. A few weeks later they swarmed in countless thousands, and I might easily have obtained a score at a shot. The reader may imagine my disgust when on my return home I found that my two birds were not the Common House-Martin after all, but a nearly-allied species, Pallas's House-Martin,* a bird so rare that the British Museum did not possess a specimen of it, and that besides

* Pallas's House - Martin (*Hirundo lagopoda*) breeds in East Siberia from the valley of the Yenesay eastwards, probably to the Pacific. It has been recorded from Turkestan and China on migration, but its winter quarters are unknown, unless the Martin described by Bonaparte from Borneo as *Hirundo dasypus* should prove to be this species. It differs from the Common House-

my two skins the species was solely represented in the British Islands by a unique skin from Japan in the Swinhoe collection.

The fine weather continued on the following day, the river went on rising slowly, the Koo-ray'-i-ka ice stopping the way; it scarcely made a verst the whole day.

There were very few birds. The Shore Larks were all gone. Only a few stray Lapland Buntings were left. Now and then a Plover or a pair of Sandpipers paid us a short visit. The Martins had a large accession to their numbers, and flew round the house like a swarm of bees. It was now possible to plough our way through the forest; for the snow was very soft, and melting rapidly. Bluethroats and Willow-Warblers were the principal songsters. The simple notes of the Redwing, the unobtrusive song of the Little Bunting, and the cheerful call of the Siberian Chiffchaff, were also very frequently heard. Both the Great Snipe and the Pintail Snipe were common enough. A couple of White-tailed Eagles flew over about noon. Now and then a few late Swans passed over, but the Geese seemed to have all gone to their breeding places. The day added only one bird to my list, the Common Sandpiper.

I had a talk with Schwanenberg about the Asiatics, as he called the natives. He said the Ost'-yaks are very friendly people. The Tun-goosks' are bad, and think nothing of shedding human blood. The Dol-gahns' again are good people. The Yu-raks are dangerous, and the Sam'-o-yades vary according to locality.

Martin of Europe principally by having all the upper tail coverts pure white. In our bird the longest upper tail coverts are black.

Matters were looking somewhat brighter at the ship. The carpenter was busy making a new rudder. At low water, when the stern was aground, he did some caulking, and as the vessel was only leaking a little we were in hopes that she might yet be made seaworthy after all.

The next morning the wind was nor-east, and changed in the afternoon to sou-west; the weather was as changeable as the wind. We had clouds, sunshine, heavy gales, thunder and rain. Scarcely a bird came near the house all day, but before breakfast I shot a very interesting one close to the door, a Pine Bunting.* I also secured a Reed Bunting, the European species, a larger and browner bird than the one I got on the 9th. I shot a Hazel-Grouse in the forest, but saw nothing else of special interest. The Siberian Chiff-chaffs seemed common enough, but snow still lay too thick upon the ground to hunt them successfully.

The river rose considerably during the following night, but during the day it fell slightly, and the current was down the Koo-ray'-i-ka. Surely, we thought, this must be the last march-past of ice. From what Schwanenberg told me, I fancy half the ice that went up the Koo-ray'-i-ka never comes down again. He said that some ten versts from our quarters the banks of the river were low. When he came back from his wild-goose chase after graphite, this part of

---

* The Pine Bunting (*Emberiza leuco-cephala*) probably breeds throughout Southern Siberia. As I never saw the bird again it is fair to assume that I was at the extreme northern limit of its range. It winters in Turkestan, North-west Himalayas, and North China. It is an occasional visitor to Central and Southern Europe in winter, but has not yet been found in the British Islands.

the country was flooded for miles on each side of the river; hundreds of acres of ice had drifted into the forests, and when the water subsided frozen blocks would probably be stranded among the trees, and gradually melt on the ground.

The villagers at the other side of the river brought us a

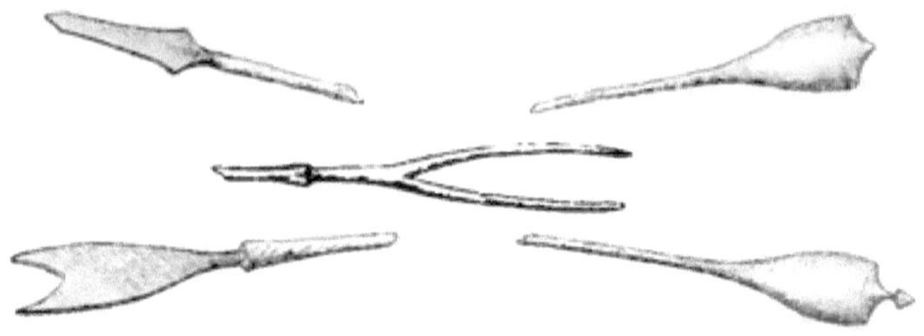

OSTYAK ARROW-HEADS

few birds which they had secured, so Glinski thought he would try how many he could skin in one day. He began at nine A.M. and finished at two the next morning. Allowing a couple of hours for meals, and a " papiross " afterwards, this would make fifteen working hours, during which he skinned forty-six birds. I labelled them all, and gave them the last finishing touch. I had arranged to pay all his expenses, and to give him besides his twenty roubles a month, ten kopeks a skin; so he made a very good thing of the bargain.

The ice was still straggling down, but slowly, on the 14th. The wind was south in the morning, with rain, but it cleared up at noon, and the evening was bright, with scarcely any wind. I had three rounds in the forest. Before breakfast

I shot a Ruby-throated Warbler.* He had a wonderfully
fine song, decidedly more melodious than that of the Bluethroat, and very little inferior to that of the nightingale.
When I first heard him sing I thought I was listening to a
nightingale; he had his back towards me when I shot him,
and I was astonished to pick up a bird with a scarlet throat.
The feathers were glossy as silk, and when I skinned him I
thought I had rarely, if ever, seen so beautiful a Warbler. It
seems that a fine voice and gay colours do sometimes coexist
in birds as well as on the stage. In the afternoon I shot
another very interesting bird, the Blue-rumped Warbler; I
did not hear his song when I came upon him; he was
busily engaged searching for insects, principally at the roots
of trees. Nor was my morning's second walk entirely a
blank, as I shot a Yellow-browed Warbler. The snow in the
forest still made walking difficult and disagreeable. I saw
a small flock of perhaps half-a-dozen birds, which, judging
from their notes, I am all but sure were Waxwings; I could
not get near enough however to identify them.

Whilst I was walking in the forest, picking my way
amongst the swamps and the few remaining snow-fields, I
was delighted once more to hear the alarm-note of the
Nutcracker. I was, however, unable to get a sight of the
bird. A fortnight before they had been common enough

---

* The Ruby-throated Warbler (*Erith-acus calliope*) breeds throughout Siberia as far north as the Arctic Circle, extending southwards as far as the extreme north of China. It winters in the Philippine Islands, South China, Burmah, and northern and central India, occasionally straying into Europe.

near our quarters. This bird seems to be well aware of the fact that offal and scraps of food of all kinds are always to be found in winter near the habitations of man. Their tameness had been quite absurd. Sometimes the Ost'-yak children shot one with a bow-and-arrow, and occasionally one was caught by the dogs. When the breeding season began they seemed entirely to change their habits. About the 7th of June they retired, apparently into the recesses of the forest. I was very anxious to secure a series of their eggs, and had carefully preserved them, feeding them with the bodies of the birds I skinned. They treated me, however, in the most ungrateful manner. As soon as the snow was melted from most of the ground they vanished, and all my efforts to discover their breeding place proved

RUSSIAN EIKON.
(Brass and enamel.)

in vain, though I offered a considerable reward for a nest containing eggs. The Russians call the Nutcracker the "Ve-roff'-ky," and both the peasants and the natives assured me that no one had ever seen its nest. With the exception of a couple of birds which I picked up afterwards in full moult, I saw nothing more of them until they reappeared in flocks on the return journey.

In the evening I spent some time watching the Great Snipes through my binocular. With a little caution I found it easy to get very near them, and frequently, as I sat partially concealed between a couple of willow bushes, I was able to turn my glass on two or three pairs of these birds, all within fifteen or twenty yards of me. They had one very curious habit which I noted. They used to stretch out their necks, throw back the head almost on to the back, and open and shut their beaks rapidly, uttering a curious noise, like running one's finger along the edge of a comb. This was sometimes accompanied by a short flight, or by the spreading of the wings and tail. The Double Snipe is by no means shy, and allows of a near approach. When it gets up from the ground it rises with a whirr of the wings like that of a Grouse, but not so loud, whilst the Pin-tailed Snipe gets up quietly. I did not succeed in finding the nest of the Double Snipe, but I have no doubt it breeds in the valley of the Koo-ray'-i-ka, as it was still frequenting the marshy ground when we weighed anchor in the ill-starred *Thames* on the 29th of June, and I noticed it in the same locality when I returned in the *Yen-e-say'* on the 2nd of August.

About this time a 'Tun-goosk' died in one of the chooms of the Ost'-yaks. He had been a servant of our landlord, Turboff. For many months he had been suffering from a chest complaint, but the disease which ultimately killed him seems to have been scurvy. Some days before he died we tried to persuade him to drink lime-juice, but it was of no avail.　Like the officials connected with our late unfortunate Arctic expedition, he did not seem to think it a matter of any importance.　I suppose he shared the opinion now getting so prevalent, that between good medicine and bad medicine there is a world of difference, but that between good medicine and no medicine there is scarcely any difference at all.　The Ost'-yaks buried the poor man; they begged from us some boards to make a coffin, and the corpse was placed in it; an axe was then waved three times up and three times down the body, the lid was nailed down, and a grave hastily dug in the forest.　At the foot of the grave a small pine-tree was growing.　It was roughly squared as it stood, a slit made in the trunk and a cross-bar inserted.

We found scurvy and chest disease to prevail a good deal here, especially amongst the natives.　The intense cold of the long winter affects the throat and lungs, and asthma, bronchitis, or consumption is the result.　During the winter also, fresh vegetable diet is very scarce.　The people preserve the cranberries, which grow so abundantly during the summer, but they are such an improvident set, that they use the berries in their tea, so long as they last, and in spring, when the need for them is greatest, the stock is exhausted.　There are no doctors.　If the government combined with the office of priest that of doctor, some good might be effected.　At present the priests are absolutely useless; their offices, in the Greek Church, are so mechanical that they might be performed almost equally well by machinery.　In many cases the priests are worse than useless; they have nothing to do, and, under the pretext of keeping holy certain days, they encourage the people in drinking to excess, and in wasting valuable time in idling. Russia stands sorely in need of an Isaiah to proclaim the truth, that the "holy days and the feast days are an abomination."

BRONZE FROM ANCIENT GRAVE NEAR KRASNOYARSK.

SUMMER QUARTERS ON THE KOORAYIKA.

CHAPTER XII.

Birds—Trip across the Yen-e-say'—The Himalayan Cuckoo—Lost in the forest—
Wood floating down the river—Two arrivals—Startling news—Spring flowers
—Second visit to the other side of the Yen-e-say'—Habits of the Great Snipe—
Song of the Scarlet Bullfinch—Number of birds—Striped Squirrels—Gull
perching—The Siberian Ground Thrush—A new bird—My new schooner the *Ibis*
—Song of the Yellow-browed Warbler—Ost'-yak fishing season—Important
observations made on the other side of the Koo-ray'-i-ka—The Dusky Ouzel—
The Mountain Hedge-Sparrow. The Siberian Pipit—Nest of the Little Bunting

FRIDAY, the 15th of June, was hot, with a south wind. The
water continued to rise, and the ice continued to straggle
down the Koo-ray'-i-ka. In the morning Glinski and I had
a row up the river. We saw some Common Sandpipers and
shot one. We also secured a female Reed Bunting and a
Siberian Chiffchaff in the willows, now half under water, and
we shot a pair of Pine Grosbeaks in the forest.

Some peasants from the village on the other side of the
Yen-e-say' rowed across, bringing us some birds. Amongst
them was a Green Sandpiper and a Curlew Sandpiper in full
breeding plumage. They gave such a glowing account of
the number of birds near their village that I went back with
them. It took us nearly two hours' rowing against wind
and tide to reach our destination. I found they had not
exaggerated; birds abounded. The country was flatter, and
thinly sprinkled over with birch-trees. There were several
lakes and pools of water, aad more grass and willow swamps.
I shot a female Hen Harrier, a bird I had not seen since the
Snow-Buntings left. I also shot a Common Gull, which
completed my identification of this species made on the 1st
inst. I saw Willow-Grouse and Black Grouse and number-
less Ducks. I added to my list both the Red-throated and
the Black-throated Divers, the Red-breasted Merganser, the
Golden Eye Duck, and the Goosander, and frequently
recognised the wild cry of the Scaup Duck. I found the
Red-necked Phalarope very abundant in the pools, and as

tame as usual. I listened to a Sedge-Warbler for some time, but did not succeed in shooting it. I also followed a Cuckoo, but could not get a shot. I supposed it to be the European bird, but it had quite a different voice. Instead of crying "cuckoo" it made a gutteral and hollow sounding "hoo'," not unlike the cry of the Hoopoe. I afterwards secured an example of this bird, and found it to be the Himalayan Cuckoo.* I had an excellent opportunity of listening to the song of the Fieldfare. The call-note of this bird, *tsik-tsak*, is continually heard, but the song seems confined to the pairing season; it is a low warble, scarcely deserving to be called melodious.

The excitement of the chase, the appearance of species new to my list, and the abundance of bird-life generally, caused me to forget that time was flying. The difference between day and night in these latitudes at this season of the year is so small that I failed to notice that it ought to be evening and that the sun must before very long prepare to dip below the horizon for an hour or so, until other sensations reminded me that it must be long past dinner-time. I looked at my watch, was astonished to find it so late, took

---

* The Himalayan Cuckoo (*Cuculus himalayanus*) breeds on the Yenesay, and probably in Central and Southern Siberia east of that river, throughout the Himalayas as far west as Gilgit, and in China and Japan; wintering in South China, Formosa, and the islands of the Malay archipelago, as far south as Flores. This species is also found during our winter in Madagascar, probably migrating there from Eastern Siberia. A similar migration is known to take place in the case of the two species of Red-footed Falcons. The western form (*Falco vespertinus*) winters in Damara Land, and the eastern form (*F. amurensis*) winters in the Transvaal. Probably the Sedge-Warblers and the Common Willow-Warblers from the Yenesay follow the same line of migration, and also winter in Africa.

out my compass, for the sky was overcast, and steered due
east with the intention of striking the Yen-e-say' and of
following the course of its banks until I reached the village.
Before long I caught a glimpse of a sheet of water through
the trees, but on reaching the shore I was astonished to find
that it was not the Yen-e-say'. Though it stretched nearly
north and south as far as the eye could reach, it had little
or no stream, and was not more than half a mile wide. Now
the Yen-e-say' had a current of at least four miles an hour
and was three miles wide. I climbed up a tree in the hope
that a distant view of the great river might be thus obtained, but it was of no use. In every direction an endless
series of tree-tops stretched away to the horizon. I realised
the fact that I was lost in the forest—a forest perhaps five
thousand miles long by more than a thousand miles wide.
I comforted myself with the reflection that it could only be
a question of time, that one end of the sheet of water before
me must be connected with the Yen-e-say', and that if I
took the wrong direction to-night I should nevertheless be
able to find the right one on the morrow. My game bag
was full, and if the worst came to the worst I could do as I
had seen the Ost'-yaks do. Fortunately, however, I discovered that in my haste to explore new ground I had
neglected to take out of my bag a pot of Liebig's extract of
meat, with which I had provided myself before crossing the
river. Sitting down on a fallen tree-trunk, I dined as best
I could on my solitary dish. I then walked for an hour
along one bank of the sheet of water without any sign of its
coming to an end. I doubled back, and had reached the

place whence I started, when I debated the advisability of having a night's rest on the ground. Visions of hungry bears just awakened from their winter's sleep floated before my imagination, and I decided that I was not tired enough to go to bed, so started to explore the creek in the opposite direction. Presently I fell in with an owl and chased it for some time. Other interesting birds then claimed my attention, until I almost forgot that I was lost in the excitement of the chase. I had wandered away from the creek, and seeing a slight elevation, comparatively bare of trees, I made for it, intending to get my bearings again from the compass. On reaching the place, however, I was surprised and delighted to find the river within sight. On reaching the bank I could just discern the mouth of the Koo-ray'-i-ka on the opposite shore, and by midnight I reached the village, and was rowed across to our quarters loaded with spoil, dead tired and a little unnerved with my adventure in the forest. When it was all over, I found that I had been more frightened than I suspected at the time. How I got right at last still remains a mystery to me.

Migration was still going on. As we crossed the river in the small hours of the morning, flocks of ducks were still flying north, and I might have shot a Short-eared Owl if I had not been too sleepy.

It was astonishing to see the quantity of wood that was floating down, but as we coasted the shore to avoid the current, we easily saw whence it all came. In many cases the banks were undermined for six or eight feet; in some places they had fallen in, and the trees growing upon them were hanging down in the water. The banks are nothing but sand and earth; the river evidently widens every year, and carries an immense quantity of mud down to its mouth.

The following day I chronicled two arrivals, the first steamer from Yen-e-saisk', and the first Common House-Sparrow. The steamer was a paddle-boat belonging to the Mayor of Yen-e-saisk'; it unfortunately did not bring the mails. It brought us, however, startling news—that Russia had declared war against Turkey, and had already taken several forts; that England was at first inclined to help Turkey, but was prevented from doing so by the outbreak of a revolution in India!

I did not go far from home in search of birds, but a peasant brought us a Bewick's Swan. A brisk breeze from the south had blown all day; it veered round to the east in the evening, when some enormous floes of ice went down the Koo-ray'-i-ka. At half-past ten P.M. we had one of the finest rainbows I have ever seen.

Spring flowers were now rapidly making their appearance. One that seemed to be our Wood Anemone was already in flower. Patches of snow were still lying in the forest, especially on the northern slopes.

During the next day the ice was still straggling down the Koo-ray'-i-ka, but not in sufficient quantity to close our little port, so I gave an Ost'-yak and his wife a couple of roubles to row Glinski and me across the Yen-e-say' in their lodka. The distance was computed to be four versts, but the current took us down a verst below the village, and this verst we had to row back up-stream. We were just over an hour making the journey. The Starrester of the village gave us quarters, and we planned to have three days' good sport. A peasant soon brought us thirteen Golden-eye Ducks' eggs, with the down out of the nest. He told us that he found the eggs in a hollow tree. He also brought two Common Gulls' eggs. The Great Snipe I found even more common than on the other side of the river. In the evening I watched numbers of them through my binocular. They stretched out their necks, threw back their heads, opened and shut their beaks rapidly, uttering that curious noise like the running of one's finger along the edge of a comb, exactly as I had heard them before.

The Scarlet Bullfinches also were very numerous. The male would be generally perched conspicuously in a birch-tree warbling a few simple notes, which sounded very like the words, "I'm very pleased to see you," with the emphasis on *see*. The Martins were busy building their nests.

I turned out at four o'clock the next morning, and had a long round before breakfast. The number of birds was perfectly bewildering. I found two Widgeons' nests, one with seven eggs and the other with five. I shot a Sedge-Warbler, and a couple of Siberian Chiffchaffs, also a small bird whose song resembled somewhat the trill of a Redpole; I was surprised to find it to be the Arctic Willow-Warbler. The Reed Bunting was there in abundance, but I did not see the smaller species.

I was well rewarded for getting up so early. There can be no doubt that ornithological observations are much more easily made in the early hours of morning immediately following sunrise than at any other period of the day. It requires some courage to turn out, ere the day has got properly aired, but an ornithologist is always well rewarded for his trouble. Birds are on the feed and can be easily approached, and in spring they are in full song. I considered that my morning's work was amply repaid by two important discoveries: first, that of the song of the Arctic Willow-Warbler; and second, the identification of the Sedge-Warbler, which I had previously only partially identified by its song. The bird I shot was, so far as I then knew, the first Sedge-Warbler ever shot in Asia, but I discovered on my return home, that Severtzow had met with it in Turkestan, though his identification was doubted by many ornithologists. I afterwards found it extremely common in suitable localities on the banks of the Yen-e-say'. Of course this bird is only a summer visitant to Siberia, and a very interesting problem presents itself for future ornithologists to solve. Where do the Yen-e-say' Sedge-Warblers winter, and by what route do they migrate?

In the afternoon we had rain, but in the evening the sun came out again very hot. I found this an excellent time to pick up the small Warblers on the banks of the *Kouria*, which forms almost an island in the summer. In a couple of hours I had shot three Siberian Chiffchaffs and a couple of Sedge-Warblers. I also recognised the Redpole-like notes of the Arctic Willow-Warbler, and secured another bird. I shot a male Shoveller Duck, and found a nest with four eggs in it, which I set down to belong to this species;

I kept the down in it, to assist its identification. The female uttered a cry like *pape* as she flew away.

I was surprised to see several small-bodied long-tailed animals in the slender branches of the hazel-trees, sometimes twelve and twenty feet aloft. As they ran along the ground or up the trunk of the tree, they had all the actions of our Squirrel. They proved to be Striped Squirrels. (See note page 72.),

The next day was dull, with heavy gales from the west, but the frequent showers did not seem to diminish the number of birds. I shot a Common Gull after having watched it perching in a larch-tree; Harvie-Brown and I had noticed this habit of the Gull in the valley of the Petchora. Two or three times I had caught a passing glimpse of a dark-coloured Thrush, with a very conspicuous white eyebrow. I was now fortunate enough to secure one, as it was feeding on the ground in a dense birch plantation. It is a most beautiful bird, the Siberian Ground Thrush, but it seemed to be very rare and very shy.*

The Fieldfares, which had hitherto been very wild, were now comparatively tame. They were in full song, if their subdued chatter be musical enough to be called a song. They often sing as they fly. That day I shot a new bird, the Mountain Hedge-Sparrow.† I also found another Widgeon's nest with six eggs in it.

---

* The Siberian Ground Thrush (*Geocichla sibirica*) breeds in the valleys of the Yen-e-say' and the Lena, between lat. 67° and 68°, and also near Yokohama in Japan. It winters in China, Burmah, Sumatra, and Java, and has once occurred on the Andaman Islands. It is met with in Europe as a very rare straggler during the seasons of passage, and has once been obtained in England in the winter of 1860–61.

† The Mountain Accentor (*Accentor*

The next morning I secured a couple more males of my new Hedge-Sparrow. They seemed wonderfully quiet birds, I did not hear them utter a note. In the afternoon we saw the steamer of Kitmanoff pass on its way to the Koo-ray'-i-ka; it had my new schooner the *Ibis* in tow, built by Boiling in Yen-e-saisk'. I had arranged with Captain Wiggins to go shares in her with me, his part of the contract being to finish her, and rig her out English fashion. In the half-wrecked condition of the *Thames* we felt it might be useful to us all to be provided with two strings to our bow. At sight of the steamer we lost no time in packing up our things and crossing the river. We had had three days' hard work. Glinski had skinned ninety-nine birds, and we were taking about thirty more with us to skin on the other side.

On our return I found that during our absence the Arctic Willow-Warbler had arrived in some numbers. Early the next morning I heard the now well-known song from the door of our house. After breakfast I had a turn in the forest, and heard many of these birds singing. The song is almost exactly like the trill of the Redpole, but not quite so rapid and a little more melodious. The bird did not seem shy, and I soon shot four. Nor did it appear to me so restless as most of the Willow-Warblers. The Siberian Chiffchaff, for instance, is a most unquiet bird; it seems always in a hurry as if its sole object were to cover as much ground as possible.

---

montanellus) breeds in North-eastern Siberia, above the limit of forest growth, where I afterwards obtained its eggs, and in a similar climate on the mountains of Southern Siberia. It passes through Mongolia and winters in North China. It is an occasional visitor to Europe, but has not been found in the British Islands.

On the extreme summit of a spruce fir I discerned a little bird shivering his wings and making a feeble attempt to sing. It began with a faint plaintive note or two, then followed the "weest" of the Yellow-browed Warbler by which I recognised the species, and lastly it finished up with a low rapid warble which appeared to be variations upon the same note. This is probably all the song of which this little bird is capable, but every particular is interesting respecting a warbler which now and again deigns to visit the British Isles.

Whilst walking through the forest I suddenly came upo a bird preparing to fly from a dense clump of trees, and was fortunate enough to shoot it before it got well on the wing. It proved to be an example of the Himalayan Cuckoo, whose extraordinary note had attracted my attention some days previously.

The heat had been great during the last two days, with scarcely a breath of wind stirring, and the snow had melted everywhere except a few patches here and there in the forests where it had drifted to an unusual depth. The river had fallen considerably, and only now and then a stray block of ice might be seen floating down the Koo-ray'-i-ka. The Ost'-yaks were busy fishing, and three chooms were pitched on our side of the river and four on the other. The season had not yet fairly commenced, the water was very cold, and fish were very scarce, but every day brought fresh signs of the rapid approach of summer, and the Ost'-yaks were very busy and evidently in high spirits at the close of the long winter. I visited each fresh family that arrived, in hopes of picking up something interesting, but they were all evidently very poor. From one man who seemed a little more enterprising than the others I procured a rude kind of spokeshave which he was using to plane his new oars into shape, and a drill which was almost the exact model of one I bought from a Samoyade in the Petchora. The Ost'-yak told me that he had made these tools himself.

The 22nd was oppressively hot, with a slight breeze occasionally from the south. It was evident that not only had summer come in earnest, but migratory birds also had come. Though I diligently took my round in the forest every morning, I found many birds conspicuous by their absence, and had no new arrivals to chronicle. The Arctic Willow-Warbler was now very common, and the principal songster. Besides its song it utters an occasional note, sometimes a single one, *dzt*, sometimes made into a double note by dwelling upon the first part, *d-z, zit*. Little Buntings were also there in great numbers. Now and then I would meet a Brambling, a Lapp-Tit, a Yellow-headed Wagtail, or a Sedge-Warbler, but the Willow-Warblers and Bluethroats, which had been so common a week back, had now nearly all disappeared. I got a Redwing's nest with three eggs.

Early on the following morning we had rain, and as we crossed over to the ship to breakfast a white fog covered the river; it cleared away before noon, and we had a warm sunshiny day. Boiling (who had come down in Kitmanoff's steamer) and I rowed across the Koo-ray'-i-ka, and we spent the day on the other side. Birds were extremely numerous, and I solved some very important problems. During the past week I had repeatedly heard the song of a Thrush with which I was not acquainted, but hitherto I had never been able to get a shot at the bird. This Thrush was a very poor songster, but he had a very splendid voice. He seldom got beyond one or two notes, but in clearness and richness of tone these notes were fully equal to those of the Blackbird. I was fortunate enough to secure a bird, which turned out to be the Dark Ouzel. It was a female with eggs large enough for a shell, so that I hoped soon to find a nest. I saw several pairs flying about. At frequent intervals I had also heard a short unpretentious song, not unlike that of our Hedge-Sparrow. It came from a bird generally perched aloft on the top of a high tree, from which, after warbling its short song, it would dart off to another. As yet I had not been able to shoot it; this time I succeeded in securing one, and found it to be the Mountain Hedge-Sparrow.

On the banks of the river where the Koo-ray'-i-ka joins the Yen-e-say', are islands and peninsulas covered with willows. These were nearly all covered with some feet of water, so that one could squeeze a boat amongst the trees. As we rowed past the willow cover, I heard a familiar song, and pointed the bird out to my companion; it was wheeling round in circles overhead, occasionally descending into the willows. I recognised it to be the Siberian Pipit which Harvie-Brown and I had discovered in the Petchora. Some hours after we first sighted it, I was lucky enough to get within shot of one, singing in a willow-tree; I had, of course, expected to find this bird in this locality, as it had already been shot east of the Lena.

My fourth important observation that morning was, however, the most valuable of all, in fact by it I attained one of the special objects of my journey. A quarter of an hour before we left the opposite shore, as I was making my way down the hill to the boat amongst tangled underwood and fallen tree-trunks, rotten and moss-grown, a little bird started up out of the grass at my feet. It did not fly away, but flitted from branch to branch within six feet of me. I knew at once that it must have a nest near at hand, and in a quarter of a minute I found it, half hidden in the grass and moss. It contained five eggs. The bird was the Little Bunting. It hovered about, so close to me, that to avoid blowing it to pieces I was obliged to leave the nest to get at a sufficient distance off. It seemed a shame to shoot the poor little thing, but the five eggs were, as far as I knew, the only authentic eggs of this species hitherto obtained, therefore it was necessary for their complete identification. The nest was nothing but a hole made in the dead leaves, moss and grass, copiously and carefully lined with fine dead grass. I can best describe the eggs as miniature eggs of the Corn Bunting.

The forest on that side of the river was principally larch, spruce, pine or cedar, and the trees were larger than upon the side where our headquarters were. The two commonest birds were the Yellow-browed Warbler and the Arctic Willow-Warbler, and the songs or notes of both were constantly to be heard. Sedge-Warblers were frequent on the banks, and Bramblings in the forest.

In the evening I had a long chase after two birds, whose song resembled somewhat that of the Wheatear. I had to take a boat at last to get to them. They proved to be two fine male Siberian Stonechats, and though I followed them at least an hour, I never once heard the call-note—*u-tzic-tzic*—which our bird so constantly utters.

The next morning Boiling, I, and one of the engineers rowed across the Koo-ray'-i-ka, and had another long round along the banks of the Yen-e-say' and in the forest. We saw no more of the Dark Ouzels, but occasionally we heard their note. The Yellow-browed Warbler and the Arctic Willow-Warbler were as plentiful as ever, but we could find no trace of their nests. These birds were both in full song, and had evidently not begun to build. I found a nest of Temminck's Stint with two eggs. In the willows near the shore Sedge-Warblers were singing lustily, and once or twice we heard the Siberian Pipit. There were several pairs of black Ducks across the river, probably Black Scoters.

In the afternoon Sotnikoff's steamer arrived. Unfortunately for us, as fate would have it, she carried as one of her passengers the Sessedatel of Toor-o-kansk'. He soon boarded us, and as a matter of course he soon began to beg. The Captain was his first victim ; from him he extracted a handsome pistol and some preserved fruit. I presented the old gentleman with a bottle of sherry and some cigars, but I absolutely refused to let him annex anything; he tried hard to cajole me, first, out of my double-barrelled gun, then of my single barrel, and lastly he made a dead set at my binocular, but I denied him everything, and he left me with a sour countenance. Certainly, in all my experience, I have

never met with so shameless a beggar as old Von Gazenkampf.   His name led one to expect that he had some
German noble blood in his veins, and his aristocratic appearance encouraged the supposition, but one soon discovered
that he belonged to the corrupt school of Russian officials
in the worst days of serfdom.   It is scarcely possible to
believe that the Government at St. Petersburg is aware of
the rascalities practised in remote corners of the empire, and
no doubt an official sent from headquarters to examine into
the administration of these distant districts, would be heavily
bribed there to keep silence.   It was lamentable to see the
universal system of plunder carried on.   The Russian
peasants plunder the poor Ost'-yaks, the Government officials
and the Yen-e-saisk' shopkeepers plunder the Russian
peasants.   Commercial honour seemed almost unknown on
the Yen-e-say'.   Let us take an instance.   During our stay
the Mayor of Yen-e-saisk' was a merchant, who had formerly
been a pedlar.   Like many of the shopkeepers of that
unfortunate town, he came from the district south of Nishni-
Novgorod.   He was at that time computed to be worth two
million roubles.   He had failed twice, dishonourably it was
said, and paid each time five shillings in the pound.   We
had a fine specimen of his mode of transacting business.
We bought sundry articles from him, paid for them, and got
a receipt.   These were of the value of seventy-three roubles,
and were to be brought down by the steamer to our ship
with other articles ordered.   When the river became
navigable, the goods were promptly delivered, and the
account hurriedly presented for payment as the steamer was

on the point of leaving to go farther down the river. Fortunately for us one of our party could read Russian. He found that the seventy-three roubles already paid down were included in the amount claimed, and their payment demanded a second time. Twenty odd casks of tallow, and about as many sacks of biscuits were also to be brought down to us by the steamer; in both cases one package less than the proper quantity was delivered. The Captain promised to have these missing packages found, and left for us at Doo-din'-ka, but I felt certain that we might as well have at once written off the value to our already sufficiently large plunder account, for, needless to say, we never heard any more of them.

It would be unfair to represent this entire absence of any feeling of commercial honour as in any way an exclusively Russian characteristic. It is Asiatic, Oriental. The moment you have crossed a line which one might draw from Königsberg to Trieste, you have ceased to be in Ethnological Europe, and as far as race and character go you are to all intents and purposes in Asia. West of this line people do frequently act dishonourably, but they are ashamed of it, and it is only the temptation of the gain which reconciles them to the disgrace which they try to hide. East of this line it gives a man far more pleasure to cheat you out of a sovereign than to earn a sovereign in a legitimate manner. So far from being ashamed of it, he glories in it, and boasts of his cleverness. I do not think this enormous difference of national character is a question of climate, race, or religion. I take it to be purely a question of free government and

just laws. The free man fears no one, and can afford to tell
the truth. Under just laws, love of justice, and contempt
of knavery rapidly develop themselves.   The commercial
immorality of Russia must be laid to the charge of its
despotic government.

RUSSIAN EIKON.
(Brass and enamel.)

CHAPTER XIII.

Birds begin to grow scarce — Absence of the Nutcrackers — Fertile hybrids between Hooded and Carrion Crows—Nest of the Yellow-browed Warbler— Birds plentiful in the early morning—Arctic Willow-Warbler—Nest of the Dark Ouzel—Second nest of the Little Bunting—Leaving the Koo-ray'-i-ka— New birds identified each week—Parting with our friends.

On Monday the 25th of June I had a long round in the forest, but met with nothing of special interest. The only nest which I found was that of a Redwing, containing four eggs. Birds were evidently beginning to become scarce again. Many had left for still more northerly breeding grounds, and those which remained had scattered themselves in the forest. The pairing season was over, and the songs with which the male birds had wooed their females were now for the most part hushed, the energies of the feathered songsters being apparently concentrated upon the engrossing duties of nidification. A few birds only seemed to have finished their nests, and occasionally serenaded their patient mates during the period of incubation. The Blue-throats had disappeared altogether. Of the four Willow-Warblers the western species was seldom heard, but the three eastern species were the commonest birds in the forest. I shot a solitary Nutcracker, a male in full moult, which I presumed from the appearances observable on dissection, might have been a barren bird. The breeding haunts of the Nutcracker remained a mystery which I was unable to solve. Probably they were quietly hatching their eggs in the remotest recesses of the forest. One of the Ost'-yaks brought me the nest of a Hazel-Grouse containing eight eggs. It was made of leaves, dry grass, and a few feathers.

On the afternoon of the following day I climbed up to the Crow's nest which I had discovered on the 11th of May. It now contained two young birds; one looked much more thoroughbred Hoodie than the other. I was unable to shoot the male, but I had often examined him through my binocular; he had a very grey ring round the neck, and showed a quantity of grey on the breast and under the wings. I shot the female; she had not quite so much Hoodie in her. The feathers on the sides of the neck and on the lower part of the breast and belly were grey, with dark centres. The fact is now conclusively proved that these hybrids are fertile.

Late in the evening Boiling and I strolled through the forest. As we were walking along, a little bird started up near us, and began most persistently to utter the alarm-note of the Yellow-browed Warbler, a note which I had learned in Gaetke's garden in Heligoland. As it kept flying around us from tree to tree, we naturally came to the conclusion that it had a nest near. We searched for some time unsuccessfully, and then retired to a short distance and sat down upon a tree-trunk to watch. The bird was very uneasy, but continually came back to a birch-tree, frequently making several short flights towards the ground, as if it were anxious to go into its nest, but dared not whilst we were in sight. This went on for about half-an-hour, when we came to the conclusion that the treasure we were in search of must be within a few yards of the birch-tree, and we again commenced a search. In less than five minutes I found the nest, with six eggs in it. It was built in a slight tuft of grass, moss and bilberries, semi-domed, exactly like the nests of our Willow-Warblers. It was composed of dry grass and moss, and lined with reindeer hair. The eggs were very similar in colour to those of our Willow-Warbler, but rather more spotted than usual, and smaller in size.

The special interest attaching to this discovery lies in the fact that the Yellow-browed Warbler has once been shot in

England, and has thus obtained a place in the list of British birds. Its eggs were previously unknown; those obtained by Brooks in Cashmere having been lately discovered to belong to a nearly-allied, though perfectly distinct species, the validity of which that keen-eyed ornithologist was the first to point out. My nest from the valley of the Yen-e-say' remains unique, no second one having as yet been found.

The next morning Boiling and I rose at one o'clock, soon after sunrise, and rowed across the Koo-ray'-i-ka, to explore the opposite banks of the river. The morning is without doubt by far the best time for birds. From sunrise to noon they were plentiful enough in the forest: the latter half of the day they were more rarely seen, and were much more silent. I secured another Siberian Pipit, and found a pair of Dark Ouzels, evidently breeding. They showed so much uneasiness at our presence, that we made a more careful search for the nest, and soon found one which I have no doubt was theirs. It was an exact duplicate of our Song Thrush's nest, and apparently ready for the first egg. I discovered afterwards, however, that it yet required a final lining of dry grass.

After breakfast I had an unsuccessful search for the nest of the Arctic Willow-Warbler. The bird was common enough, but evidently it had not begun to breed. Often four or five of them would be singing together at the same time. As they did not arrive until a fortnight after the other three Willow-Warblers, we might fairly expect them to be late breeders.

In the afternoon I had a siesta, and in the evening strolled out again into the forest. I walked for a mile without shooting anything but a Hazel-Grouse, when suddenly a Thrush flew off its nest with a loud cry, and alighted in a tree within easy shot. I glanced at the nest, snapped a cap at the bird, with one barrel, and brought her to the ground with the second. I picked her up, expecting to find a Red-wing, but was surprised and delighted to find the rare Dark Ouzel. The nest was in a slender spruce, about fifteen feet from the ground, on an horizontal branch, some six inches from the stem. I lost no time in climbing the tree, and had the pleasure of bringing down the nest with five eggs in it—so far as I know the first authenticated eggs of this species ever taken. The nest was exactly like that of a Fieldfare, and the eggs resembled small, but richly marked Black-bird's eggs.

On the following morning I felt somewhat fatigued after the previous long day's work of twenty-four hours, but could not resist the temptation of having a short early stroll in the forest. It produced a very small bag, nothing but a solitary male Bluethroat; but I found, however, a second nest of the Little Bunting containing two eggs. I carefully marked the spot, hoping to get the full clutch of five eggs should we remain long enough for the purpose. A north wind had been blowing for some days, and the Captain was taking the opportunity of getting the little schooner into order.

The next morning I returned to the spot I had marked, and took the nest of the Little Bunting, which had now three eggs in it. At noon we packed up, and went on board, towing our unfinished schooner with us. We got up steam, and cast anchor some fifty versts down the Yen-e-say'.

We were all heartily glad to leave the Koo-ray'-i-ka. The sailors who had wintered there were sick of the place; and the Captain, who had seen his ship all but lost, could have no pleasant recollections of the trap into which he had fallen. For my own part I was anxious not to be too late for the Tundra, which I looked upon as my best ground. I had been about ten weeks in the Koo-ray'-i-ka.

The following table of the number of species of birds identified during each week will show at a glance the date of the arrival of the mass of migrants:

23 April to 30 April . . .	12
1 May „ 7 May . . .	2
8 „ „ 14 „ . . .	5
15 „ „ 21 „ . . .	3
22 „ „ 28 „ . . .	3
29 „ „ 4 June . . .	13
5 June „ 11 „ . . .	33
12 „ „ 18 „ . . .	18
19 „ „ 25 „ . . .	3
	90

Comparing this list with that of the arrivals of migratory birds in the valley of the Petchora,* it would appear that birds arrive much later in the valley of the Yen-e-say': but it is possible that the difference may be an accidental one of season and not a constant one of locality. In the Petchora we found that the greatest number of migratory birds arrived between the 10th of May and the 4th of June,

* See 'Siberia in Europe,' page 301.

whilst on the Yen-e-say' the arrivals were principally between the 31st of May and the 18th of June. These dates correspond with the time at which the ice on the two rivers broke up, in lat. 65°, the 21st and 31st of May respectively.

When we left the Koo-ray'-i-ka, of course we never expected to see it again; so we took an affectionate leave of our landlord Turboff, and of the Starrester of the village on the other side of the Yen-e-say'. I believe they were sorry to part with us, although Captain Wiggins had had one or two quarrels with both of them. In one way or other they had made a considerable profit out of our long visit to their remote corner of the world. We had hired their dogs and their reindeer, paid them for labour of various kinds, bought milk, meat and firewood from them, and made them presents of all sorts of things, and yet for all that it was easy to see that they looked upon the enterprise of Captain Wiggins with great jealousy. The Russians are intensely conservative people. They look with suspicion upon anything new. Of course I never for a moment expected them to understand my object in collecting birds. From what Glinski told me they evidently considered it to be a cloak to hide some ulterior object. Captain Wiggins was perhaps a little imprudent in expatiating in broken Russ upon the wonderful benefits which the introduction of commerce was to bestow upon the country. He told them over and over again that the success of his enterprise was to open the door at once to English commerce. This naturally aroused the jealousy of the men, who had practically a monopoly of the commerce of the district. They were too short-sighted to see the advantage which such a change might bring them, and looked upon Captain Wiggins as a competitor. His scrupulous honesty in dealing with the natives, many of whom came to buy cotton goods and always received over-measure, was another cause of offence with traders, who systematically cheated their customers, and took advantage of their necessities to over-charge them on every possible occasion. Nevertheless their innate Russian hospitality and good-nature overcame much of their prejudice, and they took leave of us with every mark of affection. As for the natives, they were really grateful for what little we had done for them, and persisted in kissing our feet. We left the settlement with gloomy anticipations of its future. Debt and drink continually drain everything of value into the hands of half-a-dozen merchants, who are gradually killing off the geese that lay the golden eggs.

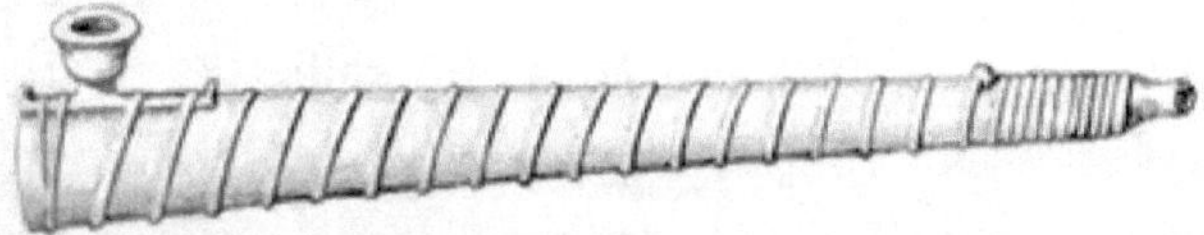

TUNGOOSE PIPE.

WRECK OF THE " THAMES."

CHAPTER XIV.

Contrary winds—Aground on a sandbank—Ost'-yaks to the rescue—Visit on shore—Nest of the Siberian Chiffchaff—Birds in the forest—Under weigh again—Wreck of the ill-starred *Thames*—Arrangements for the future.

ON Saturday, the 30th of June, we sailed down the river with a somewhat contrary wind, which obliged us to tack more or less, but the current helped us to the extent of at least three knots an hour. In the evening we cast anchor, about one hundred and ten versts below the Koo-ray'-i-ka. I went on shore and found a third nest of the Little Bunting, with five eggs somewhat incubated. The nest was lined with the hair of reindeer.   We had a heavy thunderstorm late at night, and, after we had turned in, the rain came down in torrents.

Sunday morning, the 1st of July, was almost a calm, with rising fog, which cleared off before noon.   We were crossing the river to get to the west of one of the islands, when the current unexpectedly drifted us too near the shore, and we found ourselves suddenly aground on a sand bank, with a light wind and a strong current driving us against the point of the island.   We spent the whole morning throwing overboard the ballast, and putting the wood and cargo on board the *Ibis*, but as quickly as we lightened the ship the water fell.   Every now and then we took an anchor out from the vessel in a boat, and hauled in the cable with the steam winch.   All our efforts proved vain, the anchors all came home, the bottom was evidently smooth ice, and the part of the anchor which trailed on the ground was polished like steel.   All the afternoon we worked away, without apparently the ghost of a chance.   We tossed half the wood overboard, filled the *Ibis*, hauled first at the bow and then at the stern, ran the engines full speed ahead, and then tried full speed astern, but the vessel was aground somewhere about midships, and we vibrated on a pivot, not gaining a single point.

In the evening a few Ost'-yaks came across in a boat, to see what was the matter, and we set them to work to clear the bunkers of wood, and move the remaining ballast forward, hoping thus to raise the ship by the stern.   Meanwhile the sailers took out an anchor, with three lengths of cables, and dropped it at a greater distance from the ship than they had hitherto done. It was eleven o'clock by this time, the men were exhausted, and this was our forlorn hope. We had all worked hard since five o'clock (eighteen hours), in a hot sun and amidst virulent mosquitoes (the *Culex damnabilis* of Rae); the Captain now decided that if he failed in this endeavour nothing more could be done; in the morning the ship would, no doubt, be high and dry on a daily enlarging sandbank, we must dismantle her, sell her as a wreck in Doo-din'-ka, and go down the river in the *Ibis*. To our great surprise and delight, our last manœuvre succeeded. The anchor held sufficiently to draw us off; we steamed into deep water, and at one o'clock cast anchor in safety. From the Ost'-yaks we bought a sturgeon a yard long for half-a-crown, and sterlet half that length for a penny a piece.

The following morning, whilst the Captain was taking in fresh ballast, I went on shore and had a few hours' shooting and bird-nesting. The mosquitoes were swarming in clouds; there were so many between the eye and the sight of the gun, that it was almost impossible to see a small bird. I came upon an encampment consisting of three Ost'-yak chooms, and about fifty reindeer. The shore was very muddy, and between the river and the forest was a long, gently sloping bank, sprinkled over with willows. In these trees wisps of dry grass were hanging, caught between the forks of the branches, and left there after the high water had subsided. In one of these, about two feet from the ground, a bird had built its nest, or rather it had appropriated one of these wisps for its nest. There was scarcely any attempt at interlacing stalks. It was undoubtedly the most slovenly and the most loosely-constructed nest I remember to have seen. It was not much more than a hole, about two and a half inches in diameter, with one side a little higher than the other, the entrance somewhat smaller than the greatest size inside, which was globular in form, and carefully lined with Capercailzie and Willow-Grouse feathers. The tree in which it was built was about fifty yards from the small encampment, and the feathers of both these birds would naturally be found outside an Ost'-yak's choom. As I approached, a little bird flew out of it, and began to fly uneasily from tree to tree, uttering the plaintive note, which I at once recognised as that of the Siberian Chiffchaff. I looked into the nest and saw it contained three eggs, pure white, with dark red, almost black, spots. I retired about twenty yards. The bird came back to the tree, and, having apparently satisfied itself that its treasures were safe, it began once more flying from tree to tree, still uttering its plaintive alarm-note. To be perfectly certain it was a Siberian Chiffchaff I shot it, and returned to the ship with the first identified eggs of this species ever taken. I found, besides, two solitary Fieldfares' nests, about a mile from each other, from one of which I shot the bird. So far as I could judge, the Fieldfare was rather a rare thrush there, and it did not appear to be at all gregarious. During migration they were in small flocks of about half-a-dozen birds, but afterwards I saw them only in pairs. I found, also, three nests of Temminck's Stint, from two of which I shot the birds. Sedge-Warblers were very abundant, and a few pairs of Bluethroats frequented the willow. I saw both the White Wagtail and the Yellow-headed Wagtail. In the pine forests the Arctic Willow-Warbler was very numerous. Most of these birds were in full song, and apparently thought that there was no occasion whatever to hurry about nest building. One pair, however, were chasing each other through the forest, uttering a note I had not heard before, a plaintive scream. I shot one, expecting to procure a new bird. Our Willow-Warbler, and also the Yellow-browed Warbler, were thinly sprinkled through the trees, the former preferring the birches, and the latter the pines. I shot a Scarlet Bullfinch, and heard several singing.

SAMOYADE PIPE.

On Tuesday, the 3rd of July, we weighed anchor early in the morning, with a fair breeze, which at noon became strong enough to clear the decks of mosquitoes. The cabin we made habitable by a vigorous application of brown paper smoke. We found the sterlet and the sturgeon delicious eating, the former the richer of the two. Now and then we passed, on the banks, small encampments of Ost'-yak chooms. The men were busy fishing, in their usual lazy fashion. They frequently boarded us, wanting to buy salt and to sell fish. We saw many birds as we steamed along, a large flock of Ducks, a small party of Swans, occasionally a Gull, once a pair of Terns, and once an Eagle.

After dinner I turned in for an hour's nap; when I came

on deck again I found that a serious accident had happened. In attempting to wear the ship, or box-haul her on her stern, she had refused to come round. The sails were in perfect order, each in the correct position for performing its required task. She was coming round very nicely, when suddenly, without any apparent cause, in spite of her helm, in spite of a monster patent jib, pulling hard with a fresh breeze, contrary to all nautical laws, she swung back and shot towards the shore. She was then in five fathoms of water. She soon got into three and a half fathoms, and the Captain, to save himself let go the anchor. The sails were thrown back, which had the desired effect of throwing her head off shore. By a most unfortunate accident, in coming back, she fouled her anchor in two and a quarter fathoms, in such a position that the current prevented her getting off. Steam was got up, an anchor was taken out, and the vessel was soon hauled off the fluke of the anchor under her, but only to fall back into a shoal. When we had twenty pounds of steam with which to work, the propeller was put in action, the steam winch hauled on the cable, and a fair breeze from the south-west soon got us off the shoal. In two minutes she would have been in perfect safety, when, without a moment's warning, the wind suddenly changed to nor-east, and drove her hard and fast into the shallow water, before the sails could be furled. All our efforts to get her off were vain. The ballast we had put in after the accident on Sunday was thrown out, the wood was thrown back again into the *Ibis,* anchors were tried on several sides, but all came home, one was taken upon shore and the cable strained until it broke. The men worked hard all night, but by morning she was more than a foot aground, fore and aft, and as the water was falling rapidly, it was evident the case was utterly hopeless. Everything that could be done had been done, and the Captain gave the vessel up. Thus ended the career of the *Thames*, a melancholy close to a long chapter of accidents and hairbreadth escapes. The ship seemed fated: why she refused to wear round in the first instance will probably always remain a mystery. Perhaps some treacherous under-current seized her keel, or possibly she fouled some hidden snag. Fouling her anchor in coming back was one of those accidents that will happen to the best-regulated vessels; but that, after having escaped both these dangers, a sudden and total change of wind should occur at the precise moment when she was sailing into perfect safety, was one of those coincidences that a century ago would undoubtedly have been ascribed to the agency of supernatural powers of evil. This untoward accident was a heavy blow to all of us. We realised to the full the truth of Burns's proverb, that "the best laid schemes o' mice and men gang aft a'-gley." The Captain's hopes were totally frustrated. The good ship was wrecked for that year at least irretrievably, and the following spring the ice would probably crumple her up like pasteboard. For my part I could only look forward to reaching the Tundra too late for my best work, with the cheerful prospect, besides, of facing an overland journey of five or six thousand miles, with a little mountain of luggage. There was nothing left for it but " to grin and abide."

The first thing to do was to hold a council of war. Captain Wiggins declared himself determined if possible to complete his programme. If he could not return to England in the *Thames* he was desirous of making the attempt in the *Ibis*. The question was would his men consent to accompany him. I declined to commit myself to what I could not but consider a foolhardy enterprise, but expressed myself not only willing but most anxious to go as far as Gol-cheek'-a, and proposed that the future destination of the *Ibis* should be left an open question, to be finally settled on our arrival at that port. Wiggins fell in with this compromise at once, and began to complete the half-finished *Ibis*. Now that the *Thames* was *hors de combat* we could freely rob her of spars, sails, compass, and many other little things which would make the *Ibis* as complete as possible. Boiling assisted in these arrangements with hearty good will. He was as anxious as I was to reach Gol-cheek'-a, but the men worked sullenly, and it was evident that something approaching a mutiny was in the wind. Wiggins told off four of the sailors to man the *Ibis*, but one of them refused to go on board without a clear understanding as to the ultimate destination of the little craft. Wiggins declined to commit himself to any route. The man persisted in his refusal to go on board; Wiggins threatened to put him in chains; the man would not withdraw his refusal. Mysterious entries were made in the log-book, and another man was chosen to fill his place. Order being thus restored, the completion of the *Ibis* was definitely arranged, and we returned to our bunks, none of us in the happiest of humours, but determined to make the best of a bad job.

YURAK HUNTER.

CHAPTER XV.

THE following day I went on shore for a few hours in the morning. The country was very flat, covered with stunted forests of birch, willow, and alder; pines rose in the distance.

grass had already grown as high as our knees, and wild flowers of various kinds were in full bloom. A sort of yellow pansy was the first to appear after the wood anemone, the Jacob's ladder was common, a dwarf rose was just bursting into flower, and the air was fragrant with the aromatic rhododendron-like shrub, *Ledum palustre;* the wild onion, and the wild rhubarb were flowering, and on the sand we sometimes found quantities of the graceful *Anemone pulsatilla.* Birds were abundant; I took two nests of the Fieldfare only a few yards distant from each other, showing that they were to some extent gregarious, also a nest of Willow-Grouse with three eggs. In one part of the forest, I heard a small bird flying round and round uttering a cry like *na-na-na.* Whilst I was watching it I was called away, but before leaving I fired at the bird and missed. I afterwards returned to the same place and saw and heard the bird; again I fired and missed it, I then sat down to watch; the bird came within twenty yards of me, alighted in a birch and in less than a minute dropped down on the ground. As I neither saw it nor heard anything more of it for five minutes I concluded that it had dropped into its nest. I walked up to the place; a fallen birch-tree was lying across a tussock of moss and bilberry. I tapped the birch-tree with my gun, and the bird flew out of the tussock. I soon found the nest, and turning round I shot the bird. It proved to be only our Willow-Warbler. This alarm-note was one quite new to me. The nest was as usual semi-domed, and profusely lined with feathers. The eggs were very small, and thickly marked with light red spots. I saw one or two Snipes and

shot two male Siberian Stonechats. The Martins were busy
hawking for mosquitoes; some of them had eggs in their
nests. Fortunately I brought a few home, as the species
proved to be different from our European Martin. We
had a cold north wind all the next day, with mist and rain.
I did not go on shore, but spent the whole of my time in
putting my things in order, getting the schooner into ship-
shape, blowing and packing eggs, and writing up my
journal. The wind continued the following day to be nor-
east blowing a stiff gale; but it was warm, accompanied by
occasional showers. I went on shore both morning and
afternoon. Strolling on the muddy sand by the river bank,
I came upon the recent tracks of a bear, which animal the
peasants said they had seen a week or two ago. I saw a
Short-eared Owl and a Hen Harrier, and shot a Cuckoo,
which proved to be the Himalayan species. I also took my
fourth nest of the Little Bunting, with six eggs. It was
lined with dry grass, and one or two reindeer hairs. I shot
the bird. Almost immediately afterwards, as I was crossing
a swamp, a Snipe rose at my feet, fluttering in a manner
that convinced me she had eggs. I shot her as she was
flying away; she proved to be the Common Snipe. The
nest was made in a little tussock of grass and moss, which
grew out of the water. A deep hole had been hollowed in
the moss, and lined with dry stalks of flat grass. It contained four eggs considerably incubated. A few minutes
afterwards, a Willow-Warbler flew out of a large tussock of
grass, and began to utter the alarm-note of the Arctic
Willow-Warbler: I shot it, but too hastily, and mangled it so

much that it was scarcely recognisable. **I soon** found the **nest. It was** built in a recess in the side **of the tussock. It was** semi-domed, the outside **being moss and the inside fine dry** grass. There was **neither** feather **nor hair used in the con-**struction. It contained **five eggs larger than those of the** Willow-Warbler, **and of a somewhat different character.** Before they **were blown they looked** pink, but **afterwards** the ground colour **became pure white, profusely spotted all** over **with very small and very pale pink spots; up to the** present time **these eggs remain the only authenticated eggs** of this species. **I saw several** Redpoles and Bramblings, but did not discover their **nests. I found a nest of the Fieldfare,** and another of the Redwing; **the eggs of the Fieldfare were** highly incubated, **and those of the Redwing still more so,** indeed two of them **were hatched.**

We spent the whole **of the** following day **in getting our** stores and baggage **comfortably stowed on board the** *Ibis*. A smart breeze from **the north still blew, keeping us clear of** the mosquitoes. **The river had fallen so much that the** *Thames* lay high and **dry on the sand, and we could walk** ashore without any difficulty.

The next day the **Captain mustered his men in the** cabin, and had a somewhat unsatisfactory **interview with them. I** had seen upon **my arrival at the Koo-ray'-i-ka that the** Captain was not popular with **the crew.** The British sailor is a peculiar character, for ever **exercising** the Englishman's favourite privilege of grumbling. Probably Captain Wiggins had been exceptionally unfortunate in the **selection** of his scratch crew; as far as **I could** learn the men had shown jealousy of each other, had taken every possible occasion to grumble at their food, and at their work; they certainly had laboured in the most spirited way upon the two occasions we had run aground, but now there did not seem to be a man among them who had any pluck left; right or wrong, they appeared to have lost all faith in their leader. They were in a complete panic at the idea of the Captain attempting to go to sea in the *Ibis*. The Captain and his men had evidently been at loggerheads some time; to some extent this was the Captain's fault; he had not sufficient tact. Captain Wiggins was a very agreeable travelling companion, one with whom it was a pleasure to converse; he was also a thorough Englishman. With the exception of the Yankee, I suppose John Bull is the cutest man in the world, but unfortunately he is too well aware of the fact, and relies implicitly upon his fertility of resource to get safely out of any scrape into which he may fall. He takes little thought for the morrow, but goes on blundering and extricating himself from the effects of his blunders, with a perseverance and ingenuity truly wonderful. But all this means hard work for those under his authority. Captain Wiggins had also minor faults which increased his unpopularity; he was apt to form rash judgments, and consequently was for ever altering his opinions and changing his plans. No one saw this more clearly nor criticised it more severely than the crew under him; then the Captain had another fault of still deeper dye in the eyes of an English tar; he was a teetotaler and worked his ship upon teetotal principles. In my opinion that was the fountain-head of all his difficulties.   After four-and-twenty hours' hard work, a glass of honest grog would, more than anything else in the world, have cheered the drooping spirits, revived the fainting pluck, and cemented the *camaraderie* that ought to subsist between Captain and his men, especially upon expeditions involving such rare difficulties.   Nevertheless my sympathies went rather with the Captain than with his crew : the latter when he appeared unjust, should have considered how much allowance ought to be made for a man who had seen his pet schemes frustrated, and his ship lost.   Commerce between England and the Yen-e-say' might be postponed *sine die.*   The Captain was suffering from a kind of monomania, that he had been checkmated by a secret conspiracy, but I could not detect any evidence that such was the case : if it were, then certainly the winds and the waves were amongst the conspirators.   He had a run of ill-luck, but his fertility of resource is so great, that I have no doubt he will yet, to some extent, retrieve the losses which were caused by a long series of petty blunders, and I heartily wish him success in his next undertaking.

I repeat, that with all his faults, Captain Wiggins is an Englishman to the backbone, possessing the two qualities by which an Englishman may almost always be recognised, the two marked features of the national character, which are constantly showing themselves in English private, social and commercial life, and most of all in English political and military life.   One of these is an unlimited capacity to blunder, and the other is indomitable pluck and energy in extricating himself from the consequences.

At length, after much unpleasantness, the last finishing touch was given to the rigging of the *Ibis*, and on Monday the 9th of July we were *en route* for Gol-cheek'-a. We bade adieu to our dogs and foxes and the larger half of the crew, and finally weighed anchor at three in the afternoon, in a stiff gale. Unfortunately the wind was nearly dead ahead, but we had a current of three or four knots in our favour.

MAMMOTH TOOTH.
(Upper view.)

The *Ibis* sailed far better than we anticipated; in spite of her flat bottom we could sail her pretty near the wind, and we beat down the great river very satisfactorily, leaving E-gar'-ka and the ill-fated *Thames* far behind us, and near-ing the Tundra at the rate of seven or eight versts an hour. Just before we left the scene of our last disaster three Swans alighted on the shore, a verst above the ship. I walked up to the spot and took the measure of their foot-prints on the sand. From the centre of the ball of the heel to the centre of the ball next the claw, the middle toe measured five and a quarter inches. This measurement enabled me confidently to assert that the birds I had seen were Bewick's Swans, the footprints left by the Wild Swan being at least an inch longer. Several Gulls passed us;

they had not the black tips to the wings, and were probably Glaucus Gulls. I hoped soon to have an opportunity of shooting one.

We passed Plakh'-in-a in the early morning of the following day, and made good headway with the wind north and norwest until noon. The wind then dropped almost into a calm, and in the evening we had a breath of air from the south, with a few occasional drops of rain. This weather lasted all night. After leaving E-gar'-ka the banks of the river are rather steep, and somewhat thinly clothed with larch, with an undergrowth of coarse grass, except where the innumerable water channels cut into the soil. The *Ibis* was only drawing about three feet of water, so we had no difficulty with the shoals; the water also had fallen so much that most of the dangerous sandbanks showed above it, and were easily avoided. We passed very few villages, perhaps one in every three versts; some of these were very small, consisting of but two or three houses. The population we were told decreases every year, in consequence of the rapacity of the Sessedatels, or local governors. Now and then we passed one or two Ost'-yak chooms; but this race also is decreasing, and evidently from the same cause. We saw very few birds. Large flocks of Black Ducks continued to fly northward, and occasionally we saw a few Gulls or a pair of Swans. In one part of the river we passed what was apparently a sleeping place for Gulls; the shore was flatter than usual, and there were no trees. About two hundred Gulls were assembled, apparently roosting, some down by the water's edge, and others on the grassy banks.

On the 11th we cast anchor at Doo-dink'-a at seven o'clock in the morning, and went on shore to visit the merchant Sotnikoff; as we almost expected, however, we found that he had gone down to Gol-check'-a in his steamer, to superintend his fisheries. He had built himself a large new residence, the only good house in the little village. In the winter I had sent Sotnikoff a message, asking him to secure for me complete costumes of the Dol-gahn' men and women, who visit Doo-dink'-a in the spring to trade. The costumes were waiting for me, and very handsome they were: I paid for them one hundred and forty roubles. I also bought some Yu-rak' and Sam'-o-yade costumes. I saw some fine mammoth tusks and teeth, but the former were too heavy and bulky to take home overland. Sotnikoff's stores contained an almost endless number of furs, but among them were no Black Fox nor Sable. The latter animal is now very rare; at one time it was hunted in the forests in winter, the hunter following the tracks in the snow, until he lost them at the foot of a tree; he then surrounded the tree with a net, whose meshes were too small for the Sable to pass through, and to which was attached a number of little bells. Lying down within sound of the bells the hunter waited one, two, or three days, until the tinkling warned him that the Sable had come out and was entangled in the net. Another mode of securing the animal was to smoke it out of its hole, and then to shoot it. An anecdote was related to me of a hunter, who followed the track of a Sable until it crossed the path of a Capercailzie, when both suddenly disappeared. The hunter came to the conclusion that the Capercailzie had seized the Sable, and that the bird had taken wing with the animal: he ascertained the direction in which it had flown by blood stains on the snow, and at last he shot the Sable, who had turned the tables on its captor, and was now feeding on the dead bird.

At Doo-dink'-a we saw some excellent coal, which burnt as well as any English fuel. It was brought by Sotnikoff from a mine on the Tundra, about eighty versts from Doo-dink'-a. There was also a quantity of blue and green copper ore from the same place. We understood that this had been analyzed, but had not turned out worth working, only containing 5 to 10 per cent. of metal.

Soon after leaving Doo-dink'-a the trees became more scarce upon the banks of the river. The right hand bank was still steep, and was called the rocky bank; the left shore was flat, and was called the meadow bank. We passed several islands and sandbanks. On one of the latter we got aground, but by running an anchor out in a boat from the ship we soon hauled her off into deep water.

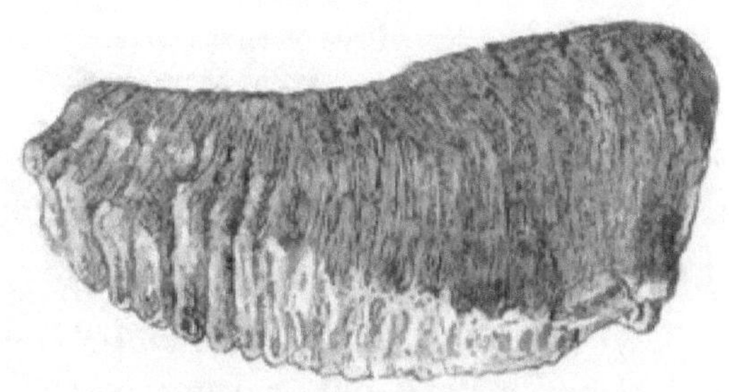

MAMMOTH TOOTH.
(Under view.)

SAMOYADES ERECTING A CHOOM.

CHAPTER XVI.

The Tundra—The dried-up Doo-dink'-a—Reception by the birds—Variety of
birds—The Chet'-ta river—Sam'-o-yade chooms—The broad nose of Tol'-sta-
noss'—Second visit to the Tundra—Asiatic Golden Plover's nest—A night on
the Tundra—The Dunlin—News of Sideroff's schooner—Winter in Siberia—
The fishing station—The King of the Sam'-o-yades—Egg of the Red-breasted
Goose—Brek-off-sky Island—Eggs of the Mountain Accentor—Various eggs—
Wearied out—Ugliness of the natives—Land on the horizon.

WE cast anchor soon after midnight, the 12th of July. I
went on shore in the morning, to ascertain what bird-life was
to be found on the Tundra. We climbed up the steep bank,
and found ourselves in a wild-looking country full of lakes,
swamps, and rivers, a dead flat in some places, in others
undulating, even hilly. This was the true Siberian Tundra,

brilliant with flowers, swarming with mosquitoes, and full of birds. In sheltered places, dwarf willows and weeping birch were growing, and (we were only some fifty versts from the forests) here and there a few stunted larches. Winding through the Tundra was the track of what had once been the bed of a river, nothing now but a small deep valley forming a chain of isolated lakes and pools. This river bed is called the dried-up Doo-dink'-a, and is about fifty versts to the north-west of the real river Doo-dink'-a. On some of the northern slopes, large patches of snow were still lying.

Most of the birds evidently had young ones. As we approached, we each found ourselves the centre of attraction of a little feathered crowd, whose constituents uttered various alarm-notes, as they flew round, or waited upon some shrub or plant, with bills full of mosquitoes, anxious to feed their young as soon as the coast was clear. I noticed the Bluethroat, the Red-breasted Pipit, the Shore Lark, and the Little Bunting; great numbers of Lapland Buntings, Redpoles and Yellow-headed Wagtails. A Willow-Grouse was sitting upon nine eggs. I took a Red-necked Phalarope's nest with four eggs; a pair of Bewick Swans had evidently a nest somewhere in the neighbourhood; several pairs of Golden Plover and Wood Sandpipers were considerably alarmed at our invasion of their breeding grounds. The Arctic Willow-Warbler, the Common Willow-Warbler, and the Siberian Chiffchaff were all in full song, and I repeatedly heard the Siberian Pipit. Several pairs of Fieldfares had nests, and I found one containing young birds. Near the shore a pair of Ringed Plover and several pairs of Temminck's Stints were very demonstrative, but my attention was devoted to more attractive game. Upon a steep sloping bank, covered with patches of dwarf birch and willows, and overlooking a flat willow swamp, close to the shore (which had evidently once formed a little delta at the mouth of the dried-up Doo-dink'-a), a pair of Thrushes were loudly proclaiming the vicinity of their nest. I shot one, and found it to be the Dusky Ouzel, whereupon I commenced a diligent search for the nest. In half-an-hour I found it, in the fork of a willow level with the ground. It was exactly like the nest of a Fieldfare, lined with dry grass, and it contained, alas! five young birds about a week old. This was very disappointing, as the eggs of this bird are unknown.

On the lakes were several Ducks and Divers, but they took care to keep out of gun-shot. After three hours' stay on land, we returned to our ship.

At noon the wind changed to sou-east with rain. In the course of the morning we passed the mouth of the Chet'-ta river, said to be the way to the Obb. In the early summer boats are towed up this river to a lake, whence a short cut across the Tundra with reindeer leads to a stream down which the boats can float into the Tazz.

During the afternoon we passed four Sam'-o-yade chooms. The inhabitants seemed well off; many reindeer sledges were lying round the tents, and five boats were on the shore. Half-a-dozen of the Sam'-o-yades came alongside of us, wishing to buy tobacco. In several places we saw huge lumps of turf, some more than twenty feet thick lying on the edge of the Tundra like rocks. They must have been floated down in days long past, when the floods rose much higher than they do now, or before the bed of the river had been channelled to its present depth.

In the evening the wind got well back into its old quarter, and it soon blew so stiff a gale, that we dared not round the " broad nose " of Tol'-sta-noss', and we cast anchor under the lee of the mud cliffs of the Yen-e-say' about midnight.

The gale continued next day with rain until noon, when I took advantage of our enforced delay, and went on shore for a few hours. A climb of about one hundred feet brought me on to the Tundra. In some places the cliffs were very steep, and were naked mud or clay. In others, the slope was more gradual, and covered with willow and alder bushes. In these trees Thrushes were breeding ; I soon found the nest of a Dusky Ouzel, with five nearly fledged young. It was placed as before in the fork of a willow, level with the ground. On the top of the bank, I found myself on the real Tundra. Not a trace of a pine-tree was visible, and the birch-trees rarely exceeded twelve inches in height. There was less grass, more moss and lichen, and the ground was covered with patches of yellow mud or clay in which were a few small stones, that were apparently too barren for even moss or lichen to grow upon. The Tundra was hilly, with lakes, swamps, and bogs in the wide valleys and plains. As soon as I reached the flat bogs, I heard the plaintive cry of a Plover, and presently caught sight of two birds. The male was very conspicuous, but all my attempts to follow the female with my glass, in order to trace her to the nest, proved ineffectual ; she was too nearly the colour of the ground, and the herbage was too high. Feeling convinced that I was within thirty paces of the nest, I shot the male, and commenced a diligent search. The bird proved to be the Asiatic Golden Plover with grey axillaries, and I determined to devote at least an hour looking for the nest. By a wonderful piece of good fortune I found it with four eggs, in less than five minutes. It was merely a hollow in the ground upon a piece of turfy land, overgrown with moss and lichen, and was lined with broken stalks of reindeer moss. The eggs resembled more those of the Golden than those of the Grey Plover, but were smaller than either. These are the only authenticated eggs of this species known in collections. I saw a small Hawk like a Merlin, a pair of Siberian Herring Gulls that evidently had a nest in the neighbourhood, a number of Shore Larks and Lapland Buntings, and a few Red-throated Pipits and some Redpoles.

I went on board again in the afternoon. The gale still continued, and squalls of rain frequently passed over us. The Captain decided that we must continue to lie at anchor for the night, so I challenged one of the sailors named Bill to spend the night with me on shore. We had no sooner landed than a couple of Peregrine Falcons revealed their nest to us by their loud cries. At a glance up the cliffs we decided the place where it would be, at the top of a steep mud promontory which stretched out to a sharp ridge beyond and above the surrounding coast. I climbed up a valley in which the snow was still lying, and came straight along the ridge to the little hollow where four red eggs were lying on a dozen small flakes of down. Bill shot the female, but she fell amongst the willow and alder bushes, and though we spent an hour in the search, we did not succeed in finding her. The time was not, however, wasted. Whilst searching for the fallen Peregrine, we started a Siberian Chiffchaff from an alder bush, and had the good fortune to secure her nest with four eggs. It was placed in the branches about four feet from the ground, and was rather more carefully constructed than the one I had previously found. It was composed of dry grass, semi-domed, and lined with Willow-Grouse feathers. The eggs were white, spotted with dark purple, and large for the size of the bird. The Siberian Chiffchaff is evidently a much later breeder than the Willow-Warbler, which is somewhat singular, as both birds arrived together from the south. Our Willow-Warbler was still there, but not common.

On the plains we passed many pairs of Asiatic Golden Plover, but as I had already secured their eggs, we passed across the Tundra to some lakes in the distance, hoping to find something new. In a marsh adjoining one of the lakes I shot a Dunlin, the first I had seen in the valley of the Yen-e-say'. A few hours later I shot a second, and secured its young in down. The old bird was in full moult. On the lake two Ducks were swimming ; Bill took them both at one shot. They proved to be two female Long-tailed Ducks, also a new species for my list. On a bare hill overlooking the second lake, I shot a pair of Arctic Terns, and soon after found their nest, containing one egg and two young in down. On a similar bare place a pair of Ringed Plover were very demonstrative, but we took no trouble to seek for their nest. We caught several young Lapland Buntings, and shot a Shore Lark in the spotted plumage of the first autumn.

Before we returned to the ship, the gale had subsided, and we hastened back to the shore. Coming down the bank, I found a Fieldfare's nest on the ground under the edge of the cliff. It contained five young birds nearly fledged. I shot the female, expecting to find one of the rarer Siberian Thrushes.

As soon as we got on board at two o'clock in the morning, the anchor was weighed, and we proceeded with a gentle breeze from the land. In the afternoon we picked up Schwanenberg's two mates in an open boat; they were on the look out for us, and from them we learned the fate of Sideroff's schooner. The little river in which she was anchored had steep banks, between which the snow drifted to the depth of twenty feet. All the sailors died of scurvy except the mate. Early in April the pressure of the snow above, and some movement, possibly in the ice below, caused the vessel to spring a leak, and she rapidly filled to the depth of six feet. The island where she was lying is called Mah'la Brek-koff'-sky, and is said to be in Lat. 70° 35′ N., and in Long. 82° 36′ E. From the mate, who wintered there, I learned the following particulars. From Nov. 22 to Jan. 19 the sun never rose above the horizon. On May 15 it ceased to set. On May 29 the first Geese appeared: the only birds seen during the winter being Willow-Grouse and Snowy Owls. On June 15 the first rain fell; on the 16th the first thunderstorm; on the 18th the ice broke up, and was all gone in five days. The river rose higher than it had been known to rise for seventeen years, the whole of the island, twenty versts long, being flooded. One house was carried away, and the other two were saved by the men standing on the roofs and staving off the ice with poles. The water came within a foot of the top of the roofs. The schooner was carried bodily away, and at the date of our visit lay high and dry a couple of versts lower down, with a large hole in her side, a more hopeless wreck than the *Thames.* The latter vessel lay near the mouth of a small but deep river, into which, it was the opinion of Boiling and some others, there was a fair chance she might be floated the following year between the rising of the water and the breaking up of the ice.

In the evening we sailed through a very narrow channel into the little creek where the fishing station was established. In various places round the creek stood the chooms of the Yu-raks'. Opposite each choom three or four boats lay on the muddy beach, the fishing nets hanging on rails and stages to dry. At the entrance to a narrow channel like a river, but which was really an arm of the great river coming to an abrupt termination, about a verst inland, was the head-quarters of Sotnikoff's agent at that station. This was the busiest place we had yet seen on the river; it contained three or four wooden houses, a couple of chooms and a yurt. The latter was a turf and mud house, nearly square, built, half under the ground, and half above it, a few larch poles as rafters supporting the turf roof, altogether making probably as good a house for the summer as one could have in this part of the world. When the cold north wind blows, the house may easily be kept warm with a small fire; and in the burning heat of the sun it forms a cool retreat, easily cleared of mosquitoes by smoke. A small steamer lay at the mouth of the Kooria, as these arms of the river are called; along with her lay a barge, and in various places Russian lodkas and Sam'-o-yade canoes were moored. On land fishing nets were piled in every stage of wetness, dryness, fulness and emptiness; fish was being salted, casks were being filled or packed in the barge. Some hundreds of White Fox skins were hanging up to dry, and men of various nationalities were going to and fro. The more information I tried to obtain about these eastern tribes, the more puzzled I became. I was presented to a Sam'-o-yade of the name of Patshka, called the King of the Sam'-o-yades. When I asked him if he were a Sam'-o-yade, he gave me a very hesitating affirmative, but freely admitted that he was a Yu-rak'. He emphatically denied that he was Ost'-yak, Tun-goosk', or Dol-gahn'. The natives did not seem to recognise the word Sam'-o-yade, except perhaps as a Russian term for an Asiatic. One told me he was a Hantah'-iski, another that he was Bear'-govoi, another that he was Karasin'-ski whilst a fourth called himself an Avam'ski. The only conclusion I could come to was, that they were all Yu-raks', and that the names by which they called themselves, referred to their respective districts.

Before anchoring in this creek, we had run aground and spent an hour or two endeavouring to get the vessel free, being obliged to send two anchors off in order to set her afloat. I went on shore about midnight. When Schwanen-berg's second mate left the Koo-ray'-i-ka I had commissioned him to procure for me what eggs he could before my arrival, and in each case to shoot the bird if possible. He and the first mate had accordingly lost no opportunity of collecting whatever eggs they could find. This collection small, as it was, proved of great value, for I had arrived at my destina-tion too late for most eggs. A very interesting egg is that of the Red-breasted Goose,* which the first mate found on the adjacent island. There were two eggs in the nest, but, shooting the bird while she was sitting, he unfortunately broke one egg.

On Sunday I spent twenty hours out of the twenty-four in exploring the island. As far as I was able to penetrate it was all swamps and lakes, with a few dwarf willows dotting it in clumps here and there. Three weeks before, the whole island had been eight feet under water; it was now about fourteen feet above the level of the Yen-e-say', so that in that time the river must have fallen about twenty-two feet. The place abounded with birds, but the variety of species on it was small. The commonest was the Yellow-headed Wagtail. What interested me most in the small collection of eggs which the two mates had procured for me was five sittings of the eggs of the Mountain Accentor, which were hitherto unknown in collections. These eggs

---

* The Red-breasted Goose, *Bernicla ruficollis*, so far as is known, is confined during the breeding season to the tundras of the Obb and the Yen-e-say'. It is supposed to winter on the southern shores of the Caspian, and occasionally strays into Europe, including the British Islands, on migration.

were blue and unspotted, and resemble very closely those of our Hedge-Sparrow. The mate took me to a nest in which were young birds. It was close to the ground in a dwarf willow bush. The next commonest bird was the Lapland Bunting, but there was no evidence of their breeding, as they had already fledged young on the Tundra. I concluded their nests had been swept away by the flood, and that they had not bred a second time. Temminck's Stints were extremely abundant; amongst the mate's collection of eggs were thirty-three of this bird. He had also secured for me some of the Red-necked Phalarope, and of the Ruff, which were not uncommon here. The only warbler I saw on the island was the Siberian Chiffchaff. This bird was always to be heard, and frequently to be seen. I took two of its nests, with eggs still unhatched in them, and received twenty-five of its eggs from the mate. The nests were on or only just above the ground. I saw a few pairs of Red-throated Pipit, and took one of their nests with five eggs, and got a second sitting from the mate. In both cases the eggs were variable in colour, forming a graduated series from dark brown to stone colour. Occasionally I heard the Siberian Pipit, and I got a sitting of eggs from my deputy collector which could belong to no other bird which I saw on the island. Redpoles were not uncommon, and the mate told me this was the earliest bird to breed. Most of its eggs in his collection were taken before the river rose. He took a few nests of a Thrush. The eggs were apparently those of the Redwing. I saw a pair of Thrushes, but failed to shoot either of them. A pair of

White Wagtails built their nest on the wreck of Schwanenberg's schooner. The mate saved the eggs for me. I took a Teal's nest with eggs, and occasionally saw Long-tailed Ducks flying past. The mate secured me three Swan's eggs. These birds were constantly to be seen. So far as I yet know, Bewick's Swan is the only species found at this place. The Siberian Herring Gull and the Arctic Tern were generally to be seen, and the same hand secured me eggs of both. Occasionally a pair of Buffon's Skuas flew over.

The following day, another twenty hours' hard work wellnigh exhausted the ornithology and ethnology of the Mah'-la Brek-off-sky Os'-troff. I was footsore with all this walking in swamps, and positively worried by mosquitoes. I think nothing short of the certainty of coming upon a Curlew Sandpiper's egg, would have tempted me on shore again that day. The natives are very ugly, not copper-brown like the Dolgahns, nor yellow like the Ost'-yaks, but almost as cadaverous-looking as corpses. The extreme irregularity of their features and the dirt of their dress add to their repulsiveness. I got a curious leaden pipe from a Yu-rak', and the mate gave me an interesting iron pipe, made by a Tungoosk', which he had got at Doo-dink'-a.

In the evening we weighed anchor, delighted to leave the mosquitoes, but at midnight we were obliged to cast anchor again and send a boat out to find water to float a ship drawing three feet. We seemed to be out in the open sea when we were, in fact, in a nest of shoals. At last we found a passage out, in one to one and a quarter fathoms, and got on fairly with a head wind and a slight current as day came on.

At noon the next day there was land on the starboard : high bold cliffs, composed, no doubt. of turf and mud extending ninety degrees on the horizon. All the rest was open water. In the afternoon two herds of Beluga or White Whale passed close to the ship. Towards evening we saw a strip of land at a great distance on the port side of the vessel. At night we made scarcely any progress, being almost becalmed, and the river so broad that the current was scarcely perceptible.

During the next morning the wind freshened a little ; the channel narrowed to perhaps six miles, which helped the current, and at noon we cast anchor at Gol-cheek'-a, close to three steamers and sundry barges.

GOLCHEEKA.

CHAPTER XVII.

Gol-check'-a—Blowing eggs—Drift-wood on the swamp—The Little Stint—Rock Ptarmigan—I secure a passage to Yen-e-saisk'—Fighting over the *Ibis*—Buffon's Skuas—Shell mounds—The Captains come to terms—Sandbanks at the mouth of the Gol-check'-a—Farewell to the Tundra.

THE village of Gol-check'-a is on an island, between the two mouths of the river of the same name; across both its arms stretches a swamp, and beyond the swamps rise the steep banks of the Tundra. In summer Gol-check'-a is a busy place; all the processes of catching, salting and storing fish, go on during a long day of twenty-four hours. The sun having ceased to rise and set, the ordinary divisions of time are ignored. If you ask a man what time it is, he will most probably tell you he has not the slightest idea. Order seems for the nonce forgotten, and people sleep and eat when inclination bids them.

Immediately after casting anchor, we took one of the boats, and paid visits of ceremony to the Russian steamers. Boiling and I had arranged to spend the night on the Tundra; but we had no sooner returned to the *Ibis* to dine than the wind, which had been freshening all the afternoon, blew such a gale that it became impossible to land with safety. The gale continued all night, accompanied by heavy showers of rain, nor did it decrease sufficiently during the next day to allow us to venture on shore in a boat. Fortunately I had on board a box of eggs, collected for me by a Sam'-o-yade, the blowing of which kept me employed. Several had been taken from the nest two or three weeks before our arrival, and were becoming rotten. The larger number were those of Gulls and Divers; there were some small eggs which were, without doubt, those of the Snow-Bunting, and there were twenty or thirty of the Sand-pipers, but none that were strange to me. There was a sitting of Red-necked Phalarope, and some eggs which I identified as those of the Little Stint. There were also two sittings of Golden Plover, and one of the Asiatic Golden Plover.

The wind having somewhat subsided during the night, Glinski, Bill, and I started at four o'clock in the morning for the Tundra. We first had to cross the swamps, which we did without difficulty, in no place sinking more than a foot below the surface; at that depth the ground probably

remaining frozen. One corner of the marsh was still bound
by a small range of ice mountains, miniature Alps, perhaps
thirty feet high at its greatest elevation. This ice would
probably survive the summer; it had, of course, been piled
up when the floes passed down the river. All over the
swamp driftwood lay scattered, old, weather-beaten, moss-
grown, and rotten. The marshy ground was then only
a few inches above the level of the sea, but immediately
after the thaw it had been, we were informed, some feet
under water. Birds were abundant. Golden Plover, Arctic
Tern, Ruffs, Red-necked Phalarope, Snow-Bunting, Lapland
Bunting, and Dunlin, were continually in sight, and I shot
a couple of female Little Stints, the first I had seen in the
valley of the Yen-e-say'. On the Tundra, the commonest
bird was the Asiatic Golden Plover. They were breeding in
every spot that we visited. My attempts to watch them on
to the nests were vain; from their behaviour I came to the
conclusion that they had young. Just as we were leaving
the swamp we picked up a young Plover not many days
old. Our Golden Plover was very rare, and we only shot
one brace. The note of the Asiatic Golden Plover is very
similar to that of the Grey Plover. Its commonest note, a
plaintive *kö*. Occasionally the double note *klëë-* is heard,
but oftener the treble note *kl-eĕ kö* is uttered. Ringed
Plover were plentiful on the barer places on the Tundra.
Wagtails seemed entirely to have disappeared; the Redpole
and the Red-throated Pipit were still found, but were not
abundant. In the small valleys running up into the Tundra
we frequently saw Willow-Grouse, and on the high ground

I shot some Rock Ptarmigan.* In some of these valleys the snow was still lying; flowers were very brilliant; but we did not come upon any shrubs more than a foot high. Occasionally Gulls, Divers, and Swans flew past us overhead, but I did not see any Skuas on this part of the Tundra until later. On the 21st of July I moved all my luggage from the *Ibis* to the steamer belonging to Kittman and Co., where I engaged a passage to Yen-e-saisk'. I secured a small cabin next the paddle-box, just large enough for myself and Glinski to work in. For this I paid twenty-five roubles. My large casks were on the barge, at a freight of sixty kopeks a pood, and we were each charged sixty kopeks a day for our meals, besides having to provide for ourselves tea, coffee, sugar, and spirits. In the afternoon I explored the island. It seemed to be about a square mile in extent, very swampy, and thinly sprinkled with rotten driftwood. I shot Arctic Terns, Red-throated Pipit, Lapland and Snow Buntings, and Temminck's Stint, and saw Red-necked Phalaropes, and a Long-tailed Duck. As I was leaving, a boat passed, towing a couple of Belugas, or White Whales; one was about six feet long, and the other nine or ten feet. Before I left, the men were already beginning to cut off the skin and blubber into strips; the skin seemed to me half an inch, and the blubber about two inches

---

* The Rock Ptarmigan (*Lagopus rupestris*) was said to be confined to Iceland, Greenland, and throughout Arctic America, until I obtained my specimens on the Yen-e-say', in lat. 71¼° —the first record of the species on the mainland of the Palæarctic region. Beyond this we have no further particulars of its range. This discovery leads to the supposition that it is a circumpolar bird.

average thickness; the former makes the strongest leather known. Captain Wiggins told me it fetched a rouble per lb. in St. Petersburg, where it is largely used for reins and traces.

On my return, I found the Captain and Schwanenberg fighting over the *Ibis*. I had offered to take six hundred roubles in a bill upon Sideroff for my half from Schwanenberg, or an I. O. U. for 500 roubles from Wiggins. Schwanenberg wanted to go in her to St. Petersburg, Wiggins wanted to go in her to the Obb. Schwanenberg's crew were on excellent terms with their captain, and were willing to risk their lives for, and with him. Wiggins, on the other hand, was at loggerheads with his men, who point-blank refused to go. It was a very unpleasant position for the Captain, but, to a certain extent, he had himself to blame for it. He had unfortunately not taken the right course to gain the affection of his sailors; and, considering the feeling existing between them, it seemed to me unreasonable to expect the men to follow him into further risks, which were never contemplated when they were first engaged. The Captain was evidently trying all he could to discover some combination by which he might be saved the humiliation of finding means for a rival to do that which as yet he had failed to do himself. In the meantime, Schwanenberg was in much suspense, fearing the boat would slip through his fingers. Both parties consulted me; I tried to give them good advice, wishing heartily the matter could be settled one way or the other. To attempt to cross the Kara Sea in a cockleshell like the *Ibis*, was a madcap enterprise, and could only succeed by a fluke, but both captains were anxious to risk their lives in the desperate attempt.   Ambition and enthusiasm seemed for the moment to have deprived them of common sense.

Boiling and I had a long round on the Tundra. The next day we saw a few pairs of our Golden Plover, and a great many pairs of Asiatic Golden Plover. I spent nearly two hours over a pair of the latter bird, trying to watch the female on to the nest. She ran backwards and forwards over one piece of ground for half-an-hour, then flew to another place, and went through the same performance. The only conclusion I could come to was that she had young, and thus sought to protect first one and then another. The male remained for a long time in one place. His object seemed to be to watch me, and to give the alarm to the female should I move.

Had I been a fortnight earlier I should no doubt have obtained many of their eggs. I had had to pay dearly for Captain Wiggins' blunders, but I could not desert him in his misfortune. I had put upon him as much pressure as I possibly could without quarrelling with him, to induce him to finish the rigging of the *Ibis*, and to let Boiling and myself proceed alone, according to our original plan.

We found the Ringed Plover very common on the bare places on the hill as far as we penetrated the Tundra. Near the river Gol-check'-a I shot two Reeves, and on the hills I shot a male Little Stint. On the same bare places which the Ringed Plover frequented, I occasionally came upon a pair of Wheatears. Redpoles, Lapland Buntings, Red-throated Pipits and Shore Larks were common, and were evidently feeding their young. On the banks of the Gol-

cheek'-a, I saw a solitary White Wagtail, and sometimes a
Red-necked Phalarope or a Temminck's Stint.   That day a
party of seven or eight Buffon's Skuas flew over our heads, out
of gunshot.   This was the only occasion upon which I saw

the " chor'-na chai'-i-ka " at Gol-cheek'-a.   One of the most
interesting discoveries we made on this trip was that of a
number of hills of shells* on the Tundra, at least 500 feet
above the level of the sea.   Some of these beds of shells

* A series of these shells was sub-
mitted to my friend Captain H. W.
Feilden, who, with the aid of Mr.
Edgar A. Smith, determined them to
be of the following species :—

Mollusca : *Pecten islandicus, As-
tarte borealis, Nactica affinis, Saxicava
arctica, Fusus (Neptunea) kroyeri,
Fusus (Neptunea) despectus.*   Cirri-
pedia : *Balanus porcatus.*   All the
species here represented, although
obtained at so great an elevation, are
now existing and common in the neigh-
bouring seas.   This can only be accounted for by the supposition of a
recent rising of the land or subsidence
of the sea in these regions.

were on the slopes of the hills, others were conical elevations of sand, gravel and shell. These latter were from 10 to 20 feet high, with a little turf and vegetation on the top; the sides were as steep as the loose materials of which they were composed would allow. I picked up four or five different species of shells in a nearly perfect condition, but by far the greater number were broken into small pieces, and bleached white. The soil in the neighbourhood of these hills, whenever it was bared from its covering of turf, seemed to be a bluish, sandy clay.

In the evening the two captains came on board, and I acted as mediator. I tried all I could to bring matters to a conclusion without allowing a final rupture. After some sparring I at last succeeded in bringing the two impracticable men to a mutual understanding on the following terms. Wiggins retained his anchors and cables, his spare sails and blocks, his stores and provisions, and Schwanenberg paid him in cash four hundred roubles, and, in a bill upon Sideroff, three hundred roubles more, whilst I took Schwanenberg's draft upon Sideroff for six hundred roubles. If it had not been for Wiggins' impracticability we might have had fifteen hundred roubles for the ship at Brek-koff'-sky, with Schwanenberg's thanks and gratitude into the bargain, but after all it did not make much difference in the long run. Wiggins had the good luck to meet Sideroff and obtain his endorsement; nevertheless the bill was not paid until Wiggins had prosecuted him from court to court, and at last got a final verdict in his favour, and an execution. As my bill was only accepted " per pro," my lawyer in St. Petersburg advised me not to throw good money after bad, and it remains unpaid to this day. I was delighted when the affair was at last settled, and the Russians could no longer accuse us of acting in a dog-in-the-manger fashion. Sotnikoff's steamer left that evening with the two captains and the *Ibis*, and, what was much more to the point, he was accompanied by the voracious Sessedatel. I paid my P.P.C. visit to him, received the Sessedatel's official kiss, and got off cheaply by giving him ten roubles for a wolf's skin worth half that sum.

When we rose the next morning we found that Ballandine's steamer had sailed during the night, leaving us with the last steamer at Gol-cheek'-a. We were told to hold ourselves in readiness to start the first moment the water rose high enough to float us, but we did not weigh anchor until the afternoon, and the evening was spent in getting on and off the shoals, at the mouth of the Gol-cheek'-a river. We did not get clear of the sand-banks until four o'clock in the afternoon of the next day, nor should we have done so then, had not a smart breeze from the north-west backed up the waters of the Yen-e-say', and raised us from two to three feet. The harbour of Gol-cheek'-a will shortly have to be abandoned, for the sand-banks at the mouth of the river increase every year. The channel through them is tortuous, and is rapidly becoming more shallow. No ships drawing more than five feet water ought to venture near it, and then they should only enter it with great care and vigilance. When the ice thaws in spring, the water rises three or four feet. The year of our visit it had risen more, and stood three feet deep in the houses; but this was an extraordinary occurrence, and, we were told, had never happened during the ten years that steamers had been in the habit of visiting Gol-cheek'-a.

My stay in the most northerly village of the Yen-e-say' lasted only six days. The weather being cold and windy, I had almost forgotten the existence of mosquitoes. I now bade adieu to the Tundra with a feeling somewhat akin to disappointment and regret. My trip might be considered almost a failure, since I had not succeeded in obtaining eggs either of the Knot, Sanderling, or Curlew Sandpiper. Nevertheless I was glad to turn my face homewards.

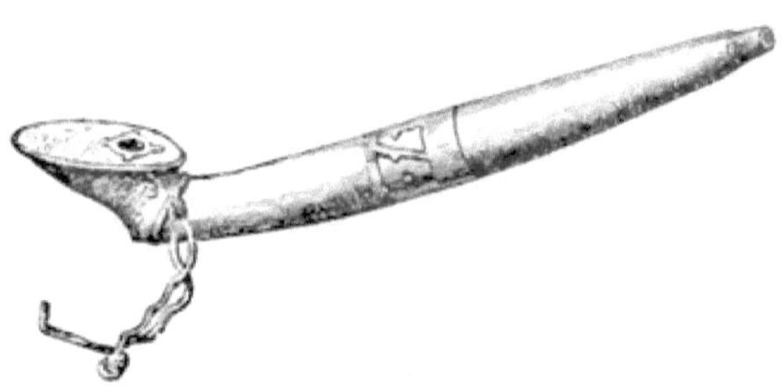

SAMOYADE PIPE.

OSTYAK BOATS.

CHAPTER XVIII.

Climate of the Tundra—Break up of the ice—Migration of birds in the south of France—Comparison between island and continental migration—Routes of migration—Grouse—Conservatism of birds—Mortality amongst migrants—Origin of migration—Glacial Epochs—Emigration of birds—Geographical distribution of Thrushes—Reports on the migration of birds.

THE history of animal and vegetable life on the Tundra is a very curious one. For eight months out of the twelve every trace of vegetable life is completely hidden under a blanket, six feet thick, of snow, which effectually covers every plant and bush—trees there are none to hide. During six months of this time at least, animal life is only traceable by the footprints of a reindeer or a fox on the snow, or by the occasional appearance of a Raven or a Snowy Owl, wandering above the limits of forest growth, where it has retired for the winter. For two months in midwinter, the sun never rises above the horizon, and the white snow reflects only the fitful light of the moon, the stars, or the aurora borealis. Early in February the sun just peeps upon the scene for a few minutes at noon, and then retires. Day by day he prolongs his visit more and more, until February, March, April and May have past, and continuous night has become continuous day. Early in June the sun only just touches the horizon at midnight, but does not set any more for some time. At midday the sun's rays are hot enough to blister the skin, but they glance harmless from the snow, and for a few days you have the anomaly of unbroken day in midwinter.

Then comes the south wind, and often rain, and the great event of the year takes place; the ice on the great rivers breaks up, and the blanket of snow melts away. The black earth absorbs the heat of the never-setting sun; quietly but swiftly vegetable life awakes from its long sleep, and for three months a hot summer produces a brilliant alpine flora, like an English flower garden run wild, and a profusion of alpine fruit, diversified only by storms from the north, which sometimes for a day or two bring cold and rain down from the Arctic ice.

But early in August the sun begins to dip for a few moments below the horizon, and every succeeding midnight sees him hide longer and longer, until, in September, the nights are cold, the frost kills vegetation, and early in October winter has set in, snow has fallen, not to melt again for eight months;

the nights get longer and longer, until towards the end of November, the sun has ceased to take its midday peep at the endless fields of snow, and the two months' night and silence reign supreme.

But wonderful as is the transformation in the aspect of the vegetable world in these regions, the change in animal life is far more sudden and more striking. The breaking up of the ice on the great rivers is, of course, the sensational event of the season. It is probably the grandest exhibition of stupendous power to be seen in the world. Storms at sea, and hurricanes on land, are grand enough in their way, but the power displayed seems to be an angry power, which has to work itself into a passion to display its greatness. The silent upheaval of a gigantic river, four miles wide, and the smash-up of the six feet thick ice upon it, at the rate of twenty square miles an hour, is to my mind a more majestic display of power, but for all that, the arrival of migratory birds, so suddenly and in such countless number, appeals more forcibly to the imagination, perhaps because it is more mysterious.

In my former work on ' Siberia in Europe ' I attempted to give the reader what information I could upon this interesting subject. My facts were principally derived from personal observation of the migration of birds on Heligoland, so that the subject was treated from an island point of view. Since then I have had an opportunity of seeing something of migration in the South of France, both in autumn and spring, and the study of the subject from a continental point of view has caused me to modify some of the views expressed in the former chapter on migration.

When we left England in the middle of October last year the Swallows had disappeared, but we found a few stragglers still basking in the sun at Arcachon. The window of our hotel looked over the bassin on to the Île des Oiseaux, and as we stood on the balcony we could see an almost constant stream of migration going on. Large flocks of Skylarks passed every few minutes, warbling to each other as they flew, and smaller flocks of Meadow Pipits were almost as frequent. Now and then we saw flocks of Dunlins and a larger species of Sandpiper which looked like Redshanks, and once a party of thirty to forty Cranes passed over, forming a line like the letter V. Flocks of Ducks, perhaps more correctly described as clouds of Ducks, so numerous were these birds, continued to pass southwards until the middle of November. In many places the farmers had put down flap nets to catch the smaller species, which were decoyed into them by call birds, and during the whole period of migration birds of all kinds were brought every day to the market.

In early spring we were at Biarritz, and here again we found migration going on apace, but the tide had turned, and the birds were all going north. Early in March small parties of Skylarks, Woodlarks, Pied Wagtails, White Wagtails, Meadow Pipits and other birds were constantly passing in succession, but only within a mile or two of the coast.

On the 11th of March we ascended La Rhune, an out-lying mountain of the Pyrenees. Just as we reached the *col* between the two peaks, we witnessed a most interest-ing little episode of migration. A flock of birds came up from the Spanish side, and, passing over our heads, continued their northerly course. This flock consisted of eight Kites, a Crane, and a Peregrine Falcon. It was a curious assemblage, and we watched them through our binoculars with great interest.

All through the winter we found the Chiffchaff very common at Pau, but it never uttered its familiar note. When we reached Biarritz it was equally common, and quite as silent; but on the 9th of March it began to chiff-chaff lustily. On the 15th Willow-Warblers arrived in considerable numbers, and were soon in full song. Newly-arrived parties were always silent, and sometimes the hedges quite swarmed with these pretty little birds, apparently tired and hungry after their migration, anxiously searching the bushes for food, and very frequently taking a short flight into the air to capture a gnat upon the wing.

The marked difference between migration at Heligoland and migration on the shores of the Bay of Biscay is, that at the former locality not a bird was to be seen in unfavourable weather, but that when the wind was propitious, birds came over with a rush, whilst at the latter post of observation a gentle stream of migration seemed always to be going on, in almost all weathers, from early morn to late at night. The natural inference from such observations is, that in the middle of a long land journey they simply travel slower in unfavourable weather, and rest at night; but when a sea journey has to be made, they wait for favourable wind and weather, and consequently it often happens that, when the right time comes, a crowd of birds has accumulated.

which comes over *en masse*, with what ornithologists call a "rush."

Another result of my Bay of Biscay experience is, that I must recall my suggestions that too much has been made of the great lines or routes of migration. I made many excursions inland, both from Arcachon and from Biarritz, but a very few miles from the coast took me out of the range of migration. On the west coast of France, both in spring and autumn, birds appeared to me to migrate low, principally by day, and to follow the coast-line. I am inclined to think that I must also recall the doubts, formerly expressed, that birds follow ancient coast-lines. The migration from the south of Denmark over Heligoland to the coast of Lincolnshire seems to correspond so exactly with what geologists tell us must have been the old coast-line, that it is difficult to believe it to be only a coincidence. If we admit the theory that migration became a fixed habit during the glacial period, we must also admit that the difficulty of proving that the old coast-line disappeared after the formation of the instinct, is removed. The fact that the British Red Grouse is entirely confined to our islands, and is replaced by a very nearly-allied, but perfectly distinct species on the continent, the Willow-Grouse, seems to prove, that in all probability, after the extermination of bird-life from the corner of Europe now occupied by Great Britain, by the ice of the glacial epoch, it was again repeopled with Grouse from the main land. During the warm period which followed the glacial epoch, we may fairly assume that the absence of the present ice at the North Pole, and the presence of an additional amount of ice at the South Pole, might so alter the centre of gravity of the earth as to leave the shallow portion of the German Ocean dry land, and then the Grouse might again find a home in England without difficulty.   It is obvious, however, that whether the land-connection between England and the Continent were formed by a difference in the level of the water, or whether it were formed by a greater former elevation of a part of the bed of the German Ocean, the severance of Britain from the continent of Europe must have taken place sufficiently long ago to allow for the differentiation of the two species which has subsequently taken place.   The reader may perhaps be inclined to think that it is quite unnecessary to assume any such land-connection, in order to account for the existence of Grouse on our island.   The Grouse is a bird, and can fly, and pretty quickly too, as any one who has shivered behind a butt in the inglorious sport of Grouse-driving knows to his cost.   Why cannot the ancestors of our Grouse have flown across the Channel?   The answer to this supposed doubt on the part of the reader for the necessity of the assumption of a former land-connection is, that there is no instance on record of a Red Grouse having been captured on the Continent, or of a Willow-Grouse having ever strayed to our islands ; and it is a well-known ornithological fact, that in a great many instances a very narrow channel of deep sea bounds the geographical range of birds.   Migration across the sea seems to take place only where it has become a fixed habit, formed ages ago.   Birds are very conservative. To an immense extent they do as their forefathers did.

One cannot expect a very high development of the reasoning faculty in them. The lower the power of the reason the greater is the blind force of hereditary instinct. Like other conservatives, birds have to suffer the penalties of not being able to adapt themselves to the changed circumstances of the times. There can be no doubt that thousands of birds perish in their attempt to follow the old routes which their ancestors' took. I have been assured repeatedly by naval officers that they have seen many instances of flocks of birds being drowned at sea, and I have myself picked up birds that have been washed ashore after a storm.

The origin of migration does not probably date back to a period before the glacial epoch. As birds gradually began to increase and multiply to an extent sufficient to produce a struggle for existence, in the form of a fight for food, they seem to have adopted a custom, which they still retain, of leading away or driving away their families every autumn to seek food and a home elsewhere. As the circle of bird-life constantly widened, in due time the abundance of food tempted many birds to stray into the Arctic regions, to breed during the long summer of those climates at that period. Probably during the darkest months of midwinter, if the cool season of the pre-glacial period may be called winter, some local migrations took place, and birds wandered back again for a month or two into the adjoining districts, but these little journeys can scarcely be dignified with the name of migration.

In process of time, however, the temperature of the earth appears to have cooled to such an extent that as each pole came to be in aphelion during winter, the winter became so severe that those birds who did not learn to migrate to southern climes perished for lack of food during the cold season. These periods of severe winters lasted for 10,500 years, and were followed by similar periods of mild winters when the cold was transferred to the opposite pole, the complete revolution of the precession of the equinoxes taking about 21,000 years. Then came the glacial period, a period supposed to have lasted 120,000 years, when the relative positions of the various planets in the solar system so increased the eccentricity of the earth's orbit, and so exaggerated the severity of the winters, that in consequence of the effects of cold being cumulative (ice and snow not running away as water does) the severity of the winter became at length so great that summer was unable to melt the whole of the previous winter's snow and ice. A permanent glacier having once been formed at the North Pole, and having once bridged over the Arctic Ocean to the continent, would rapidly increase so long as the cause of its existence continued; and the evidence of geology goes far to prove that, at the height of the glacial epoch, the field of ice measured five or six thousand miles across. As this immense glacier marched southwards the palæarctic birds were driven before it, and whilst most of them still came annually to breed in the semi-arctic climate which hung around its skirts, all had to winter as best they could in the already overcrowded Indian and Ethiopian regions, and a few species seem to have made, not simple migrations for a season, but absolute emigrations for good and all into distant lands, and thus their descendants have become almost cosmopolitan. The migration or irruption of Sand-Grouse in 1863 was probably an emigration of this nature.

It must have been a curious state of things in south Europe at this time, when reindeer were destroyed by tigers within sight of a glacier such as now exists at the South Pole.

After the glacial period had passed its meridian, and the edge of the ice gradually retreated northwards, carrying its climate, and its swamps, and its mosquitoes with it, the great body of the palæarctic birds followed it, returning every summer farther and farther north to breed. Here and there a colony was left behind, and formed the tropical allies of so many of our species—birds which no longer migrate, but which have the powers of flight, the pointed wings of their ancestors, though they no longer require them.

The extraordinary emigration of Sand-Grouse alluded to is without doubt only one of many such great movements which have, from time to time, taken place. The disturbance of bird-life produced by the temporary extermination of it in the northern half of the palæarctic region during the glacial epoch must have been very great. The countries to the south of the great glacier must have been overcrowded, and the natural cure for such a state of things must have been emigration on a large scale. It is not difficult to trace some of these movements even after such a lapse of time. Their history is written indelibly on some of the palæarctic genera. The reader may be interested in hearing upon what data such theories are based. Let us select the Thrushes as an example. They are almost cosmopolitan. They are found on all the great continents, on many of the Pacific Islands, and almost all over the world except in New Zealand, Western Australia, the greater part of New Guinea, and Madagascar, and we must remember that these countries are by no means fully explored yet. But in spite of their near approach to being cosmopolitan, they belong to a palæarctic genus or genera. A large proportion of their nearest allies are palæarctic, and the formation of their wings—flat, long, pointed, and with the first primary very small—is such as is principally found in palæarctic birds who acquired wings capable of powerful flight to enable them to migrate during the glacial epoch. Before this time we may assume that the Thrushes were residents in Europe and North Asia.

The Thrushes are divisible into three tolerably well-defined genera. The genus *Geocichla*, or Ground Thrushes, contains about forty species. The genus *Turdus*, or true Thrushes, contains about fifty species, and the genus *Merula*, or Ouzels, contains rather more, about fifty-three. Zoologists have come to the conclusion that the history of the individual is more or less an epitome of the history of the species. Now the young in first plumage of all Thrushes have spotted backs, but the only Thrushes which retain this peculiarity through life are to be found in the genus *Geocichla*; and we therefore assume that the Ground Thrushes are the least changed descendants of their pre-glacial ancestors. In fact we come to the conclusion that before the glacial period

there were no true Thrushes and no Ouzels, and that the
Ground Thrushes inhabited Europe and North Asia, whence
they were gradually driven south as the polar ice extended
its area. The European Ground Thrushes took refuge in
Africa, and overspread that continent. A small part of
them remained Ground Thrushes, and their descendants now
form the African species of the genus *Geocichla*. But by far
the larger portion developed into true Thrushes, some of
whom permanently settled in Africa, whilst others crossed
the then warm South Pole and spread over South America,
some even emigrating as far as Central America and South
Mexico. We thus find that the true Thrushes of the
Ethiopian and the Nearctic regions are very closely allied,
and have by some writers been separated from the genus
Turdus, and associated together under the name of *Planes-
ticus*. During the warm period at the North Pole, which
followed the glacial epoch, the true Thrushes of North
Africa appear to have followed the retreating ice, and to
have spread over Europe, penetrating eastwards into Turkestan and Cashmere, and northwards across the pole into
North America as far south as Mexico.

In Asia a similar emigration must have taken place. The
original Ground Thrushes of Siberia were driven across the
Himalayas into the Indo-Malay region, where a few of them
still retain their original generic character. It would
appear that one or two species found a retreat across
Behring's Straits into America, one being found in Alaska
and one in Mexico. The Alaska species probably crossed
over after the glacial period, as it is very nearly allied to

the East Siberian species. The Mexican species is nearly allied to that found on Bonin Island, and probably crossed over before the glacial period, and was driven southwards by the ice never to return. The greater number, however, of Asiatic Ground Thrushes appear to have developed into Ouzels, which filled India and the Malay peninsula, and many of whom emigrated eastwards to Java and the Pacific Islands, some even reaching across the Pacific Ocean, and forming a colony of Ouzels in Central America and north-western South America. After the glacial period had passed away from the North Pole, some of the Ouzels seem to have followed the ice northwards, and again to have spread over Siberia, two species even reaching into and spreading over Europe.

Such is a brief outline, so far as we can guess it from the present facts of geographical distribution, of one of the greatest emigrations or series of emigrations which the world has probably ever known, and comparable only to those of the Aryan race of men. The fact most observable in these movements seems to be that birds are guided by something very nearly approaching reason; their habits are not merely the result of their capabilities; there is method in their migrations. Whilst we find that a narrow channel is frequently the boundary of a bird's distribution, we must admit that in most cases it is a self-imposed boundary. It is not that the birds cannot migrate across the sea; the fact is simply that they do not because they have no adequate motive.

The more one sees of migration the less it looks like an

instinct which never errs, and the more it seems to be guided by a more or less developed reasoning faculty, which is generally right, but occasionally wrong. The stream of migration, which we watched for weeks whilst waiting for the opening of navigation on the Yen-e-say', was almost always from due south to due north, but at the commencement many parties of Wild Geese, too eager to reach their breeding grounds, overshot the mark, and although the ice broke up at the rate of a hundred miles in the twenty-four hours, they overtook and passed the thaw, and finding no food, had to turn back. The records of migration which have been kept on the British coast seem also to show that similar blunders are committed in autumn, and that many birds which ought to reach our northern and eastern shores have apparently in like manner overshot the mark, and have had to turn back, some from the sea and others from the continent, and consequently arrive on our western or southern shores.

It has been remarked in this country that migration takes place in autumn in greater flocks or " rushes " than in spring. This is probably caused by the birds lingering at some favourite feeding grounds, and accumulating in increasing numbers until a sudden frost warns them that they are over-staying their time, and they " rush " off *en masse*, helter skelter, for summer climes. A somewhat similar accumulation of birds apparently takes place on the skirts of the frost in spring, for when the ice broke up we had a " rush " of various sorts of birds, which suddenly swarmed on all sides.

In the valley of the Yen-e-say' the stream of migration follows the course of the river from north to south instead of from east to west as at Heligoland. Very few, if any, birds appear to cross the deserts of Mongolia. In South Siberia the stream of migration divides, part of the birds probably following the Angora, and part the smaller stream which retains the name of the Yen-e-say'. Among the birds which take the eastern route are the Yellow-browed Warbler, the Arctic Warbler, Blyth's Grass-Warbler, the Pin-tailed Snipe, the Petchora Pipit and many other birds, whilst amongst those which appear only to take the western route are the Willow-Warbler, the Sedge-Warbler, the Great Snipe, the Fieldfare, and many others. Occasionally, however, a bird, or a small party of birds, which ought to take the eastern route, accidentally get wrong, take the western turning, and find their way into Europe, where some of them are caught, and are justly considered as great rarities. Most of these little blunderers who have taken the wrong road are birds of the year, who have never migrated before, and have not yet learnt their right way, and may be excused for having gone wrong.

The facts of migration, as observed from an insular point of view, lead to theories which will not hold water when we come to compare them with observations made on a great continent. It must be conceded that birds have certain recognised routes or highways of migration which they follow with remarkable pertinacity. But different species of birds have in many cases different routes. Some of these routes have been mapped out by Palmen, Middendorf, and Severtzoff, but it would be a great mistake to suppose that all birds migrating from any given locality choose the same route. These highways are complicated, and the route chosen by one species of birds often crosses at right angles that selected by another species. In Cordeaux's interesting book on the birds of the Humber district, many interesting facts connected with this subject are given.

The subject of migration is one which is receiving much more systematic attention than has ever been given to it before. For the last year or two printed forms with schedules of instructions how to fill them in with facts observed connected with migration have been forwarded to more than a hundred and fifty lighthouse stations on the coasts of England and Scotland, by two gentlemen interested in this branch of the study of ornithology, J. A. Harvie-Brown, Esq. (my companion on my trip to the valley of the Petchora), and John Cordeaux, Esq. The returns from these stations, a summary of which is published annually (W. S. Sonnenschein & Allen) under the title of 'Report on the Migration of Birds,' are extremely interesting, and ought to be studied by every ornithologist.

BRONZE FORK FROM ANCIENT GRAVE NEAR KRASNOYARSK.

CHAPTER XIX.

Ornithological spoils—My three companions—The native tribes—Birds on a little island—Dol-gahn' names for various articles of clothing—An island rich in birds—The Siberian Pipit—Temminck's Stint—The Arctic Accentor—My doubts cleared concerning the Thrush seen at Brek'-off-sky—"Die Wilden "—Evil influences—Need of a hero in Siberia—The two curses of Russia—Baptized natives retaining their charms and idols—The strange hours we kept—Marriage ceremonies—Funeral ceremonies—Diseases—Birds seen on approaching Doo-link'-a—Vair'-shin-sky—Golden Plover frequenting the summit of larch-trees—Gulls—Mosquitoes—The *Thames*—An impenetrable island—Koo-ray'-i-ka in its summer aspect.

THERE is a great deal of truth in the old proverb that " it is an ill wind that blows nobody any good."   If my visit to the Tundra had not been delayed by the blunders or the misfortunes of Captain Wiggins, I might still have missed my birds. As it was, I brought home eggs of three species of Willow-Warbler which had never been taken before; besides eggs of the Dusky Ouzel and the Little Bunting, which were also new to science. Had my original programme been carried out, I should certainly have missed all of these, except the eggs of the Siberian Chiffchaff. Of my other novelties, the eggs of the Mountain Accentor and of the Asiatic Golden Plover, I should probably have obtained a more abundant supply. Then again, the voyage across the Kara Sea would probably have been somewhat barren of ornithological results, whereas my journey home overland, though a somewhat fatiguing one, was, as I hope the reader may learn for himself, extremely interesting, and not wanting in important ornithological and ethnological results.

We left Gol-cheek'-a on Tuesday the 24th of July. There were three persons on board with whom I could converse. Besides my aide-de-camp Glinski, I had Boiling's company as far as Yen-e-saisk'. Boiling was a well-read man who could talk sensibly on almost any subject, and who had lived many years in Siberia. As far as Vair'-skin-sky we were to enjoy the society of Uleman, a native of Saxony, who had emigrated to Poland, and was exiled thirty years ago. He lived by himself at Vair'-skin-sky with no other companions than his dogs and his birds; at one time he had amused himself by rearing foxes, wolves, and birds of different kinds.

In the summer he went down to Gol-cheek'-a to fish, and in the winter he carved boxes, cigarette-holders, studs, combs, &c., out of mammoth ivory, and the horns of the wild goat or sheep which inhabits the rocky mountains of the Tundra. He was also somewhat of a doctor, and was friendly with all the Asiatic tribes who frequented that country. During our journey he gave me some interesting information concerning the natives, which I looked upon as more reliable than any I had hitherto obtained.

The Sam'-o-yades, Yu-raks', and Ost'-yaks, in Uleman's opinion, are three distinct races, having more or less distinct languages, and each occupying an intermediate position between the European and the true Mongol. The similarity between their numerals leads me, however, to the conclusion that they are very closely allied, and that their languages are merely dialects of a common tongue.

The true Mongol races are much darker in colour, their eyes are more oblique, and less capable of being opened wide, they have flatter noses and higher cheek-bones. Several Mongol races speak dialects of the same language — for instance, the Tartars of Perm and Kazan, the Dol-gahns', and the Yah-kuts' are all closely allied, and can understand each other without much difficulty, and are all near relations of the Turks.

Early on the morning of the 25th, the rough sea and the contrary winds made it impossible for us to proceed, so we cast anchor in lat. 71°. Late in the evening the river was calm enough to make it safe to land, and I went on shore for a couple of hours. On a small island, in one of the numerous lakes, Gulls were evidently breeding; and Long-tailed Ducks and Divers were common. The Wheat-ear was very abundant on the clay-cliffs, and I saw many

Little Buntings, Bluethroats, Shore Larks, Lapland Buntings, and Red-throated Pipits. I shot a Dotterel, and found one of its young in down. I also found two Thrushes' nests, built on a small ledge of the nearly perpendicular mud- or clay-cliff, where the ground had slipped. One contained eggs, and the other young birds. I was not able to secure the old birds of either nest. They were too wild and shy to come within gunshot. The nest and eggs were like those of the Redwing, to which species they doubtless belonged.

From Uleman I got the following Dol-gahn' names for their various articles of dress. The outside coat with the hood is called *să-kŏŏ'-y̆*. The under coat *mă-khăl'-kă*. The trousers *chŏr-kĕĕ'*. The stockings *chăy̆-zhĕĕ'*. The boots *bŏk-ăr ĕe*. The cap *chŏ-băk*. In very cold weather a pair of over-boots are worn called *chĕrt-ă-kŏ'-dĕĕ*. The girdle round the waist is a *pŏy'-ăss*. The men wear a belt across the shoulders for their powder, &c., and a highly-ornamented front or breast-cloth ; but the names of these he could not remember. I afterwards ascertained that of these names those for the trousers, the boots, and the girdle, were Russian names, which the Dol-gahns' appear to have adopted.

We cast anchor on the following evening at Nik-an'-drin-a in lat. 70½°. I spent a few hours on shore, and was well rewarded for my trouble. The island was about twenty versts south of Brek'-off-sky, and very similar to it in character. It was nearly dead-flat, not many feet above the level of the river, and (judging from the drift-wood of various ages scattered on the surface) must be entirely under water when the river is at its height in June. The lowest flats are swamps covered with *carices*, in which Reeves and Red-necked Phalaropes are found. At a few inches greater elevation stretch swamps covered with willows, about a foot high; there the Yellow-headed Wagtail and the Siberian Pipit breed. Of the latter I secured eight specimens. Hitherto I had found this bird very difficult to shoot, for the female would lie hidden in her nest among the willows, and the male soar lark-like, singing in the air out of gunshot. Now both parents were feeding their young with mosquitoes. My attention was attracted to them by hearing repeatedly the call-note of a Pipit, so loud that I at first mistook it for that of a Thrush. I soon found out that it proceeded from a comparatively short-tailed bird flying round me in the company of half-a-dozen long-tailed Yellow-headed Wagtails, whose breeding-haunts I was invading, much to their con-sternation. Every now and then the Pipit alighted on a willow-tree, where it uttered an alarm note like *wit, wit*. By watching my opportunity, I secured five males and three females.

On slightly higher ground, the swamp was nearly dry, the willows were growing in isolated clumps, and the soil was bare or covered with short grass and moss. Great numbers of Temminck's Stints were there breeding, and were soon flying round me in all directions. Many of their broken egg-shells lay about, and I found one of their young in down. Lap-land Buntings were also common on this piece of ground.

Another slight elevation brought me to different ground, where the willows were four or five feet high, and the open space was gay with the brilliant flowers of the Tundra. The

Red-throated Pipit, the Lapland Bunting, and the Yellow-headed Wagtail abounded, and occasionally I saw a Reed Bunting, a Siberian Chiffchaff, or a Thrush. I shot one of the latter birds. It was a Redwing, with the spots on the breast more developed than usual, and the belly perhaps less spotted. I had no doubt that this was the same species of Thrush that I had seen at Brek'-off-sky, and at the place where we had stopped the preceding night. Its note and appearance at a distance were the same. I also saw a Fieldfare on this island, and shot several examples of the Mountain Hedge-Sparrow. The cold wind with occasional showers keeping the mosquitoes down, I was able to shoot without a veil, and consequently to see, and to shoot birds with much greater ease than heretofore.

The Mountain Accentor was a silent bird, but now and then I could hear a tit-like note, *til-il-il*, proceeding from a willow-bush. It was some time before I was able to see the bird that uttered the cry, as it frequented the thick of the willow-bushes, sneaking from one to another like a Grass-hopper Warbler. This bird should not be called the Mountain Accentor, a much better name would be the Arctic Accentor. Like the Lapland Bunting on the Dovrefield, when it gets out of its Arctic latitude it has to ascend a mountain in order to find a climate cold enough to suit its constitution. Yet it is essentially a bird of the plains, the willow-swamps are its natural habitat, and there the female lays her blue eggs, and rears her young, only a few feet above the level of the sea.

Turning into bed at four o'clock in the morning I slept

until noon.   When I awoke a steady rain was falling,
which continued till night.   Meanwhile a boat arrived from
Brek'-off-sky, bringing me the Thrush I had failed to secure
at that place; Schwanenberg's mate had sent it.   It also
turned out to be a Redwing.   I now considered this matter
settled, and all the doubtful points cleared up.

We got under weigh at 4 P.M., and steamed steadily up
the river.   The rain cleared off about midnight, but the sky
was still cloudy, and we had no sunshine.   Boiling, Uleman,
and I spent the night chatting about "die Wilden," as
Uleman called the Mongolian races there.   He had had a

BRONZE MIRROR FROM ANCIENT GRAVE NEAR KRASSNOYARSK

rare opportunity of observing them, having been there five-
and-twenty years, and having lived eight of these years
amongst them on the Tundra, as Sotnikoff's agent.   He had
seen more of the Dol-gahns' than of the other races.   When
he first went there, he told us, all the native tribes were
virtuous, honest and truthful, and they still live very peaceably amongst themselves, and quarrel rarely.   The selfish-
ness of civilisation is unknown; thus, when one buys or
begs a bottle of vodka he shares it with his companions, the
oldest man or woman being always served first; even the
children get their share.   Amongst themselves the rights

of property are still strictly observed.   In the Tundra, or on the banks of the river, sledges are frequently to be seen laden and covered over with reindeer skins; they are perfectly safe, and are often thus left for months.   The natives used to be truthful in their dealings with strangers, and their word was formerly as good as their bond; now they have become corrupted by intercourse with the Russians.   Siberia is largely peopled with exiles, and even a political exile, isolated from his own set, and removed from the restraints of society, after a while loses the conscience which formerly governed his conduct towards those who formed his surroundings; smarting also, perhaps, under a keen sense of injustice, he gradually conforms his thoughts and actions to the low standard of morality sure to be found amongst exiled criminals.   Truth and honour are, at best, scarcely known in Russia.   Like the Greek, the Russian lies without shame, and looks upon cunning as the highest virtue.   Siberia is sorely in need of a hero, a man who, having made a fortune honestly by energy, enterprise and ability, is capable of spending it wisely.   In a country where the rouble is worshipped as devoutly as the almighty dollar is said to be in the United States, such a man might do much to raise the tone of society, infuse fresh intellectual life amongst the better educated few, and establish a new standard of honour and morality in commercial intercourse.   I believe the only hope for Russian society lies in its merchants.   They alone may be able to rise out of the corruption of the officials, and the superstition of the clergy. The two curses of Russia are its church and its state staff.

The one sells justice, and the other palters with morality. The Emperor is said to be anxious to reform these fatal errors in the administration; but, in a remote corner like the one to which I allude, he has practically no power. The Russo-Greek Church is nominally Christian, but what the elements in it of Christianity are, I am unable to say. Its outward appearance is simple buffoonery, savouring more of Cagliostro than of Christ. It has never had any real influence upon the natives. Many of them have, indeed, gone through the ceremony of baptism, and wear crosses of silver or brass as charms, but none the less do they retain their old faiths, or seek the aid of the Shammanski in their troubles. Every native family has a special sledge set apart for its household gods, drawn by reindeer, which are also set apart for this purpose, and covered in by a "clean" reindeer skin, that is, a skin upon which no man has ever slept. The images or idols are made of wood, stone, iron, anything in short that can be carved to resemble a human being or an animal. These idols must be looked upon more in the light of charms than of gods. They are never prayed to. Their only use seems to be to act as a centre of magnetic or spiritual influence. The Sham'-man arranges them, walks round them, beating incessantly on his drum, whilst the people dance around, until he, and probably they, become more or less ecstatic, or under the sway of frenzy. It is said that under this excitement the Sham'-man will often foam at the mouth. In this state they believe a certain supernatural influence is exerted, through which information is obtained, supposed also to be of a supernatural character. It principally relates to the weather, or to success in catching fish, or trapping or shooting foxes, &c. No other use is apparently made of these idols. This superstition seems to be common to all the Asiatic tribes of Siberia, and I could not discover that they had any other religion, beyond a hazy notion of the existence of a Good Spirit and of happy hunting grounds.

As we discussed these customs of the natives we were steaming up the river with a slight head wind and a cloudy sky. We had drifted into keeping curious hours. We rose at noon and took a cup of tea together; at 4 P.M. we had a substantial breakfast, followed by a cup of tea at eight. At midnight we dined, and at 3 A.M. we had again a cup of tea, and turned in soon afterwards for the night.

From day to day I lost no opportunity of obtaining scraps of information from Uleman about "die Wilden." It seems that there are little, if any, ceremonies observed with regard to marriage. The chief point to be settled is the number of reindeer the bridegroom will give to the father of the bride, in exchange for his daughter. Those natives who have been baptised have only one wife, but the others sometimes have two, and, if they be rich, even three. The wives of the natives are said to be always faithful to their husbands. There is more ceremony observed in the funerals. Those who are not baptised do not bury their dead. The dead man is laid out upon the Tundra in his best clothes, his bow and arrows, his knife and other personal effects, placed around him. Some of the fleetest reindeer that belonged to him in life are killed and left by the corpse; bread and fish are also laid near, so that in the next world he may arrive provided with the necessaries of life. The principal diseases from which the natives suffer are fevers of various kinds. Consumption and scurvy, so common among the Russians, are almost unknown to them. No doubt their fondness for raw flesh, coupled with their active open-air life, prevent the latter malady. Since their increased intercourse with the Russians, syphilis and small-pox have, unfortunately, appeared among them.

About fifty versts before we reached Doo-dink'-a, we noticed several Red-breasted Geese, with their young broods, on the banks of the river; but I could not persuade the Captain to stop to give me the chance of a shot. Occasionally we saw a pair of Peregrines and a small Eagle, which I took to be the Rough-legged Buzzard.

I went on shore on Sunday at Vair'-shin-sky, walking three versts on the banks of the river to the place where the steamer stopped to take in wood for the engine fires. I crossed a succession of little valleys full of alder and willow-trees, and frequently having a small charming tarn in their hollow. The high land was Tundra, with abundance of reindeer moss, and thinly scattered over it were stunted and weather-beaten larches. Vair'-shin-sky is the most northerly point at which I met Pallas's House-Martin, in lat. 69°. I shot a young Little Bunting, and White and Yellow-headed Wagtails. The Little Bunting was unusually common. I saw both the Arctic and Common Willow-Warblers, and also several pairs of Golden Plover. The latter were very anxious to entice me away from their young. Occasionally they uttered their plaintive cry from the ground, but oftener from the topmost branch of a larch-tree. I shot one, perched at least fourteen feet aloft. Another bird which frequented the tops of the larch-trees was the Wood Sandpiper. I shot a pair of Redwings and some young Fieldfares; Bluethroats, also, had fully fledged young. In some of the more sheltered valleys patches of snow were still lying unmelted. The wild flowers were very brilliant, and, after I had shot off all my cartridges, I gathered a few and pressed them. Rhubarb and a species of thyme were abundant there. One of the passengers on board was my friend, the second priest of Toor-o-kansk', and he gathered a quantity of each for medicinal purposes, saying that the natives were ignorant of their uses.

Early in the morning of the 30th we stopped an hour at an island to take some barrels of salt-fish on board. I went on shore and found a large colony of Siberian Herring Gulls sleeping on the sand. By far the largest proportion were immature birds, that apparently do not go further north. I shot one, and the rest flew off to a distance. The day turned out very wet, and we did not go again on shore. We had scarcely had a fine day since we left Gol-cheek-a. We were told that this was an exceptionally cold summer; and for one great blessing we had to thank the keen winds, they banished the mosquitoes. We had indeed almost forgotten their existence until the preceding day. When I was on shore it was a dead calm, the clouds were black as before a thunderstorm, and the bloodthirsty insects were swarming in thousands. I had neglected to take my gauntlets, and was, in consequence, much bitten on the wrists, causing me some slight suffering; the irritation of my hands prevented my sleeping; it was accompanied by little or no swelling. Either the mosquitoes had exhausted their stock of poison, or my blood had grown so thin, that they did not care to expend much virus upon it.

In the evening we stopped an hour at E-gar'-ka to take our leave of the ill-starred *Thames*. The water had fallen away some distance since we had abandoned the vessel, but the sand in which she lay had a considerable slope; still it seemed the general opinion that she might yet be got off before the season was over. In a few days the Captain was expected down with the Sessedatel to hold an inquest on the ill-fated vessel; the result of which could not be foretold, except that one might be perfectly sure that a certain imaginary friend in Omsk would be considerably enriched thereby. It was grievous to see so fine a craft thrown away. The Captain had no doubt done his best by her; but he was a man lacking administrative skill, whose actions always seemed guided by the impulse of the moment. Nevertheless his crew, who half hated and half despised him, were obliged to confess that he was every inch a sailor.

The first real summer day we had had for a long time was August 1st. We steamed up the river under a cloudless sky, and with scarcely a breath of wind. We passed a large colony of Sand-Martins about noon. In the evening I landed for half an hour on an island. The shore was bare sand. Higher up it was covered with a dense growth of *Equisetæ*, which soon ended in impenetrable willow thickets. The island was some miles long. Boiling said he remembered the island fifteen years ago without a tree or a green leaf upon it, nothing but bare sand. Birds were not abundant. I saw Yellow-headed and White Wagtails, old and young, and heard the cries of Ducks and Divers, and Terek-Sandpipers, beyond the willows. Temminck's Stints were common. The absence of grass prevented other birds frequenting it.

The following day we cast anchor at the village of Kooray'-i-ka, at four in the morning, to take in wood, and I availed myself of the opportunity to go on shore and have an hour's shooting on our old hunting grounds, and to take a cup of tea with old Jacob the starrester. The trees being now in full leaf, the short grass having grown to a height of two feet or more, and the level of the rivers and lakes having fallen five or six feet, the aspect of the place was utterly changed. The Arctic Willow-Warbler was very common, and still in full song. Wagtails appeared to be less numerous, but the Redpoles and the Lesser White-throats still frequented the birches. Young Fieldfares were abundant, and I heard the song of the Scarlet Bull-finch. The Great Snipe was also there, and must have been breeding. The House-Martins were swarming in countless numbers. We seemed to have almost got below the mosquito region, for the weather was warm, and yet we scarcely saw any of these insects. On the other hand, a small midge was occasionally abundant, and irritating.

It was interesting to see the familiar place once again, every feature of which was stamped upon our memories by the monotony of our long, weary waiting for summer. It was almost impossible to believe that only two months ago the banks of the Koo-ray'-i-ka were still white with snow, and the possibility of the shipwreck of the *Thames* scarcely dreamed of. So much had happened in the interval, that it seemed to be years ago.

DOLGAHN AND SAMOYADE BOOTS.

KAHMIN PASS.

CHAPTER XX.

AT sunrise on the morning of the 3rd of August the barge
was anchored at Sil-o-vah'-noff to take in more wood, whilst

the steamer went to 'Toor-o-kansk' and back. I went on shore to shoot, and to inspect the extraordinary inhabitants of the village. It was evident at a glance that the people here were a different race from the Yen-e-say' Russian. The place looked quite English! Order reigned, and a hundred little details betokened industry and civilisation. The boats were larger and better finished; instead of being hauled up to shore through the mud, a wooden landing-stage was provided for them, with a revolving wooden roller at the head. Instead of having to climb a muddy inclined plain to reach the houses, a flight of wide and easy wooden steps led up to them, with a neat gate at the bottom to keep the cows from coming up. The surrounding space was clean; the cows being railed off on every side. (To reach an ordinary Russian peasant's house one has to pick one's way across a dunghill.) The inhabitants were most hospitable. Although it was only half-past two the women-folk were stirring. Soon the samovar came in steaming, and tea, sugar, bread and butter, and smoked herrings, were laid before us. "That says more than it looks," as the German idiom has it: tea and butter are kept in store for strangers only, and are never tasted by the inhabitants. The house we were in was far better than any we had visited between Yen-e-saisk' and the sea; the rooms were lofty, the windows large, well glazed and double; there was a large and well-built stove in it, and due provision made for ventilation. A special stove was erected to smoke out mosquitoes. A clock hung upon the wall, and there were positively books on a shelf! The carpenters' work was excellent, evidently planed, and not merely smoothed with an axe. There was also ample evidence about that the village possessed a competent smith. Outside, the same signs of honest toil prevailed: casks were being made, and boats were being built. Several fields, carefully railed off, were planted with potatoes. Everything betokened order, industry, and comparative wealth. In sooth, a model village, without crime, where idleness and drunkenness were unknown. And yet the people did not look happy. There was no fire in their glance, no elasticity in their step, there seemed to be no blood in their veins. They were as stolid as Sam'-o-yades; their complexions were as sallow, and the men's chins as beardless. Strange to say, there was not a living soul in the village under forty years of age. It was the village of the Scopsee, a sect whose religion has taken an ultra-ascetic form—teetotalism carried out to the bitter end, an attempt to annihilate all human passions, not only their abuse but their use as well. All the men were castrated, and in all the women the milk glands were extracted from the breasts. They ate no animal food except fish. They did not even allow themselves butter or milk. All intoxicating and exciting drinks were forbidden, such as spirits, wine, tea and coffee. On the other hand they had a very mild beer called quass, which, coming up from the cold cellar on a hot day, was very refreshing. It was a very mild beer indeed, certainly not XXXX, nor even single X. Possibly its intoxicating properties might be represented in terms of X by the formula $\sqrt[4]{X}$. I was not able to procure a Scopsee pipe, for tobacco in all forms was prohibited. Although the population of the village numbered under a score, yet there were two sects of Scopsee among them; one drank milk, the other did not. They kept all the holidays of the Russian church, but had no priest, saying that every man was a priest, and could perform priestly offices only for himself; so curiously do eccentric errors and half-forgotten truths grow side by side. The Scopsee have been justly banished to this island by the Russian government, Uleman said principally from the neighbourhood of the iron mines near Ekatereenberg. They told me there were formerly seven or eight hundred of them, but that they were literally dying of starvation, and they petitioned the Emperor to send them elsewhere, to some region where they could cultivate the land and grow vegetables. They were consequently sent to a place near Yakutsk', where some thousands of these amiable but misguided people now live. After breakfast we spent some hours in the forest, then enjoyed the luxury of a commodious Russian bath, and were afterwards invited to dine. We had, of course, a fish dinner. First a fish pasty of tcheer, then sterlet, followed by a refreshing dessert of preserved cranberries. A pint of quass each completed a by no means despicable repast.

In the forest birds were abundant, Fieldfares and Red-wings had fully-fledged young. I saw several Three-toed Woodpeckers, and shot a Lapp-Tit. Redpoles were very numerous. The song of the Arctic Willow-Warbler was continually to be heard, and occasionally that of the Common Willow-Warbler. The Siberian Chiffchaff was carefully tending its newly-fledged brood, and only its alarm-note was now to be heard. Martins were swarming like bees under the eaves of the houses, and a flock of Siberian Herring Gulls, mostly immature, were watching the fishing boats. On the pebbly beach young and old White Wagtails were running about. I shot a young Bluethroat and a young Redstart. The latter was a new bird for my list. As in the Petchora I did not find it so far north as the Arctic Circle.

The forest behind Sil-o-vah'-noff was very luxuriant and very picturesque, and I enjoyed my solitary rambles in it beyond measure. Now and then I came to a charming swamp abounding with Waders, and ever and anon glimpses of Thrushes excited my hopes as the wary birds frequented the thick underwood. I was specially on the *qui vive* for rare Thrushes. I had shown my friend the priest the skin of the Siberian Ground Thrush, the solitary example of which rare bird I had obtained at Koo-ray'-i-ka, and he had immediately recognised it as the *chor'-na drohst,* and told me that it was more abundant in the district round Toor-o-kansk' than anywhere else. I searched far and wide in the forest, but in vain. I was not fortunate enough to obtain a second example. A good specimen of the Dark Ouzel in its first spotted plumage was, however, some compensation for my trouble. In my efforts to explore the country I nearly lost myself a second time. I had been wandering for some hours in the forest when my appetite warned me that it was time to return home. I took out my compass and steered west, but the further I went the more impassable the forest became. I found myself in a swamp so deep that I could only make slow and uncertain progress by struggling from one fallen tree-trunk to another, and finally I stuck fast altogether, and had to turn back. The question to decide was, should I try to round the swamp to the north or to the south. I had not the least idea which way I had come, but fortunately I had a good map in my pocket and succeeded in striking the Yen-e-say' without making any very serious detour.

When the steamer came back from Toor-o-kansk' we heard that it had had sundry misadventures on the way. Once or twice it had run aground on a sandbank, and had got off not without difficulty. To provide against these accidents twenty or thirty long poles are kept on board, and it is very amusing to see them in action. The moment the ship grounds all is noise

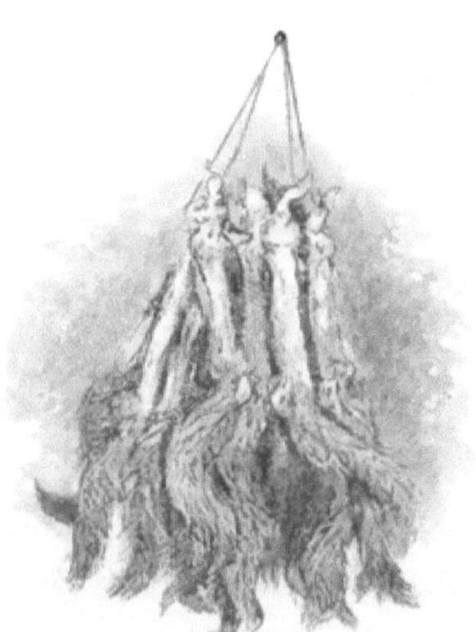

BUNCH OF SQUIRRELS' SKINS.

and confusion. The Captain shouts to the two men who, one on each side of the bows of the ship, are constantly calling out the depth of the water (which they measure with long poles), *chat-cer'-a, trace-pol-a-veen'-a,* &c., and in a moment all is hurry-skurry and bustle, and the shallow side of the' steamer suddenly develops a score or more legs like a centipede, the men straining on the long poles till they bend again, organising a strong push and a push all together by the most unearthly screams and yells.

When we left Sil-o-vah'-noff we were minus one passenger, Michael Susloff, the second priest of Toor-o-kansk', by far the most active and intelligent Russian I had met. He was sent by the Archbishop to visit the Ost'-yaks on the Tazz, and he at the time was busy writing a report for his Eminence. He promised me a copy of it. It contained much interesting ethnological information, and a number of valuable historical facts regarding the ancient town of Man-ga-zay, extracted from the archives of Toor-o-kansk'. Susloff told me that he did his best to prevent a rupture between the late Sessedatel and Wiggins and Schwanenberg when the two captains passed through Toor-o-kansk' in the previous autumn, but the Blagachina and the Postmaster edged them on for private reasons of their own; Sotnikoff and Ivanoff were also among the conspirators for obvious considerations.

At the monastery the Blagachina of Toor-o-kansk' came on board to install his mother as a passenger on the ship; he was, however, so inebriated that he could hardly speak, and he speedily left without taking leave either of Kittmanoff or of myself.

We did not get a chance of going on shore till late the following evening, when it was too dark to shoot. Boiling and I had a long talk about Siberia, and the anomalous facts in its domestic history. It presents the spectacle of a healthy race of people, living in a healthy because dry climate, continually replenished by emigrants and exiles, and yet the population remaining almost stationary; a country "with capabilities of becoming rich beyond the dreams of avarice" continuing poor. Report affirms that scarcely one merchant in ten in it is solvent, and that not one bank in ten could pay more than ten shillings in the pound if wound up. The question arises, to what cause is this extraordinary state of things to be attributed? Boiling ascribed it all to the gold mines. The land, he said, cannot be cultivated; manufactures cannot be successfully carried on, because the peasants and workmen are continually tempted away by advances on account of wages, and by having the opportunity of pocketing gold. Arrived at the gold mines they are overworked. A certain task is allotted to each man to perform every day, and he must work until it be done. Not unfrequently it takes twenty hours out of the twenty-four to finish it, and then, after insufficient rest, he has to turn to work again, often in wet clothes. The miners have to "work the dead horse" for perhaps a year; that is to say, the advance of wages which they received on being engaged having been speedily squandered, it usually takes them a year to save sufficient from their pay to clear off their debt. They do not like to return to their village empty handed, so they steal gold as fast as they can. When at length they have made a purse they come home, possibly with ruined constitutions, probably utterly demoralised with extravagant habits, unfitting them for their former life. Many never reach home at all. Some die on the way, and others are robbed and murdered in the forest for the sake of the gold on their persons. The Russian law prohibits the purchase or sale of gold, and compels the owners of mines to sell to the Government only. Nevertheless a large trade in the precious metal, principally in that which has been stolen, is carried on, and considerable quantities find their way to China, or are bought by the Kirghis. This is well known to the police, who are, nevertheless, seldom able to detect it. Siberia is rich in gold mines, but its true wealth is to be found on its soil, not under it.

We had an hour on land the following afternoon. We were now in lat. 64°. I went first into the deep forest, the pines of which had evidently been burnt some years ago. Only a few charred trunks remained ; the forest had become a dense mass of birch-trees. Under foot spread a thick soft carpet of moss, lichen, and liverwort, thinly sprinkled over with cranberries, laden with unripe fruit, the aromatic *Ledum palustre*, the graceful *Equisetum sylvaticum* and the *Lycopodium annotinum*. I found there also three ferns, the first I had seen for some time : the *Polypodium dryopteris, Athyrium filix-fæmina*, and *Lastrea multiflora*. During half-an-hour's walk we saw only one bird, a Capercailzie or a Black-Cock. The thickness of the forest prevented our identifying the species. On the bank, among some willow thickets, the birds were more numerous. I shot two young Siberian Chiffchaffs out of a family noisily flying from tree to tree like a brood of Tits. Young Bluethroats were also on the wing. During the evening we saw several birds, two pair of Grey-headed White-tailed Eagles, and a pair of smaller birds with apparently a slightly longer tail and somewhat narrower wings. The wings appear to be darker in colour than the tail and the rest of the body. I took the larger bird to be the White-tailed Eagle, and the smaller the Rough-legged Buzzard.

We stopped a couple of hours about noon the next day at Verkh-nah'-ya An-bat-ski-a. This place used to be the great rendezvous of the Ost'-yaks: a kind of yearly fair was held in it, to which they brought the tribute of skins annually paid to the Government, and at the same time purchased meat and other necessaries. The fair was held as soon as the river was free from ice. At the beginning of this century about two hundred large boats would be moored on the banks of the small river which here joins the Yen-e-say'. Thirty years ago the number had dwindled down to eighty, and at the time of my visit they did not exceed a score. This decline of traffic may be partly accounted for by meat depots having been established in other villages, but there can be little doubt that the Ost'-yaks have largely decreased in numbers and in wealth. They have been plundered and demoralised by the Russian merchants. One of those wealthy arch-robbers still lived here, carrying on a contraband trade in spirits with the unfortunate Ost'-yaks. The Government had tried to trap him, but hitherto he had eluded the grasp of the officials. I bought three sable skins of him for twenty roubles each, fine black sable with white hairs, the only good skins I saw in Siberia. The Ost'-yaks' boats are unique in form, built without nails, and very picturesque. Their canoes are light and extremely elegant, and are made of one, or sometimes two pieces of wood.

Around the village undulated pa-ture land, sprinkled over with spruce fir, and fragrant with white clover in full bloom. Birds abounded there. I shot a Nutcracker, one of a flock of seven or eight. Young White and Yellow-headed

Wagtails were numerous, but I devoted most of my attention to the young Thrushes. Two species, with different voices, frequented the spruce firs. I secured two of one, and one of the other. One species proved to be the Dusky Ouzel, whose eggs I discovered at the Koo-ray'-i-ka; and the other was a new species of bird for my list, the Black-throated Ouzel.* This was probably the northern limit of its breeding range. On the shores of a small lake the Green Sandpiper was very noisy. On the banks of the river, both the House-Martin (doubtless the Siberian species) and the Sand-Martin swarmed. I watched them pursue and finally drive away a Merlin, who pertinaciously approached too near their nests. The alarm-note of the young Dusky Ouzels was very much like the *u-tic* of the Wheatear, but louder; it might be expressed by *tick-tick*. On the stones on the bank of the Yen-e-say' were several of the latter bird.

As we steamed up the river on the following day, we discussed the subject of the forest-trees of the Yen-e-say', and, to the best of our ability, we thoroughly ventilated it. So far as I can ascertain, there are five trees belonging to the Pine group. They are as follows:

Larch (*Pinus larix*). This well-known tree extends

---

* The Black-throated Ouzel (*Merula atrigularis*) breeds in the pine forests of the valley of the Yenesay, between lat. 60° and 63°. It probably also breeds in a similar latitude in the valley of the Obb, and also in the pine regions of the Himalayas and Eastern Turkestan. It winters in Western Turkestan, Baluchistan, and North India, occasionally straggling westwards into Europe, where it has been obtained in Russia, Germany, Denmark, Belgium, England, France, and Italy. Eastwards it has occurred on migration as far as Lake Bykal, and in winter as far as Assam.

further north than any of the others, and is abundant, though small, as far north as lat. 69½°. Further south it attains large dimensions. At Yen-e-saisk' a larch-pole, suitable for the mast of a ship, 36 inches diameter at the stem, and 18 inches diameter at the point, and 60 feet long, may be bought for a sovereign. This hard dark wood looks well for the walls and ceilings of the peasants' rooms.

Spruce fir (*Pinus obovata*). This elegant tree, with branches growing out of the trunk down almost to the root and trailing on the ground, extends nearly as far north as the larch, say to lat. 69°. It is a very important tree for commercial purposes. Its wood is white, of very small specific gravity, extremely elastic, and is said not to lose its elasticity by age. It makes the best masts for ships, and is for oars the best substitute for ash. Snow-shoes are generally made of this wood. The quality is good down to the roots, and it makes the best "knees" for ship-building, knees which do not require to be cut out of the solid, or artificially bent. It is, however, subject to very hard knots, and care must be taken not to blunt the edge of the axe.

Siberian spruce fir (*Pinus sibiricus*). This tree differs from the common spruce in having a smooth bark of an ash-grey colour; its leaves are also of a much darker blue-green. We did not meet with it further north than lat. 63°. It has little commercial value, being soft and apt to crack and decay. The ease with which it is split causes it to be used for firewood and for roofing.

Pine or Scotch fir (*Pinus sylvestris*). This well-known tree scarcely extended so far north even as the preceding, say to lat. 62½°.

Cedar (*Pinus cembra*) is very similar in appearance to the Scotch fir, but its timber is said to have a much higher marketable value.   It is dark, but not so dark as larch, and there is very little of the white inferior wood next to the bark.   If stacked too long in the forest, it is liable to be attacked by worms, but for furniture and in-door use, it is the best timber to be found in Siberia.   It is reputed never to rot, shrink, warp, or crack.   Soft and easy to work, it has nevertheless a fine grain, and is almost free from knots.   The Ost'-yaks build their ships of it.   They hew down a trunk two or three feet in diameter, split it, and of each half make a wide thin board; the rest is wasted, for the axe is an extravagant tool.   This tree is found up to lat. $67\frac{1}{2}°$.

We found the common birch up to lat. $69\frac{1}{2}°$, and in various places we noticed that where a pine forest had been burnt or cut down, it appeared to be immediately replaced by a luxuriant growth of birch.   The creeping birch and two or three sorts of willow were common in suitable localities on the Tundra as far north as we went, i.e. lat. $71\frac{1}{2}°$.

The alder was abundant at $69\frac{1}{2}°$ and the juniper at $69°$.

I did not observe the poplar at the Koo-ray'-i-ka in lat. $66\frac{1}{2}°$, but it was abundant at Sil-o-vah'-noff in lat. $66°$.   The Ost'-yaks hollow their canoes out of the trunk of this tree.

As we conversed upon this interesting topic of northern trees, a pair of Peregrines loudly protested against our approaching so near the shore, and in the afternoon I twice noticed a large, very dark, and long-tailed Hawk sail majestically between the ship and the shore, apparently taking no notice whatever of our noise and smoke.   Possibly it might have been a female Goshawk.

The next day we steamed through much more picturesque scenery than any we had hitherto seen on the Yen-e-say'. The banks were much more hilly, and the course of the river much more winding. For some few versts we steered due north ; the river not being more than half-a-mile wide here ; its character resembled that of lake scenery.

We stopped for two hours at Sam'-or-o-koh'-va in lat. 62°. Birds were not abundant; they were as a rule in full moult, and were very silent and retiring. Nearly all those we shot were birds of the year. I added two fresh ones to my list, the Tree Pipit and Blyth's Reed-Warbler.* The latter was making a sound like "*tick-tick*." Sand-Martins were breeding in great numbers on the banks of the river ; they evidently had unfledged young. As I walked on the top of the bank, they flew at me uttering a shrill harsh cry, which I do not remember having heard in England. The Siberian Chiff-chaff and the Arctic Willow-Warbler were also common, the latter in full song, the former uttering its plaintive alarm-note only. For some days the Common Sandpiper had frequented in large numbers the sand at the water's edge. The Common Gull frequented the river, and we rarely saw the larger species. In the evening the vessel stopped an hour to take in wood, just outside the Pod-kah'-min-a Tun-goosk' river ; in the fir-trees behind the village I shot a couple of Black-throated Ouzels, female and young.

---

* Blyth's Reed-Warbler (*Acrocepha-lus dumetorum*) breeds in the Central Palæarctic Region, from St. Petersburg eastwards at least as far as the valley of the Yenesay. It also breeds in the Himalayas from Cashmere to Nepal, wintering in India as far south as Ceylon. It does not appear to have been observed in the Burma peninsula.

In the dusk of the following evening we steamed up to the entrance of the Kah'-min Pass, and there anchored for the night, the pilots being unwilling to risk the navigation of that part of the river without daylight.

Soon after four we got under weigh again. The scenery now passed was certainly very fine. It looked very different on a sunshiny summer's day from what it had done on a blustery winter's morning. Many of the rocks appeared to be limestone, conspicuously veined with quartz. In one place high up the cliff was a large colony of Swallows, no doubt House-Martins.

The peasants told us that the mountains are frequented by a kind of Ibex, which they call Kabagar; they described it as having very small horns, long hair, and told us that it produces musk. This animal must not be confounded with the Khalkoon, a kind of goat found on the mountains of the Tundra towards the Kat-an-gar river. The latter is much larger, has also long hair, but has heavy horns.

The next day we did not get a chance of going on shore until nearly midnight, when it was too dark to shoot. The last few days had been oppressively hot, and we had all found it difficult to sleep. Our food was ill adapted to the weather. Beef, fish, and bread, with no vegetables, are at best a somewhat heating diet, and when the fish is sturgeon and sterlet, delicate as salmon and rich as eel, melting in the mouth, the heating properties of the regimen are increased. There scarcely stirred a breath of air, the thermometer must have been 80° or 90° in the shade, and we continually felt a stray mosquito busily employed injecting poison into our veins. No wonder the blood gets hot and feverish under such conditions, and that we tossed upon our hard bunks and wooed the fickle goddess of sleep in vain. In a state of mind, the result of these circumstances, Boiling and I went on shore at midnight, the anchor having then been dropt to allow a boat-load of fire-wood to be stored in the barge. Our engine fires burnt a great quantity of wood, twelve sar-zheens a day, costing a rouble and a half each. A sar-zheen is a stack three arsheens high and as many long, the width of the length of each log, say one to one-and-a-half arsheen; each arsheen measures twenty-eight English inches. We had to stop once or twice every four-and-twenty hours, to get the requisite supply of fire-wood on board, and with the occasional additional delays in getting casks of salt fish, we lost nearly a third of our time. I always took advantage of these stoppages to go ashore and pick up a few birds, but upon this occasion it was dark, and I did not take my gun. Boiling and I went out in the village to forage. We hoped to find some peasant who, from the recesses of his cellars, would bring up milk and fruit to cool our hot blood. We met an old acquaintance of Boiling's, and went home with him. Curiously enough, his house happened to be the one at which we had stopped to change horses in the winter. The man's wife was in bed, but when she heard of our visit and of our need, she got up at once, and in a few minutes we were luxuriating in the large basin of deliciously cold milk and the plate of freshly gathered bilberries she set before us. We ate so much that I was really afraid that we should be ill, but the acid of the fruit had the desired effect upon our fevered condition. We returned to the steamer, and that night enjoyed a more healthy sleep than we had had for a week or more, awaking the next, morning cool and refreshed.

Next day I had a couple of hours in the forest about noon, but did not get a bird; my bag consisting of one Grey Squirrel only. I caught a far-off glimpse of a Woodpecker, and occasionally saw a Nutcracker or a Tit out of shot. I suppose that most birds were then in full moult, and were hiding away. The oak-fern was very abundant, and I noticed for the first time the beech-fern. Bilberries were ripe and plentiful; cranberries grew in less numbers and were scarcely ripe. On the banks of the river we had seen several birds of prey; occasionally three or four had passed us on the wing together. It was the first occasion on which I noticed a Kite,* a large bird with a long forked tail, his colour dark brown; when one could see the body underneath, a broad pale band across the tail and across each wing was visible. In the forests the mosquitoes were at this time

---

* The Black Kite (*Milvus ater*) breeds throughout Europe, south of the Baltic, occasionally wandering as far north as Archangel. It has only once been caught in England. It also breeds sparingly in North-Western Africa. It winters in Africa, south of the Atlas mountains, occasionally wandering as far as the Cape. Eastwards it breeds in Asia Minor and Palestine, Persia and Turkestan. In the latter country it is found in company with a nearly-allied form which some writers consider specifically distinct, *M. melanotis*, which extends through Southern Siberia into Japan and China. The Black Kite of India also shows some very slight variations such as would be expected to occur in a tropical climate, and has been considered distinct, under the name of *M. govinda*, but in Australia and the Malay regions the western form reoccurs on a very slightly smaller scale, and has been named *M. affinis*. The difference between these forms is, however, very slight, and intermediate examples are not rare in collections.

very common and virulent, but on board we escaped them and the midges, thanks to a cool breeze from the north. That afternoon we passed the mouth of the Tass, a river which it may be hoped some day will be turned into a canal to the Obb. Three expeditions have successfully made the passage. The river rises from a marsh, across which boats may be pushed to the source of a tributary of the Kett, which flows into the Obb.

At noon, on the 12th of August, we passed the village of Yair'-mak, once the San Francisco of Siberia. The gold mines lie some two hundred versts up the mountains that rise behind Yair'-mak towards the watershed of the Yen-e-say' and Lay'-na. Yair'-mak used to be five versts in length; it was once the centre of the head offices of the gold mines, and the emporium of Siberian gold. At that time large houses were built in it, handsomely furnished billiard-tables erected in them, French cooks were brought over to prepare for the inhabitants the delicacies of a European table, and champagne flowed like water. Thousands of horses filled the stables of the city, its granaries overflowed with corn, and every thing that money could buy was to be found in its stores. At the time of my visit all this had disappeared. Each gold mine has its offices on the spot, and the miners are provisioned by contract. On the whole one cannot regret the change. Such centres of luxury and riot do much to deteriorate a nation; and the more their dimensions can be contracted and the site removed from the haunts of peasant life, so much the better for the morality and ultimate prosperity of the country.

I find recorded in my journal of that day the first sight of Barn-Swallows since shooting the solitary example of the species at the Koo-ray'-i-ka. Cranes passed us going northwards. Eagles and Kites, and now and then a small Hawk, were the principal birds we met as we steamed along.

TUNGOOSE FETISH.

KARMIN PASS.

CHAPTER XXI.

ON the morning of the 14th of August, soon after tea, we reached Yen-e-saisk', having been twenty-two days on the road, which was considered a good passage. I was busy all the afternoon getting a large empty room in Boiling's house fitted up to unpack and dry all my skins. I found them

R

in better condition than I had expected, but nevertheless, far too damp for me to venture travelling with them for a month longer, without running great risk of injuring them, unless artificially dried.

My skins being laid out so that the process of drying might go on, I devoted most of the next day to exploring the banks of the Yen-e-say'. The country I found almost flat, and for miles there stretched an extent of meadow land that had recently been cut for hay. It was intersected with numerous half-dried-up river beds, running parallel to the Yen-e-say'. These beds were full of tall *carices*, various water plants, and were almost concealed by the willow-trees; occasionally the water was open, running between muddy borders. On this meadow land Wagtails were numerous, especially near the town; but I saw only one species, the Masked Wagtail.* It was, however, very hard to get good specimens of any bird. Nearly all being in full moult, they did not sing and remained concealed in the herbage, making it difficult to shoot them, and when shot they proved very imperfect. Many of the young birds also were not yet fully fledged. Kestrels† were very abundant, and I frequently saw as many as a score on the

---

* The Masked Wagtail (*Motacilla personata*) breeds in the highlands of Persia, Turkestan, and Cashmere, also in the mountains of Southern Siberia as far east as Krasnoyarsk, ascending the valley of the Yenesay to lat. 60°. It winters in the plains of India and in the valleys of Afghanistan and Persia.

† The Kestrel (*Falco tinnunculus*) breeds, south of the Arctic Circle, throughout the whole of the palæarctic region from the Atlantic to the Pacific, being replaced in North China and Japan by a very nearly allied species, *T. japonicus*. In the basin of the Mediterranean it is a partial resident, and winters in great numbers in the plains of India.

wing together.   Richard's Pipit* was also common, frequenting the newly-mown meadows; I shot both old and young. Occasionally I saw a Shrike which appeared to be the Great Grey Shrike†, but I did not succeed in bringing one down. Magpies were numerous, especially near the town.   Singularly enough, we did not see any before reaching Yen-e-saisk', yet

---

* Richard's Pipit (*Anthus richardi*) is not known to breed anywhere except in Central Siberia, in the valley of the Yen-e-say'. I found it extremely abundant near Yen-e-saisk', and Dybowsky found it equally so near Lake By-kal. As none of the travellers to the Amoor have observed this species, the main stream of migration apparently crosses Mongolia into China, where this bird is very numerous in winter, whence it ranges into Burma and India.   As appears to be the case with several other Siberian birds, which are in the habit of migrating eastwards in the autumn, a number of individuals, principally birds of the year, apparently accidentally join the western stream of migration and find their way into Europe. It has occurred in Persia, passes Heligoland regularly every year on migration, frequently occurring on the southern shores of our islands, and is found every autumn in Spain, and occurs more or less regularly in other parts of South Europe and North Africa.

† Since my return home I have received a series of skins of Grey Shrikes, collected by M. Kibort at Krasnoyarsk. They are of two species, Pallas's Grey Shrike (*Lanius major*) and the White-winged Grey Shrike (*L. leucopterus*). The first of these two birds breeds in Southern Siberia, from Vladivostok on the coast westwards across the Northern Urals to Scandinavia. Here it meets with the European Grey Shrike (*L. excubitor*), with which it apparently interbreeds, as intermediate forms are not rare. *L. excubitor* breeds throughout Central and Southern Europe, but becomes much whiter on the wing in South-east Russia. Across the Southern Urals the white spots on the wing increase still more in size, and the rump becomes white, which variety of plumage is known by the name of *L. homeyeri*. In Turkestan the secondary quills of the wing have become pure white, with the exception of an occasional spot near the centre. This form is known as *L. leucopterus*, and extends northwards into South Central Siberia, where its range overlaps that of *L. major*. In this district the birds appear to breed true, having become so widely separate as not to cross. Nevertheless they are connected by a complete series of intermediate forms enumerated above, and consequently we must assume that both of them interbreed with *L. excubitor*. Pallas's Grey Shrike has been several times obtained in the British Islands.

Uleman told me that rarely a summer passed without one or two being seen at Vair'-shin-sky. Crows abounded, but I saw no Jackdaws. I shot both the Great-Tit, and the Cole-Tit. Amongst the willows one of the commonest birds was Blyth's Grass-Warbler,* mostly young not yet fully fledged. I shot one Siberian Chiffchaff, but did not see any young. My attention was frequently attracted by small parties of young birds among the willows, uttering a loud *tic-tic-tic*. These proved to be Pallas's Grasshopper-Warbler.† On one occasion I heard a similar sound, very loud and harsh, emanating from some *carices* from a pool. Presently the bird came in view perching on a reed, and I felt sure I had a large Reed-Warbler. It turned out, however, to be a male Ruby-throated Warbler. Frequenting the willows I also found the Yellow-breasted Bunting‡ and the Tree-Pipit. In the neighbourhood of the running water and muddy banks, Sandpipers were numerous. Three species were almost equally abundant: the Common Sandpiper, Temminck's Stints, and the Green Sandpiper.

There did not appear to be much actual migration going

---

* Blyth's Grass-Warbler (*Lusciniola fuscata*) breeds in South-eastern Siberia and Japan, passes through South-eastern Mongolia and North China on migration, and winters in Formosa, South China, Assam, Burma, and near Calcutta.

† Pallas's Grasshopper-Warbler (*Locustella certhiola*) breeds in Central and Eastern Siberia, passes through China on migration, and winters in India, Ceylon, the Burma peninsula,

and the islands of the Malay archipelago. A specimen of this bird has been obtained on Heligoland.

‡ The Yellow-breasted Bunting (*Emberiza aureola*) breeds throughout Siberia, and in Europe as far west as Archangel, and as far south as lat. 60°. It winters in China and Northern India. It appears accidentally in winter in Europe, and has been obtained on Heligoland, but not in the British Islands.

on. Starlings were collected together in great flocks, but they would probably remain until driven away by cold weather. Now and then a small party of Cranes passed overhead, generally flying south. Boiling told me that the Swallows ought to have left before our return to Yen-e-saisk'. When we first arrived House-Martins were swarming and breeding on the church-towers, a few lingered for a week, but their number appeared to diminish daily. Occasionally I saw a Barn-Swallow, which did not seem to be a common bird at that time. On the other hand Sand-Martins flew over the meadows, or skimmed over the Yen-e-say' in thousands. Both the Common- and Tree-Sparrows congregated in large flocks. Hawks were very numerous ; there was a large brown Buzzard, a dark coloured Kite, and several small Hawks.

Boiling meanwhile was busy superintending the unpacking of Nordenskiöld's goods. It was remarkable the little damage they had suffered, after having lain for a year at Kor-e-o-poff'-sky. On the whole the various articles imported seemed to give satisfaction. Nordenskiöld, however, had put 50 per cent. on to the original cost-price in Sweden, to cover the expense of freight, insurance, and agents' commission ; the merchant who bought them here would require at least 25 per cent. profit on an average, so that ultimately double the Swedish price would probably be demanded for them. This would make some of the articles too dear for the Russian market, for instance sugar, for which nine roubles a pood would be asked, was sold at the last fair in Eer-beet' at seven roubles. Other articles, on the other hand, were scarcely good enough for the Siberian market, such as nearly all the glass-ware.

The Russian Government had granted entrance to these goods, and a further shipment duty free. The English manufactures gave the most satisfaction, and no doubt a still better quality of these would have been still more appreciated.

I spent most of the day of Saturday, the 18th of August, in

DOLGAHN LADIES' BONNET.

P. P. C. visits. This was a holiday; a harvest it must have proved to the Isvoschicks, or cabdrivers. The merchants and the various official personages sat in state to receive visitors, and occasionally slipped out to pay calls themselves. On a

side-table in each house, Vodka, Sherry or Madeira, dishes
of cold meat, sardines, dried fish, &c., were laid out, but no
plates, and very little cutlery, were to be seen. The visitors
took a mouthful and a glass of wine standing, chatted a few
minutes, and then left. I paid my visits with one of the
Telegraph officials in uniform, who kindly translated for me.
He had just got two months' leave of absence, and was going
to Warsaw, so we arranged to travel together. I spent the
whole of the next day finishing the packing-up of my birds.

A dinner at the Ispravnik's on the following Monday furnished me with a curious example of Yen-e-saisk' customs.
I received a written invitation in French to dine at two
o'clock. Soon after that hour I made my appearance, and
found three other gentlemen, officials from Kras-no-yarsk',
making up a party of half-a-dozen, including host and hostess.
After being introduced to the other guests, I was requested
to help myself from the side-table to a glass of Vodka or
Sherry, with a morsel of bread and cheese, or a sardine. A
card-table was soon after placed in the centre of the room,
and the four gentlemen sat down to play a game resembling
whist, whilst I chatted in French with Madame. Sometimes
Madame took a chair at the card-table, then the Ispravnik
and I would hold a laborious conversation in Russian with the
help of a dictionary. This continued until half-past three,
when soup was brought in and laid upon a side-table. The
Ispravnik and I alone sat at this table; the card-players did
not stir from their post; a plate of soup was placed beside
each; they quickly dispatched it and resumed their game.
Courses of roast beef, fowls, pudding, &c., followed, and

between each course the card-playing went on as usual. Half-an-hour after dinner coffee was served, and after coffee cards were continued as before, so I made my adieu highly interested and amused. In the evening (Monday the 20th of August) we left Yen-e-saisk' in a post povoska, with our heavy luggage in a tyelega. The luggage being almost all mine, I paid for three horses, and M. Sprenberg, my companion, the young telegraph officer, for one.

We went along very pleasantly, progressing without any accident. The country looked very different from what it had done in winter. From the tops of some of the hills we could see a great distance, and many of the views were striking. The fine road, with the long line of telegraph posts, descended into the valley through a strip of partially cleared country, like an English park, and then lost itself in the forest. In the middle distance we could catch glimpses of the winding Yen-e-say'. On its banks was a large village, conspicuous by its two white churches, whilst far away rose the distant mountains, almost as blue as the sky. As we neared Kras-no-yarsk' the country became barer and bleaker. the villages larger and more numerous, and considerable patches of black land were under cultivation, growing oats, wheat, rye, and hemp. Our road for miles extended in some places through meadows where horses and cows were grazing in great numbers. Birds were plentiful for the season of the year. Starlings were in large flocks. In the villages Sparrows and the three common species of Swallow abounded. Wagtails were also numerous, all apparently the Masked Wagtail. Birds of prey were frequently to be seen perched upon the telegraph posts; of these the larger number were Kestrels, and occasionally a large brown Buzzard. A Grey Shrike likewise affected the telegraph wires. Magpies, Carrion Crows, and Ravens also abounded. We reached Kras-no-yarsk' on Friday the 24th of August, at ten o'clock at night, having been about fifty-two hours on the way. The journey cost me thirty-eight roubles.

Here we spent three days very agreeably at the family hotel of Madame Vis'-o-ko-voi'. There is an excellent club in Kras-no-yarsk', where English bottled beer and stout may be obtained at three roubles the bottle. The club is situated in a large garden, where sometimes two or three Orange-legged Hobbies may be seen together on the wing.

The engineer of the telegraph-office here is a German, from Berlin, and he gave me some interesting information about the line, which is leased to a Danish company. It frequently happens when some of the Indian cables are out of order or overcrowded with messages, that from 500 to 1000 English telegrams pass through Kras-no-yarsk' in a week. The fact of my travelling companion being a telegraph official, and dressed in the government official uniform, gave us free access to all the telegraph offices, and it was great fun chatting freely from time to time with the friends we had left behind us a thousand miles or more. I found in Kras-no-yarsk', in consequence of the quantity of baggage I was bringing home, that I should be short of money, so I wired to St. Petersburg for five hundred roubles, and forty-eight hours afterwards had the notes in my pocket.

I found in Professor Strebeloff a most interesting and

highly educated man, and enjoyed his hospitality more than once. To find a scientific man who could read English and speak German was a treat. He gave me a small collection of Siberian spiders for an entomological friend.

The most interesting event which happened to me in this town was, however, the purchase of a small collection of bronze and copper celts and other instruments which had been dug out of the ancient graves between Kras-no-yarsk' and Min-o-sinsk'.

The most interesting of these bronzes are figured as tail-pieces in this volume. So far as I know, this little collection is unique in this country. In Erman's 'Travels in Siberia,' published in 1848, in an English translation (vol. ii. page 139), a description will be found of a similar collection from the same district. In an ethnological periodical published at Toulouse, entitled *Matériaux pour l'histoire primitive et naturelle de l'homme* (1873, page 497), a very similar collection is described and figured (plate xvi) by Mons. E. Desor, the bronzes having been forwarded to him for that purpose by Mons. Lapatine, a Russian engineer residing in Kras-no-yarsk'. As I passed through St. Petersburg on my return journey, Mons. Russow, the curator of the Anthropological Museum in that city, showed me, in their almost unique series of Siberian objects of ethnological interest, a collection very much like my own, from the same valley, and I also discovered a case of bronzes in the Imperial collection in the Hermitage in St. Petersburg, evidently having the same origin. All authorities agree that these bronzes are the remains of a race antecedent to any of the present races of Siberia.   Mons. Lapatine states that he obtained his bronzes from nomad Tartars, who collected them in the steppes whilst feeding their flocks; and Erman mentions that they "are found in graves which, as the present Tartar inhabitants of the circle maintain, belong to a race now extinct and totally different from theirs."

Doctor Peacock presented me with a complete suit of Tun-goosk' summer clothes, a quiver full of arrows, and the pipe and belt which he had got from a Tun-goosk' at the gold mines.   In one of these districts Dr. Peacock was for some years a physician; he told me that he had found, on his arrival, out of a population of five thousand men under his charge, no less than eighteen hundred suffering from scurvy; he soon discovered that they were in the habit of bleeding themselves twice a-year, in spring and in autumn.   To this he put an end, and the following year the number of patients afflicted with scurvy was reduced to eight hundred, and the year following to two hundred.

Kibort, the Pole, who had promised to get me skins and eggs of birds, I found had done nothing, so after blowing him up sky high, I left 100 roubles with Dorset, the Kras-no-yarsk' "Vet," who vowed to look after the delinquent; and in consequence I have received many interesting parcels of birds from this district.

During our stay at Kras-no-yarsk' the weather was very unsettled; one day we had to put up with showers of rain, and another with clouds of dust.   The country in the neighbourhood looked charming—mountain, river, rock, and forest alternating with grassy plains and naked hills; birds abounded.   The White Wagtail which we saw was the Masked Wagtail. Jackdaws were common, together with plenty of Carrion Crows, but no Hoodies.

We left Kras-no-yarsk' on Saturday evening at eight o'clock, and reached Tomsk on Wednesday morning, August the 29th, at ten o'clock, travelling two only out of the four nights. The weather was fine, broken but by one thunder-shower; in the afternoon, however, we found it very hot, with the sun striking in our faces. The roads were generally good, but dusty, and it was only now and then that we came upon a short stretch of corduroy road, which is certainly one of the most diabolical inventions for breaking the backs of poor travellers that can be conceived. The scenery was very fine. We seemed to be constantly driving through an English nobleman's park; the autumnal tints of the trees were wonderful, the same that I have seen in the fall in the American forests. The range of colours was exactly those of the finest Newtown Pippin, going from the richest chrome-yellow to the deepest madder red. Some of the villages we passed were very large; occasionally we went through a Tartar village, where the crescent occupied the place of the cross on the church spire. We frequently came upon gipsies who had pitched their wigwams outside the gates. Now and then we met a Boor'-ry-at, a Trans-by-kal Mongolian. Birds were very numerous. The Carrion Crow was common for perhaps the first two hundred versts; during the next one hundred and fifty versts it was still found, but the Hooded Crow, and the Hybrid between the two, abounded, and for the last two hundred versts the Hoodie only was found.

The migration of Hoodies appears to have gone across country to Yen-e-saisk', leaving Kras-no-yarsk' to the south-east. A Pole, whom I met at one of the villages, a zealous Jäger, and therefore an observer of birds, told me that the Hooded Crow had been there as long as he had—that is, thirteen years. The Green Wagtail was common, but the White Wagtail appeared to me to be the Indian or European White Wagtail, and not the Masked Wagtail.

This journey cost me forty roubles. We might easily have made it in twelve hours less, but the steamer from Tomsk leaving only at 3 A.M. on the morning of the 30th, we preferred to take it easy. We were never absolutely stopped for horses, but we travelled under difficulties, for six horses had been reserved by telegraph at each station for General Sievers, who was on his way from Irkutsk, bent on catching the steamer for which we were bound. Early one morning we were told at one of the stations that there were no horses, not even for our crown padarozhna. We had, however, long ago reached that chronic state of stoical imperturbability into which all old travellers finally drift, and had ordered the samovar, and were discussing our second *stakkan chai*, when a cossack rode up full gallop, bearing orders from the Ispravnik of the town lying thirty miles behind, to the effect that the General might go to Hong Kong, but the Englishman must have the horses.

At Tomsk we found a capital hotel, the " European," kept by a one-armed Pole, and we spent a pleasant evening with one of the telegraph officers with whom my travelling companion was acquainted. Here we learned that Captain Wiggins had sold the wreck of the *Thames* for six thousand roubles. I afterwards learned that the Yen-e-saisk' merchants who bought her were successful in saving her in the spring, but that they made the mistake of attempting to tow her up to Yen-e-saisk.' After a series of disasters she was finally stranded on a sandbank, where it was impossible to save her when the ice broke up, and she was dismantled, and what was left of her abandoned.

TUNGOOSK SUMMER DRESS.

VILLAGE ON THE OBB.

CHAPTER XXII.

From Tomsk to Tyu-main'—An old acquaintance—Cost of steamboat travelling—
Cooking—Tobolsk—Contrast between Russian and Tartar villages—Threading
the labyrinth of the Toor-a—The Black Kite—Cormorants—Asiatic White
Crane—Notes of Sandpipers—Tyu-main'—Russian hotel accommodation—Bad
roads—Ekatereenburg—Recrossing the Ural—Iron works—Kongoor—New rail-
ways—The big village.

WE left Tomsk on Thursday the 30th of August. The water
in the river was so low that the steamer was not able to
come up to the town, so we were obliged to hire a droshky to
drive us three miles to the station on Wednesday evening,
when we got into a small tug steamer which weighed anchor
at three o'clock in the morning. The *Kos-a-goff'-sky* was
lying about forty-five versts down the river, and we were

comfortably quartered on board of her in time for a late breakfast. She was a smart iron vessel, built in Tyu-main', and would not have disgraced an English dockyard. As we were going on board we met an old acquaintance, the secretary of old Von Gazenkampf of Toor-o-kansk', and we arranged to take a private second-class cabin for us three. The price was fifty roubles (about £2 each at the then rate of exchange), which, for a journey of 3200 versts, or upwards of 2000 miles, was very cheap. For our luggage, we paid at the rate of one rouble per pood, or about eight shillings per cwt. Our meals were served in our own room, and we had an excellent dinner, consisting of five courses, for a rouble each.

We had an excellent cook on board, and had an opportunity of tasting the celebrated Siberian fishes to perfection. Fried sterlet is undoubtedly one of the finest dishes that can be put upon the table; it reminds one both of trout and eel, but possesses a delicacy superior to either. Nyelma, or white salmon, is, I think, an overrated fish ; to my taste, it is immeasurably inferior to pink salmon. What it might turn out in the hands of an English cook I do not know. Our cook on board was the best I had met in Russia; indeed, I might say, the best I had met out of England. He could fry to perfection, but his roasts and his boils were not up to the mark; they evoked a suspicion that our *cordon bleu* had tried to kill two birds with one stone. His boiled meat had been stewed with an idea of making as much soup out of it as he dared, and his roast joints never underwent *destructive combustion* in any part ; they were only a shade better than boiled meat browned with some piquante sauce. It is the fashion to praise French cooking to the skies. For my part, I must plead guilty to enjoying a dinner prepared by a good Yorkshire cook beyond all others. There is a delicacy of flavour, a fineness of bouquet attainable in meat and vegetables, cooked *au naturel,* which is quite as impossible to attain by sauces as it is to imitate the aroma of Prince Metternich's Schloss Johannisberg by doctoring a common Rhine wine with liqueur. The French cooks excel in entrées; but you can no more live upon entrées than you can upon cake. A French dinner is nothing but a succession of **entrées.** The joints are cooked so execrably that one has no alternative but to pass them by, and consequently it becomes the old story of *toujours perdrix* over again. Our *cordon bleu* was an artiste. His dishes, as they were sent up to table, looked enchanting. Like most French cooks, he was, beyond imagination, clever in concealing his ignorance of the art of cooking. It was obvious that, according to his philosophy, it was the eye and not the tongue who was prime minister of the dinner-table.

On the 3rd of September we had left the Tom and the Obb and were steaming up the Eer'-tish, before long to enter the To-bol' and afterwards the Toor'-a. At noon on Wednesday we spent a couple of hours at Tobolsk, a fine old city with many interesting churches. Part of the town is built upon a hill, and part on the plain. It was formerly the capital of western Siberia, but since the removal of the Government offices to Omsk, it has declined in importance. Its streets are wide, and paved with thick planks or battens laid longitudinally, which have rotted away in places, and a drive through the city is an experience to be endured rather than enjoyed. We found a second-class photographer in Tobolsk, from whom I bought some photos of Ost'-yaks and Sam'-o-yades.

The next day we steamed up the To-bol' accompanied by a small steamer, which was to take us on to Tyu-main' when the river became too shallow for our vessel to navigate. The country we passed continued to be very flat; there was seldom any view to be had from the deck, but that of the interminable willows on either bank. Whenever we stopped for wood in the neighbourhood of a village, its inhabitants came out with milk, cream, eggs, raspberries, and cranberries to sell. These Russian hamlets looked as usual, poor and dirty : many houses in them falling to ruins. On the other hand, the Tartar villages were clean and orderly.

We were nine days and nights steaming from Tomsk to Tyu-main'; but although the scenery was generally very monotonous, for the most part a low sand-bank, and the edge of an interminable willow swamp was all that could be seen, we nevertheless enjoyed the change. It was something to be able to enjoy a "square" meal. Occasionally we were able to go on shore at the villages, where we stopped to take in passengers or fire-wood. The stacks of the latter at some of the stations were enormous. Our engine-fires consumed forty sar-zheens' a day, more than two hundred cubic yards. Twice before reaching Tyu-main' we had to change into smaller steamers, which alone were able so late in the season to thread the shallow labyrinth of the

Toor'-a. This river winds like a snake; we seemed to be perpetually describing a circle ; the normal appearance was that of circumnavigating a clump of willows, surrounded by a narrow strip of green grass, which gradually lost itself in a a sloping bank of yellow sand. The monotony of the journey was, however, wonderfully relieved by the abundance of bird life. To lounge on deck with binocular at hand ready to be brought to bear on any interesting bird or group of birds was pleasant pastime.

Birds of prey were very numerous. On the meadows around Tomsk the Black Kite was as common as it is in the Golden Horn at Constantinople. Hooded Crows and Magpies were constantly seen on the banks of the river; and near the villages we noticed Jackdaws, Tree-Sparrows, and White Wagtails. After we had entered the labyrinth of the Toor'-a, large flocks of Rooks appeared for the first time. Wading and swimming birds were of course the most abundant. Soon after leaving Tomsk, I noticed about forty Cormorants * on a sand-bank. Whenever we passed a fishing party, Gulls and Terns were sure to abound; probably the Common Gull and the Common Tern. Ducks abounded everywhere. Cranes passed over occasionally in small flocks, and whilst steaming up the Toor'-a, I had a fine view of four or five Asiatic White Cranes † as they flew leisurely over

---

* The Cormorant (*Phalacrocorax carbo*) is a common resident on the coasts of the British Isles. It is almost a cosmopolitan bird, but in Western North America and South America it is represented by allied species.

† The Asiatic White Crane (*Grus leucogeranus*) is only a rare straggler to Eastern Europe, but is found throughout Siberia, North-east Mongolia, and Japan, wintering in India and North China. It breeds in the marshy forests as far north as the Irtisch.

our vessel. During flight they appeared to be pure white all over, except the outside half of each wing, which looked jet-black.

Sandpipers were the commonest birds of all, and the most noisy. The Redshank was the loudest of all, though perhaps the least numerous. His *tyü, tyü* is well known to every ornithologist. · The note of the Wood Sandpiper is very similar, but softer. This bird abounded. A less noisy and less common but more conspicuous bird was the Green Sandpiper, whose *tyĕ, tyĕ* was frequently heard. The Common Sandpiper was also by no means uncommon, and its meek *iss, iss* did not pass unnoticed. As we neared Tyu-main' a small flock of Peewits * appeared, feeding on the water's edge and flying before us from bank to bank of the river. In one of the villages I examined a peasant's stock of Swan's skins; they were the Wild Swan and Bewick's Swan in about equal numbers; so that there can be no doubt that both species are found in the valley of the Obb.

We reached Tyu-main' just as the sun was setting, and went to the best hotel. The town was one mass of mud, and the streets full of deep holes; no provision being made for lighting them, when darkness fell they became utterly deserted. No doubt it was the business of some official to see something done to improve matters. No doubt also he

---

* The Lapwing (*Charadrius vanellus*) breeds throughout the central and southern portions of the palæarctic region, from Japan to the British Islands, occasionally straggling to Iceland, and even Greenland. It is a resident, except in the coldest portions of its range, the Siberian birds wintering in India and China.

was paid so much a year by the inhabitants to permit
nothing to be done, and so long as he could fill his own
pockets he was perfectly satisfied, I doubt not, and the
streets might go to the dogs. The "Wirthshaft" in the
hotel was not much better; if a guest was provided with
a lofty room having
plenty of windows and
a large door, it was
evidently considered all
that was needful for his
comfort. A card-table,
a sofa, and a couple of
chairs was furniture
abundant. If he had
neglected to bring his
bed and bedding he had
better not undress, but
lie down upon the sofa
and sleep as best he
could. Russian hotel-
keepers apparently
labour under the de-
lusion that travellers
are subject to hydro-
phobia, and must upon
no account be allowed
to see more than a pint

DOLGAHN QUIVER.
(Border of Yurak Soveek in background.)

of water at a time. When we asked to wash after a
dusty journey, we were conducted to a brass machine

containing when full about a quart of water. This mysterious looking receptacle was fixed against the wall. On lifting a valve at the bottom about a wine-glass full of water would ooze out and fall upon our hands, and this was called washing! To convert the dust into mud such an arrangement sufficed, but to do anything else than this was out of the question. On other occasions, when we asked that the necessaries for performing our ablutions might be brought to our rooms, a dirty flat-bottomed basin made of brass would be carried in to us, and placed upon the floor; over this we were expected to stand and wash, whilst the servant from time to time poured water upon our hands from an ancient looking vessel, also brass, and highly ornamented with a long narrow spout like a large coffeepot. You are expected to have your own soap and your own towel. The only explanation I can suggest for these curious customs is that they may have first originated in the desire to avoid the communication of infectious diseases, brass being popularly supposed, in the East, to be incapable of conveying contagion. In Athens, Constantinople, or Smyrna, for example, the mouthpiece of your private nargilleh or chibouque will be made of amber, but in a public restaurant, if you call for a nargilleh, the mouthpiece of the one handed to you will be of brass; should you ask why it is not of amber, the answer will probably be given you that amber is dangerous, being capable of conveying infection.

We left Tyu-main' at sunset on Saturday night, and made the first station in four hours, over a road which was a disgrace to the town. No ditches bordered it, and the rain that fell had to lie until the sun or the wind dried it up. We could not discover the slightest evidence that the road was ever mended. At the first station we slept four hours, simply to recover from the effects of the wretched journey over this highway, and then we travelled the whole of the following day without any improvement in the condition of our route.

The next morning, however, after a six hours' night rest, we came upon excellent roads, and reached Ekatereenburg at eight o'clock in the evening. The presence of rock on the roadside, a few stations before, indicated our near approach to the Ural. I saw no birds of special interest on the journey. The peasants we passed were busy stacking their corn. We got very comfortable quarters at the American Hotel, and spent an interesting day. Mr. Onesime Clerk was kind enough to do us the honours of the place. He took us to see the Emperor's private manufactory of works of art executed in the various valuable stones found in the Ural. We saw huge blocks of material and several unfinished vases, but as it was a holiday the men were not at work.

We visited the observatory, from which their is a panoramic view of the town, and were much astonished to learn there that the average rainfall per annum for the last forty years has been eleven inches only (278 millemeters). The town looked very different now in the summer time from what it had done in the winter season. It was by far the handsomest Siberian city that I had seen, being in some parts very picturesque.

We left Ekatereenburg the following morning at ten o'clock, and crossed the European frontier, soon entering the range of hills and valleys called the Ural mountains. The roads were not so bad as we had expected to find them, and we made the fourth station by nine o'clock, putting up there for the night. We had been warned at starting that many robberies had lately occurred on this route, and we were recommended not to travel after dark, and to wear our revolvers by day as conspicuously as possible. The story ran that some convicts, after murdering the soldiers who had escorted them to Siberia, had made their escape, and were now in the Ural forests, living by plundering the caravans that passed through. In many places the roads over which we travelled were mended with white quartz, and we met many "tyel-ay-gahs" laden with granite, probably destined to be used for the same purpose. The scenery all around was very fine, alternate hill and forest, but we saw nothing that could possibly be called a mountain. The next morning we were up by four o'clock, and accomplished five stations during the day, over roads that did not deserve to be much grumbled at. We passed the Vassilyova Iron Works, and took with us a sample of the iron ore, which is so magnetic that a needle clings to it with considerable force.

Our way still lay through hills and valleys covered with forest, and from some of the ridges we had fine and extended views. The next day we travelled from 5 A.M. to 8 P.M. The last thirty versts before reaching Kon-goor were very heavy work, the roads almost reaching the point when it is impossible for roads to become worse; they were a thick mixture of gravel and mud, with deep ruts into which our wheels sank nigh up to the axles. To add to our misery, we were overtaken by frequent showers of rain. We seemed generally to be on high land, only occasionally descending into the valleys. Rooks were very abundant, and we constantly passed colonies of their now deserted nests in the birch-trees on the road-side. The Hooded Crows seemed to live very peaceably amongst them. We often noticed birds of the two species amicably feeding together, but there was not the slightest evidence of any interbreeding between them. The Rook is probably only a summer visitor here as it is in Tyu-main', and the Hooded Crows may possibly pair before the Rooks arrive. Jackdaws were also equally abundant, some having grey necks, others marked with a ring almost pure white. As soon as we arrived at Kon-goor an *Isvoschik* drove us to the house of Mr. Hawkes. Unfortunately he was from home, attending the great fair at Nishni Novgorod, but his manager entertained us most hospitably, and we enjoyed some English porter, which to us was as great a treat as champagne would have been. Kon-goor was the most easterly town we had visited, whose streets were lighted at night; no attempt, however, being made at paving, we found them transformed into rivers of mud. The four remaining stations to Perm occupied us fourteen hours. The road was simply diabolical, and had it not been that we could frequently leave it and travel on the grass bordering it, we should have been much longer on the way. Attempts to improve this highway have been made to little or no purpose. The amount of traffic upon it is enormous. We no sooner passed one caravan than we came upon another; and frequently, as far as the eye could reach, there defiled before us one long line of "tyel-ay-gahs," laden with goods, *en route* for Siberia. In the other direction the traffic was less.

We were told that the railway was to be opened between Perm and Ekatereenburg the following autumn. Another mode of transit and conveyance in this direction will be a boon to the overworked horses, and ought to prove a profitable speculation to all concerned in it. When the enormous traffic is removed from this road, the chances of mending it will improve.

The railway has since been opened, and my friend Mr. Wardroper informs me that the price of wheat has doubled in Tyu-main' in consequence of a concession having been granted by the Government to a company to form a line of rail from Ekatereenburg to that town. When this line is completed there will be steam navigation in summer from St. Petersburg to Tomsk, a distance of 6,630 versts, or 4,200 miles.

It was an immense relief to think that we had paid off our last yemschik, and should finish our long journey by steam. The distances that are travelled by horses in Siberia are enormous, and yet there is probably no country in the world where so much travelling is accomplished by the merchants, who are obliged to visit the great fairs regularly if they wish to buy in the cheapest and sell in the dearest market. In the course of conversation with one of these merchants Siberia was half-jokingly described to me as a big village the main street of which, extending from Nishni Novgorod to Ke-akh'-ta, was about five thousand miles long, where there were always half a million horses on the road, and where everybody knew everybody from one end of the street to the other.

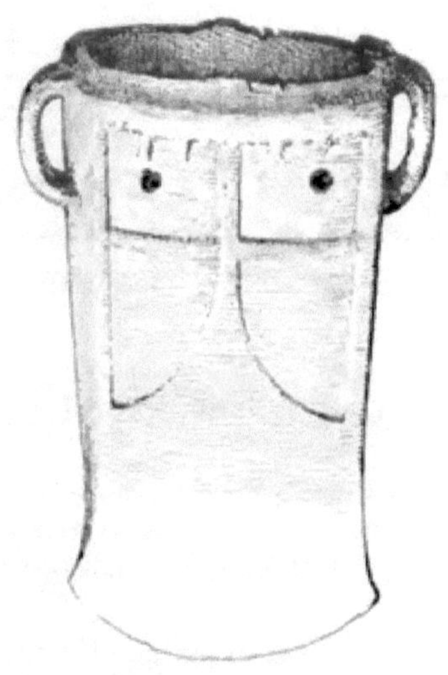

BRONZE CELT FROM ANCIENT GRAVE NEAR KRASNOYARSK.

OSTYAK CHOOM ON THE OBB.

CHAPTER XXIII.

It was quite dark when we reached Perm, on Saturday the 10th of September, and we at once drove to the steamer *Samolot*, or "self-flyer," delighted to bid a long adieu to tarantass, tyel-ay-gah, and Tartar yems-chik, and to find ourselves once more directly steaming towards Europe and civilisation.

Russia has made enormous progress since the abolition of

serfdom, yet the moment you cross its frontier you still feel that you have left Europe and European ideas behind, and are, to all intents and purposes, amongst Asiatics in Asia. The Mongols are at home there, but you are a foreigner. The late Emperor, no doubt, did much to de-Tartarise his vast realm, and, from what I can learn, with, if comparatively slow, yet with sure, results. I am told that the most European town in all the Russias is Irkutsk. Some day, doubtless, this city will be a second New York, the capital of an Asiatic United States, a free Siberia from the Ural to the Pacific. This change will probably not be brought about by revolution. The Russian is too law-loving a man to try and free himself by force from the mother country. He will trust to the accidents of diplomacy. Siberia will some day be free. Every Siberian imbibes the notion of freedom with his mother's milk. Though born in Russia, or the child of Russian parents, he repudiates his nationality, calls himself a Siberiak, and is proud of his country. He looks down upon the Russian as the Yankee scorns the Britisher.

We left Perm in the morning of the 16th of September; a strong sou-wester blowing, which, during the afternoon, ended in a deluge of rain. A day later on the road we and all our goods would most likely have been drenched through. From the river we did not see much of the town; the banks were steep, and we only saw that part built in the valleys, which came down to the water's edge. At a distance the lower valley seemed to be full of public buildings, and the upper one of factories.

We had heavy gales and showers all the next day. Only

at intervals could we enjoy a walk on deck. The banks of the Kama are hilly and well wooded, and the trees were then in all the brilliancy of their autumnal tints. I have only seen in America any hue approaching the chrome-yellows of the birches, or the fire-red of the poplars. This was thoroughly Siberian, yet we were enduring all the miseries of the worst season of European climate. In the morning rain and wind, in the afternoon wind and rain. Another feature in the landscape showed that we had left Siberia : the much greater extent of land under cultivation, and the increased number of villages. What struck me most was the immense amount of traffic on the river; we were continually meeting steamers towing two, three, four, and in one instance ten large barges laden with goods *en route* for Siberia.

We ought to have reached Kazan at eleven o'clock the next morning, but a driving hurricane of wind and rain, in our teeth, delayed us until three in the afternoon. The town lay some four versts inland, and was connected to the river by a tramway. We bargained with an Isvoschik to drive us direct to the University, a huge pile of buildings surrounding, in a rambling fashion, a large courtyard, possibly intended for a garden, where confusion reigned supreme. Six hundred students from all parts of Russia and Siberia are educated at this University, where, no doubt, the elements of disorder everywhere so rife in the Russian character, are thoroughly inculcated. I had a letter of introduction from an eminent ornithologist in St. Peters-burg to Professor Peltzam, whose acquaintance I was most anxious to make, as he had visited the Petchora the year before Harvie-Brown and I were there. After seeking in vain in various official buildings, we at last found an old woman, who conducted us to the Professor's house in the University grounds. Madame Peltzam came to the door, and the following colloquy took place: "Is the Professor at home?" I asked. "No." "Is it possible to send for him?" "No." "Can Madame inform me where we might find him?" "No idea." "Can Madame tell us when the Professor will be at home?" "Possibly late at night, or early to-morrow morning!" I explained that I had letters of introduction to the Professor, and intended to leave for England early the following morning, and was most anxious to see him. Madame was sorry she "could give us no further information." Nothing more was to be said, yet what was to be done? Fortunately I remembered that I had another letter to a Professor in Kazan, Professor Kovalefsky. The Isvoschik drove us to his house. The Professor was at dinner, but most kindly came at once to see us. I explained my vain attempts to find Dr. Peltzam, and asked if he could arrange for me to see the ornithological museum. He at once offered to conduct me thither in half-an-hour, and promised that Dr. Peltzam should be there to meet me. When I called again, at the expiration of the prescribed time, the Professor was waiting to escort us to the museum, and informed me that Dr. Peltzam was already there. This was the second time that a Russian lady had denied to me all knowledge of the whereabouts of her husband, of whom I was in quest, and on both occasions the denial was given in a manner that convinced both myself and those who accompanied me, that its object was to prevent us finding the gentleman in question. The only explanation I can suggest for this strange reception is, that, as my companion travelled in the uniform of the Russian service, we were mistaken for members of the secret police, who have power of arresting any individual at a moment's notice, without granting him any form of trial or explanation, and transporting him there and then to Siberia; a monstrous exercise of tyranny which only a chicken-hearted nation, like the Russian, would endure for a day without a revolution.

In the ornithological museum I found very little to interest me. The birds were without localities, and consequently without scientific value. Dr. Peltzam told me that since the retirement of Dr. Bogdanoff, no one had taken up ornithology as a speciality. He showed me what he believed to be hybrids, between the Capercailzie and black game, and a couple of female Black Grouse, which had partially assumed the male plumage. The latter were interesting from the fact that, upon dissection, the ovary in each case was found to have been injured by a shot, and the birds in consequence rendered barren. Although three years had elapsed since Dr. Peltzam's visit to the Petchora, he had not yet prepared the scientific results of it for the press. Whether this delay was the result of Russian dilatoriness, or of German " Grundlichkeit," carried to a pedantic extreme, I cannot say.

In the ethnological department the prevailing disorder

reached its climax; considering the locality, also, the collection was meagre in the extreme; I saw, however, one or two things of great interest. A complete suit of summer clothing, was said to be 'Tun-goosk', from the east of Lake By-kal. This dress was semi-transparent, and made of bladder or fishes' skin. Another most interesting object was the dress of a Sham-man, the front covered with many pounds' weight of iron, wrought into images of fishes and animals of all kinds. It was evidently Siberian. The curator told me that the Sham-man was the doctor of the tribe, and that each image was a present from a patient whom he had cured. I was shown everything that could interest me, and I am much indebted to Professor Kovalefsky, Dr. Peltzam, and the other curators, for their kindness and attention. I can only regret that they are buried alive in such a God-forsaken place as the University of Kazan.

I had now seen much of the Tartars. By their appearance they would seem to belong to a much higher race than the Dolgahns or Tungoosks. More or less copper-coloured, with high cheek-bones, small noses, sunken eyes, and large jaws, their features are yet much more regular than those of their supposed relations, and their beards more developed. This may be the result of their more civilised life in a more genial climate. Yet it would seem to make them indebted to the Arabs for something more than their religion. Probably the change of faith was not made without some admixture of Arab blood, or perhaps, like the Turks, the Tartars have undergone a national change of feature through the importation of Aryan blood into their harems.

T

We ought to have left Kazan at eight o'clock the next morning, and we were at the station punctually at that hour, but we waited and waited in vain—no steamer came. At eleven a telegram arrived with the news that our vessel had been injured by collision with another. A spare steamer was now made ready for us, and the Kazan passengers departed, leaving the Kama passengers to their fate. I was told that

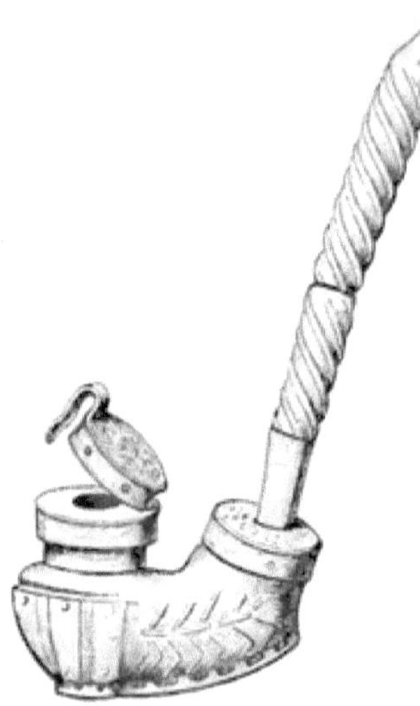

RUSSIAN PIPE.

three hundred steamers ply the Volga and the Kama, and considering the darkness and storminess of many of the nights, and the narrowness of the navigable channels in some parts of the river, an occasional collision is no matter for surprise. The scenery of the Volga was very similar to that on the banks of the Kama, but the river was wider, the country somewhat flatter, and the towns larger. Formerly the church was the only stone building to be seen, now there were stone dwellings in most of the villages we passed.

We reached Nishni about five o'clock in the afternoon of Thursday, the 20th of September, our progress having been delayed by the strong westerly gales that continued to prevail. The fair was over, but still the brisk atmosphere of business pervaded the town, the streets and bridges were crowded with traffic, and everything denoted activity and prosperity. In a couple of hours we had transferred our luggage to the railway station, delighted once more to see a locomotive, and to feel ourselves dragged over rails after having sat behind about fifteen hundred horses, to say nothing of dogs and reindeer.

We reached Moscow in good time on Friday morning, September the 21st, and I lost no time in presenting my letters of introduction to M. Sabanaeff. From him I learnt that he had ceased to pursue his ornithological studies, and had given away his collection to one of the Moscow museums.

The next day I spent an hour at the museum of the University, looking over Sabanaeff's collection of birds' skins from the Ural. In the University of Kazan I thought disorder reigned supreme; but in that of Moscow I was obliged to admit the final triumph of chaos. There was a collection of more than a thousand skins of birds, specially interesting, being collected on the boundary of the Eastern and Western Palæarctic regions. These skins were all mixed up, the land-birds with water-birds, the large with the small, crammed into drawers and cupboards, with no covering over them, not even a sheet of paper to keep out the dust. Delving for information in such a mine was almost a hopeless task; but I succeeded, owing to the indefatigable kindness of M. Sabanaeff, in gaining some interesting facts.

I left Moscow on Saturday at half-past eight in the evening, and arrived at St. Petersburg at half-past ten the next morning. I remained a few days in this interesting city, and reached home the afternoon of Wednesday, the 10th of October, having accomplished the following mileage.

Sheffield to Nishni Novgorod by rail 2,560
Nishni Novgorod to Koorayika by sledge 3,240
Koorayika to Golcheeka by ship 1,000
Golcheeka to Yenesaisk by steamer 1,810
Yenesaisk to Tomsk by pavoska 590
Tomsk to Tyumain by steamer. 2,134
Tyumain to Perm by pavoska 460
Perm to Nishni Novgorod by steamer 800
Nishni Novgorod to Sheffield by rail 2,560
——————
15,154

Shortly afterwards Captain Wiggins also returned, though he had to abandon part of his baggage on account of the badness of the roads across the Ural mountains. Of the adventures of the crew all I know is that they arrived safely in England at last. Captain Schwanenberg weighed anchor in the *Ibis* on the 13th of August, and by a fluke arrived without accident on the 11th of September at Vardö, whence he was towed to Stockholm, and crossed the Baltic, arriving at St. Petersburg on the 13th of December.

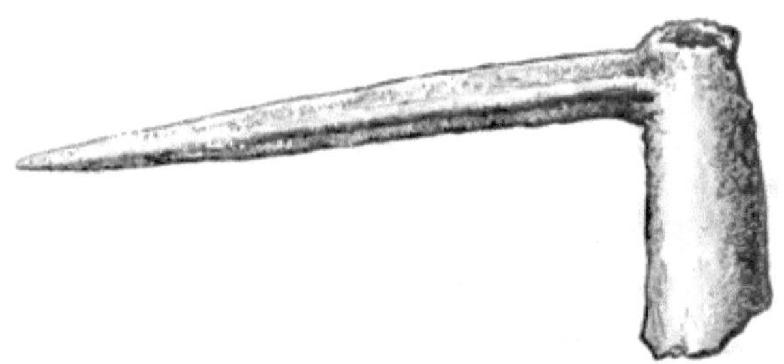

BRONZE FROM ANCIENT GRAVE NEAR KRASSNOYARSK.

TARTAR GIRL.

CHAPTER XXIV.

WHEN we arrived in St. Petersburg we found, as might naturally be expected, that the one topic of conversation was the war. Everybody from the Emperor downwards was dis-

appointed. No one imagined that there could be any difficulty in the matter if the enemy was not assisted by
European allies. The conquest of Turkey was expected to
be a mere walk over the course, a march past, with a few
victories to give *éclat* to the Russian army. The Emperor
soon discovered his mistake. Like Louis Napoleon in the
Franco-German war, he found that his generals had deceived
him as to the state of the army. In every department of
the government corruption had reigned supreme so long
that disaster was the inevitable result. It was commonly
reported that official incapacity and dishonesty reached their
climax in the War Office, and every post brought fresh
narratives of blunders and defeat. The commercial world of
St. Petersburg were chuckling over a cartoon in Kladdera-
datsch, in which the Russian Army was depicted with lions'
heads, the officers with asses' heads, and the generals with
no heads at all. Of course the number of the Berlin 'Punch'
containing this lampoon was forbidden entrance into Russia,
but many copies were surreptitiously introduced. There can
be little doubt that, had not the Turkish army been equally
mismanaged, Russia would have been ignominiously defeated
by her plucky little foe. But after all, the less said about
Russian blunders by Englishmen the better. Our fiascos in
the Crimea, and recently in Zululand and the Transvaal, have
been quite as disgraceful, possibly, if the whole truth was
known, much more so.

The corruption of Russian officials is beyond all conception.
Some time ago an attempt was made by the Government to
clear out the Augean stable of Railway management. It was

found on one of the lines that for years the head office had been debited with an annual sum for the repairs of a building which had never been built, both the original sum paid for the purpose, and the subsequent annual grants for imaginary repairs, having been embezzled by the local officials. The administrative staff was cashiered in a body, but the result was unsatisfactory in the extreme. Formerly the railway was managed by corrupt and dishonest men, who had at least the merit of knowing something of their business. After the change, the railway was managed by corrupt and dishonest men, who knew nothing of their business.

There is, perhaps, scarcely anything in the whole range of Russian social politics more hopeless than the universal official corruption. Half the Nihilism in Russia may be traced to this source. The Russian official is very impartial in the selection of his victims. He plunders the Government, he plunders the people, and he plunders his fellow-officials; but this is not all, his worst feature is that he helps the rich to plunder the poor. If by any chance an honest official is placed in any position of trust, and tries to act justly, the rich merchants of the district combine together, and move heaven and earth to have him displaced, so that their own petty schemes of plunder may be renewed.

The cause of this corruption is not difficult to trace. In a nation so recently emancipated from serfdom a high standard of honour cannot be expected. All oriental nations are corrupt, not because they are oriental, but because they are governed more or less despotically. Theft and falsehood are the natural resources of slaves. It is only the free man who can afford to be honest, and to tell the truth. It is unreasonable to expect a sense of honour in the bureaucracy of any country unless it is supported by public opinion. Russia is passing through a stage which all nations have had to pass through, or will have to pass through,—an intermediate stage between serfdom and freedom. Serfdom has been abolished by the decree of the late Emperor, but the vices of serfdom will only be abolished by a gradual development, which it will take generations to complete. At the present time the Russian peasant has little or no sense of honour. A merchant does not lose caste by doing a dishonourable action. So far from feeling any sense of shame from having acted dishonourably, he feels a sense of complacency. It gives a Russian far more innate pleasure to cheat somebody out of a rouble than to earn a rouble honestly. He feels that he has done a *clever* thing by earning a rouble dishonestly, and despises the honest man as *weak*. Nevertheless there are in the Russian character may elements of future greatness, and it is impossible to live amongst the Russians without liking them. Those who know Russia best will respond most heartily to the sentiment: "Russia, with all thy faults I love thee still." It is impossible to look upon the dishonesty and incapacity of the Russian officials without feeling both anger and contempt; but we must not confound the Russian nation with its governors, nor can we condemn the latter without remembering that many of their vices are fostered by, if not inseparable from, the miserable system of despotism under which Russia still groans. The Russian is a child, with a child's virtues and a child's faults, and naturally claims from any right-minded person the pity and affection which childhood demands. The faithfulness of a Russian servant is something wonderful. He never tires in your service. If he has worked for you all day, he will gladly work for you all night if required. Nothing is too difficult for him to attempt. He is your right-hand man in every case of need. He can mend your carriage or your harness, and repair your clothes or your boots. Give him a good axe, and there is no joiner's or carpenter's work which he cannot do, nay, if need be, he can build you a new house almost single-handed. He can shoot your game, kill and cut up an ox, or do any plain cooking you may require.

He is the soul of punctuality; and if you order him to wake you at four o'clock in the morning, you may sleep soundly to the last moment, in the full confidence that, at five minutes past that hour, it will be your own fault if you have not made considerable progress with your toilet.

He is honest if you trust him; but for all that, to earn a glass of vodka, he will lie without shame, and commit a petty theft without remorse.

There must be a great future in store for a nation with so many virtues. The Russians will surely not always remain children. At present we may consider them to be in a state of arrested development. A generation or two of education would, doubtless, develop both the intellectual and moral possibilities of the Russians, as it has done those of his western cousins. Russia is at this moment only beginning to rise out of the darkness of the Middle Ages. The Russian, as well as the Turkish patriot, must devoutly pray for the coming time, when "the last king shall be strangled with the sinews of the last priest." The Russian can at least congratulate himself upon the fact, that there are two worse governments than his own in Europe, the Turkish and the Greek. The former government is probably the worst in the world; and it is a scandal to Europe, and a shame to England, that it should have been propped up so long. The Turkish *government* is nothing but a band of robbers, plundering Moslem and Christian alike, a horde of banditti, whose only desert is the gallows. The Turk, on the other hand, is in some respects the best Christian in Europe. He is, in fact, too Christian. He carries his Christianity to such an extreme that it becomes a vice. No other nation, unless it be the Russian, would submit to such misgovernment without a revolution.

Like the Russians, the Turks are hospitable to a fault; and, as in Russia, so in Turkey or Asia Minor, you may travel in safety into the remotest corners, and in the wildest districts. I remember passing an orchard in Asia Minor laden with ripe cherries. Because I was a stranger, the Turk to whom it belonged asked me to enter and take my fill. As we steamed down the Yen-e-say', and passed a "lodka," the poor fisherman flung us a brace of sterlet on board, because we were strangers. How different to the English boor! "Who's him, Bill?" "I don't know—a stranger." "Then heave half a brick at him."

In some respects the Turk is the superior of the Russian, for he never lies, and his word is as good as his bond. The

Turk, too, can live where the Russian would starve. The Russian is kept in comparative poverty by the rapacity of his Ispravnik, and the venality of the police; whilst the Turk thrives under far greater robbery and more shameless injustice. How is this? Because the Russian, like the Englishman, is a spendthrift, and too fond of his glass; whilst the Turk, like the Frenchman, is a sober, saving man. On the other side, again, the Turk has a touch of the Spaniard or Italian about him. It is always wise not to quarrel with a Turk. A Turk makes a good friend, but a vindictive enemy. With a Russian you may quarrel to your heart's content. He has this noble trait in his character, that he never bears malice; and however violently you may have quarrelled the night before, everything is soon forgiven and forgotten, and he meets you in the morning with a smile on his face, and a hearty shake of the hand, as if nothing had happened. If you escaped being murdered last night in the heat of passion, you may be sure that you are in no danger to-day, or in the future, on the score of that quarrel.

Something of the good nature, the childishness, the happy-go-lucky feeling of the Russian, which forms such a marked feature in the national character, is doubtless attributable to the fact that in the country the necessaries of life are extremely cheap, and in the towns the demand for labour frequently exceeds the supply. Although commercial affairs appeared to be in a chronic state of depression, and the peasant was said to be taxed to the last rouble note that he could possibly realise, we saw nothing approaching destitution. Whatever may be the case in the more densely populated districts of South Russia, wherever we travelled there appeared to be a superabundance of land. Bread, meat, milk, and potatoes generally abounded at fabulously low prices, and the heavy taxation did not appear, after all, to be such a very terrible thing. Neither the peasant nor his children had any occasion to starve. They might possibly have to go on short rations of their favourite tea, or be obliged to drink it without sugar; or they might be compelled to let their wardrobes run to seed, and have to make up for the thinness of their old clothes by putting an extra log on the fire. On Sundays and on holidays the rouble which the government or its representative had annexed, would be most missed. The poor peasant might be obliged to forego the luxury of getting drunk, but possibly his inability to purchase vodka is a blessing rather than a curse. The struggle for existence in the parts of Russia which we visited is very easy, and the rate of development of the Russian mind can only be proportionately slow. The uneducated Russian is a child, with a child's virtues and a child's faults. The uneducated Englishman is a brute, a savage, with nothing of the child about him. The Englishman has learnt many a bitter lesson in the school of adversity. He has had many a battle with the wolf at the door—terrible battles—of the anguish and desperation of which the Russian can form no conception whatever; battles which have dried up his milk of human kindness, and made him naturally as savage as the wolf, with which he has metaphorically fought. There

are plenty of wolves in Russian forests, but they seldom
come to a poor man's door, as they do in England. When
they do come, the man becomes a Nihilist.

During both my journeys in Russia, as on a subsequent
visit to St. Petersburg, Moscow and Warsaw, at the time
of the assassination of the late Czar, I made many inquiries
respecting Nihilism. I found no difficulty whatever in
entering into conversation on the subject, but considerable
differences of opinion as to its nature and extent prevailed.
One set of opinions, which I found principally held by
the foreign residents, represented Nihilism as being confined
to a handful of half-crazy fanatics. I was told that the
Russians were the most conservative nation in the world,
that when there has been another revolution in France, and
a revolution in Germany, and when England has become
a republic, that then, and not till then, the Russians will
inquire whether their turn has not come. There is some
truth in this idea. There is a strong party, whose head-
quarters are in Moscow, which are very conservative, and
who attribute all the troubles of Russia to the introduction
of Western civilisation and Western ideas, and who would
gladly go back to the days before Peter the Great.

The other class of opinions which I found held by many
influential and well-informed Russians, represent Nihilism
as a much more important and wide-spread influence, which
is said to be especially rife in the army, and is being rapidly
disseminated in the country by the soldiers who have served
their time and have been dismissed to their homes. The
pessimist party naturally look upon the optimists as living

in a fool's paradise, and think that a revolution, which will sweep away every vestige of rank and wealth, may happen any day. I cannot think that any such movement is possible in any part of Russia with which I am acquainted, but the condition of the people in South Russia may be quite different, and a blaze once lighted, the fire would probably sweep across the whole country, and carry everthing before it.

The financial condition of Russia is most unsatisfactory. The Crimean War, by increasing the indebtedness of the nation to foreign countries, brought down the value of the paper rouble from 38*d.* to about 32*d.* The Turkish War, from similar causes, still further reduced it to 25*d.* The philosophy of the Exchange is easy of explanation. Russia has to export every year, in gold, an amount said to be fifteen millions sterling, to pay the interest of the national and private debts held out of the country. After exhausting the produce of her gold mines, roughly estimated at seven millions sterling, the balance must be the excess of exports over imports. If this be not enough, the price of bills on Russia (payable in paper roubles) must fall until they are low enough to tempt merchants to buy them for the sake of purchasing with them Russian produce, which they can sell in Europe at a profit, and thus make up the exports to the required amount.

Under these unfavourable circumstances Russia is obliged to discourage imports as much as possible, and cannot adopt Free Trade. The finances of the country are in a diseased state, and cannot digest the wholesome food of Free Trade, but must resort to Protection as a medicine.   Some plausible physicians suggest a different remedy.   They assert that Russia should honestly admit her bankruptcy, and offer her creditors a fair composition, as other bankrupts do or ought to do.   They say that if Russia was to pay her interest for the future in paper roubles, and adopt Free Trade, that her commerce would develop to such an extent that the country itself would benefit enormously, and that in the long run, by the rise in the value of the rouble, the bondholder would be better off than he will be when the inevitable break-down of the present system comes.

There can be no doubt that the internal resources of Russia are immense, and that under a wise government, which made their development possible, Russia would soon become one of the wealthiest nations of Europe.   Unfortunately the present Emperor has not the courage to attempt to govern his country justly.

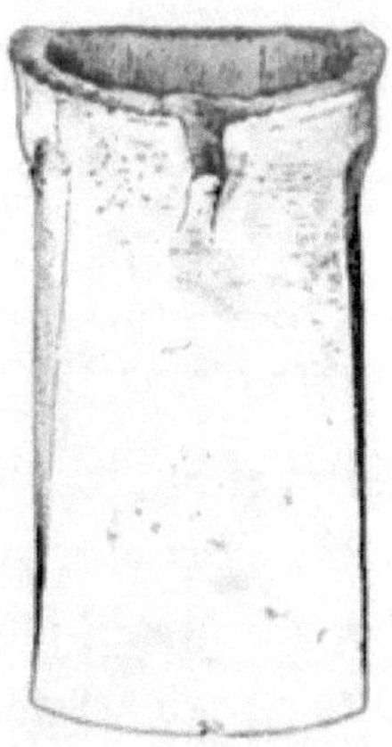

BRONZE CELT FROM ANCIENT GRAVE NEAR KRASNOYARSK.

CARRION AND HOODED CROWS
AND HYBRIDS.

CHAPTER XXV.

Ornithological results of the trip—Siberian forms of birds — Discoveries of Pallas— Comparison of European and Siberian birds—Interbreeding of allied species— Affinity of European and Japanese species—Sub-species—Conclusion.

THE ornithological results of my trip to Siberia in Asia were on the whole satisfactory.   It was a great disappointment to me not to get to the coast, and still more so to miss the birds of the Kara Sea, and to arrive on the Tundra too late for most of the eggs I was in search of.   The enforced delay in the pine forests produced, however, some very interesting results, and, take it altogether, the excursion must be pronounced a success, although I did not solve the problems which our expedition to Siberia in Europe left open. It is very seldom that the first expedition to a strange land is successful. The pioneer can do little more than discover the localities where future researches may be successfully made. My great mistake was that I wintered too far north. Had I waited the arrival of migratory birds at Yen-e-saisk' instead of on the Arctic Circle, my ornithological bag would have been increased fourfold in value. On my return journey my time was necessarily very limited, and I was obliged to husband my ammunition. It was also the most unfavourable time of the whole year for making ornithological observations. During the breeding season many birds forsake the neighbourhood of the villages and the cultivated land, and scatter themselves through the forests; and whilst they are moulting in the autumn they seem to be fully aware that their powers of flight are limited, and that, consequently, they are an easy prey to their raptorial enemies, and therefore they seem afraid to trust themselves on the wing. For the most part they are silent at this season, and skulk amongst the underwood, and it is only by chance that one can obtain a shot at them.

My plans were also considerably disarranged by the two shipwrecks, which did not form a part of my original programme; nevertheless an enumeration of the most important observations which I made may not be without interest to the reader.

Authentic eggs of the Asiatic Golden Plover had never before been taken, nor the habits of the bird at its breeding grounds recorded.

The interbreeding of the Carrion Crow with the Hooded Crow had never been noticed on such a large scale, nor had the fact that the hybrids between these two species are fertile been satisfactorily ascertained.

The nest and eggs of three species of Willow-Warbler, the Arctic Willow-Warbler, the Siberian Chiffchaff, and the Yellow-browed Warbler, were absolutely unknown before my visit to the Yen-e-say', and my specimens of these eggs still remain unique.

The Sedge-Warbler had never been found in Asia before (except in Turkestan); nor had our Willow-Warbler ever been known to breed there, the only previous record of the latter bird on the Asiatic continent being from Persia, where it seems that the Willow-Warblers which breed in North-East Russia winter.

The nest and eggs of the Little Bunting had been described by Middendorf, but it was not known that any examples of these beautiful eggs existed in any collection.

The eggs and nesting habits of the Mountain Accentor were previously unknown and undescribed.

The young in first plumage of the Dusky Ouzel, the Dark Ouzel, and the Black-throated Ouzel, were all un-described.

The geographical range of the Siberian Pipit and the Siberian Herring-Gull, two birds which Harvie-Brown and I may claim to have almost rediscovered, was extended, and, by the help of the skins in the museum at St. Petersburg, completed.

The eggs of the Red-breasted Goose were only previously known from a drawing in Middendorf's Travels in Siberia.

The additional eggs of Bewick's Swan and the Little Stint which I obtained were very valuable, as the eggs which Harvie-Brown and I obtained in the valley of the Petchora were the only eggs of these birds then known in collections.

The examples of the Rock Ptarmigan which I obtained were the first which had been found on the mainland of the palæarctic region.

The example of the male in breeding plumage of Middendorf's Reed-Bunting which I obtained, and which was figured in the Ibis for 1879, plate 1, was new.

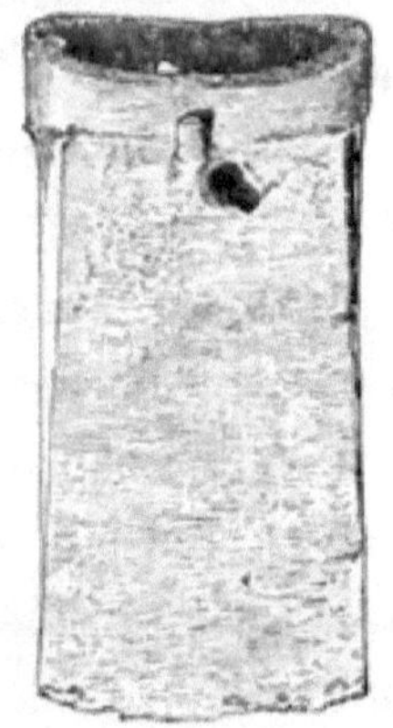

BRONZE CELT FROM ANCIENT GRAVE NEAR KRASNOYARSK.

Besides these results, there are one or two generalizations which I was only able to make when my Siberian plunder had been carefully compared with collections from Europe and China. These investigations have also been much increased in value and importance by small collections, which M. Kibort (the Polish ornithologist whom I discovered in Kras-no-yarsk') has from time to time sent me.

The pioneer of Siberian ornithology was Pallas, whose 'Zoographia Rosso-Asiatica' was written in 1806, though.

in consequence of the Napoleonic wars it was not printed until 1809, only published in 1826 and scarcely known until the re-issue in 1831. Pallas was a very keen observer, and finding that many species of Siberian birds though closely allied to West European species were nevertheless distinguishable from them, he gave them names of his own. Modern writers on European ornithology have treated Pallas's names with scant courtesy. In some cases, where they have had an opportunity of comparing examples from Siberia with West-European skins, they have admitted the validity of his species; but in other cases, where they have also had access to East-European skins, the existance of intermediate forms has been alleged as a reason for denying the validity of the species, and the Siberian forms have been passed by with a contemptuous sneer, as beneath the notice of science. In the majority of cases, however, the writers have never seen a Siberian skin, and Pallas's name is consigned to the limbo of synonyms without note or comment. With these writers a species is either a species or it is nothing. They attempt to draw a hard and fast line where nature has drawn none. They profess to believe in the theory of the development of species, but they never dream of looking at birds from an evolutionary point of view. In their hearts they still cling to the old-fashioned notion of special creations. Their dogmatic criticism of Pallas's species, " we consider this a good species," or " we cannot admit the validity of this species," reads like a satire upon their own ignorance.

The fact is that most Siberian birds which are common to

Europe do present marked differences in colour, not only amongst resident birds, but also amongst migrants. If we consider the European forms as the typical ones, then the Siberian birds are Arctic forms. It may be interesting to enumerate some of these.

The Siberian form of the Three-toed Woodpecker, which Bonaparte (adopting a manuscript name given to it by Brandt) called *Picus crissoleucus*, has the under parts almost snowy-white, whereas the European form has the feathers of most of the under parts conspicuously striated with black. Some of the Siberian examples, probably young birds, show some of these striations.

The Siberian form of the Lesser Spotted Woodpecker, to which Pallas gave the name of *Picus pipra*, has the whole of

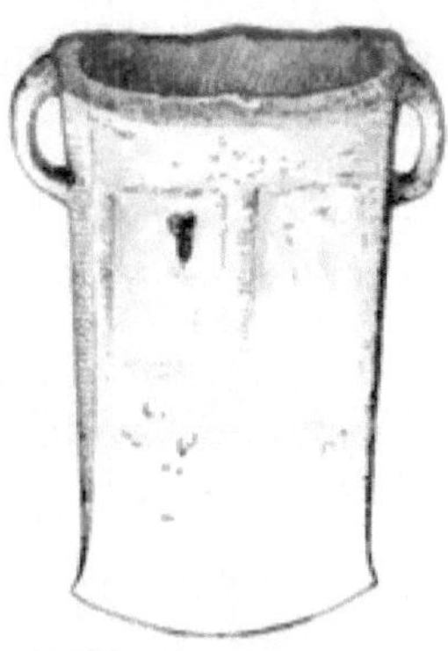

BRONZE CELT FROM ANCIENT GRAVE NEAR KRASNOYARSK.

the under parts unspotted silky-white, with the exception of the under-tail coverts, which are very slightly streaked with black. The transverse bars on the back and rump are also nearly obsolete. It is larger than the South European form, the wing measuring 3·75 inches, and the tail 2·5. I have shot it at Archangel and in the valley of the Petchora, and in addition to skins from the valley of the Yen-e-say'. I have examples from Lake By-kal, the Amoor, and the islands of Sakhalin and Yezzo, north Japan. Specimens from Norway and Sweden are, however, somewhat intermediate, being as large as the Siberian form; but in the colour and markings of the back and under parts they are only very slightly paler than the South European form.

The Siberian forms of the Lapp-Tit, to which Cabanis gave the name of *Parus obtectus*, are much less rusty on the flanks than Norwegian examples. It is, however, easy to find a complete series from the Scandinavian bird, through Archangel and Petchora skins, to the extreme Siberian form.

The Siberian form of the Marsh-Tit, to which Bonaparte gave the name of *Parus camtchatkensis*, is an extreme term of a somewhat complicated series. English skins are the brownest, and have the black on the head extending only to the nape, and are scarcely distinguishable from examples of *Parus palustris*, from the South of France, Italy, and Asia Minor. This form turns up again in China. Examples of *P. borealis* from Norway differ in having the back grey instead of brown. Examples from Archangel are greyer still, and have the black on the head extending beyond the nape. Both these characteristics are more pronounced in skins from the Petchora, the Obb, and the Lower Yen-e-say', and still more so in those from the Upper Yen-e-say', the true *P. camtchatkensis*; whilst in Japan a fourth form, to which I have given the name of *P. japonicus*, is found, which combines a greyish-brown back with the great development of the black on the head.

The Siberian form of the Nuthatch, to which Lichtenstein gave the name of *Sitta uralensis*, is another case in point.

Examples from the Yen-e-say', and also from the north island of Japan, have the under parts almost pure white.

Other examples of slight variations between our birds and those of Siberia might be given, in some cases where intermediate forms are known to exist, and in others where they have not yet been discovered, or may possibly not exist. The subject of the interbreeding of nearly-allied birds in certain localities where their geographical ranges meet or overlap, and the almost identical subject of the existence of intermediate forms in the intervening district between the respective geographical ranges of nearly-allied birds, is one which has not yet received the attention which it deserves from ornithologists. The older brethren of the fraternity have always pooh-pooh'd any attempt to explain some of these complicated facts of nature by the theory of interbreeding, and have looked upon the suggestion that hybridisation was anything but an abnormal circumstance, as one of the lamest modes of getting out of an ornithological difficulty. The fact is that these pre-Darwinian scientific men have adopted the theory of evolution only theoretically, and have not yet been able to overcome the effects of early education sufficiently to adopt it practically, and to look upon the facts of nature from the new standpoint.

The explanation of these Siberian forms of our well-known species of birds, whether they be or be not connected together by intermediate links, must be sought for in Japan and North China. When we get back into a temperate climate again, we find the familiar forms of temperate Europe reappearing, or nearly so. For example, the Great-

Spotted Woodpecker of South Europe is almost identical
with that of Japan, whilst that of Siberia is white instead of
pale-grey on the under parts.   The Short-eared Owl of
South Europe is also identical with that of North China,
whilst the adult male of the Siberian form is, what ornithologists unmeaningly call the "pale phase" of the species.
The same remarks apply to the European, Siberian, and
Japanese forms of the Ural Owl. The Nuthatch of China
only differs from ours in being a trifle smaller. The more
one examines this subject the more evidence one finds of the
existence of forms, the extremes of which are very distinct,
but which must be considered as only subspecifically sepa
rated, inasmuch as a series of intermediate forms from intervening localities connects them with each other. Many
birds have, in addition to the typical or temperate form, an
Arctic form, in which the white is highly developed, a desert
form, in which the yellowish-browns are predominant, and a
tropical form—in localities where the rainfall is excessive—
which appears to be highly favourable to the production of
reddish-browns. It is very difficult to determine the precise
cause of these variations.   At first I was inclined to ascribe
it to the direct chemical influence of climate upon the
colouring-matter of the feathers, but a larger acquaintance
with these Siberian forms, which are much more numerous
than I supposed, the fact being that it is the rule and not
the exception for Siberian forms to differ from European
ones, has convinced me that the explanation must be sought
in the theory of protective colouring gradually assumed by
the survival of the fittest.

Here again the confirmed habit of the older ornithologists of either treating these little differences as specific, or of ignoring them altogether, is much to be deplored. I venture to suggest, as a punishment for their delinquencies, that they should be exiled to Siberia for a summer to learn to harmonise their system of nomenclature with the facts of nature. Dr. Dry-as-dust and Professor Red-tape have committed themselves in the pre-Darwinian dark ages of ornithology to a binomial system of nomenclature, which does not easily lend itself to the discrimination of subspecific forms; and although the American ornithologists have emancipated themselves from the fetters of an antiquated system, English ornithological nomenclators still groan under the bonds of this effete binomial system, and vex the souls of field naturalists with capricious change of names in their futile efforts to make their nomenclature subservient to a Utopian set of rules called the Stricklandian code—laws which are far more honoured in the breach than in the observance, and have done great harm to the true study of birds. It is devoutly to be wished that the rising generation of ornithologists would have the courage to throw the binomial system to the dogs, and trample the Stricklandian code under foot, and once for all study nature, and make their nomenclature harmonise with the facts of nature.

One of the great charms of the study of ornithology is the amount of work which still remains to be done. The pleasure which comes from labour of any kind is pretty much in proportion to its results, and there are very few, if any, countries in which ornithological field work is not

amply repaid by interesting discoveries. I trust that when
the reader lays down my book he will agree with me that,
in spite of its reputation for dreariness, there are few countries in the world more prolific of objects of interest than
Siberia in Asia.

BRONZE EIKON.

ARCTIC OCEAN
Kara Sea
RUSSIAN EMPIRE
CHINESE EMPIRE
TURKESTAN
Map to illustrate
SIBERIA IN ASIA

INDEX.

LONDON: PRINTED BY WILLIAM CLOWES AND SONS, LIMITED, STAMFORD STREET
AND CHARING CROSS.

50 Albemarle Street, London,
January 1882.

MR. MURRAY'S
LIST OF WORKS
IN
GENERAL LITERATURE,

CONTAINING

The Speaker's Commentary on the Bible.

History, Ancient & Modern.

Biography, Memoirs, &c.

Geography, Voyages, and Travels.

Handbooks for Travellers.

Theology, Religion, &c.

Science, Natural History, Geology, &c.

Art, Architecture, and Antiquities.

Educational Works.

Poetry, the Drama, &c.

Naval and Military Works.

Philosophy, Law, and Politics.

Rural & Domestic Economy.

Field Sports, &c.

Miscellaneous Literature and Philology.

Home and Colonial Library.

Dr. Wm. Smith's Atlas of Ancient Geography.

THE SPEAKER'S COMMENTARY.

Medium 8vo.

THE HOLY BIBLE, according to the Authorised Version, A.D. 1611, with an EXPLANATORY and CRITICAL COMMENTARY, and a REVISION of the TRANSLATION. By BISHOPS and CLERGY of the ANGLICAN CHURCH. Edited by F. C. COOK, M.A., Canon of Exeter, Preacher at Lincoln's Inn, and Chaplain in Ordinary to the Queen.

THE OLD TESTAMENT. 6 VOLS. 8VO, 135s.
Vol. I.—30s.

GENESIS—Bishop of Winchester.
EXODUS—Canon Cook and Rev. Samuel Clark.

LEVITICUS—Rev. Samuel Clark.
NUMBERS—Canon Espin and Rev. J. F. Thrupp.

DEUTERONOMY—Canon Espin.

Vols. II. and III.—36s.

JOSHUA—Canon Espin.
JUDGES, RUTH, SAMUEL—Bishop of Bath and Wells.

KINGS, CHRONICLES, EZRA, NEHEMIAH, ESTHER—Canon Rawlinson.

Vol. IV.—24s.

JOB—Canon Cook.
PSALMS—Dean Johnson, Canon Cook, and Canon Elliott.

PROVERBS—Dean of Wells.
ECCLESIASTES—Rev. W. T. Bullock.
SONG OF SOLOMON—Rev. T. Kingsbury.

Vol. V.—20s.

ISAIAH—Rev. Dr. Kay.

JEREMIAH AND LAMENTATIONS—Dean of Canterbury.

Vol. VI.—25s.

EZEKIEL—Rev. Dr. Currey.
DANIEL—Archdeacon Rose and Rev. J. Fuller.
HOSEA and JONAH—Rev. E. Huxtable.
AMOS, NAHUM, and ZEPHANIAH—Rev. R. Gandell.

JOEL and OBADIAH—Rev. F. Meyrick.
MICAH and HABAKKUK—Rev. Samuel Clark and Canon Cook.
HAGGAI, ZECHARIAH, and MALACHI—Canon Drake.

THE NEW TESTAMENT. 4 VOLS. 8VO, 94s.
Vol. I.—18s.

GENERAL INTRODUCTION—The Archbishop of York.
ST. MATTHEW & ST. MARK—Dean Mansel and Canon Cook.

ST. LUKE—Bishop of St. David's.

Vol. II.—20s.

ST. JOHN—Canon Westcott.

THE ACTS—Bishop of Chester.

Vol. III.—28s.

ROMANS—Canon Gifford.
CORINTHIANS—Canon Evans and Rev. J. Waite.
GALATIANS—Dean of Chester.
PHILIPPIANS, EPHESIANS, COLOSSIANS,

THESSALONIANS, and PHILEMON—Rev. F. Meyrick, Dean of Raphoe, and Bishop of Derry.
PASTORAL EPISTLES—Bishop of London and Prof. Wace.

Vol. IV.—28s.

HEBREWS—Rev. Dr. Kay.
ST. JAMES—Dean of Rochester.
ST. JOHN—Bishop of Derry.

ST. PETER and ST. JUDE—Canon Cook and Prof. Lumby.
REVELATION of ST. JOHN—Archdeacon Lee.

With a Preface on the Completion of the Work. By the EDITOR.

THE STUDENT'S EDITION OF THE SPEAKER'S COMMENTARY on the Old Testament, abridged and edited. By J. M. FULLER, M.A., Vicar of Bexley, late Fellow of St. John's College, Cambridge. 4 vols. Crown 8vo, 7s. 6d. each.

Vol. I. GENESIS to DEUTERONOMY.
Vol. II. JOSHUA to ESTHER.

Vol. III. JOB to SONG OF SOLOMON.
Vol. IV. ISAIAH to MALACHI.

HISTORY ANCIENT AND MODERN.

Ancient History.

History of the Ancient World; from the earliest Records to the fall of the Western Empire, A.D. 476. By PHILIP SMITH. Plans. 3 vols. 8vo, 31s. 6d.

Student's Ancient History of the East. From the Earliest Times to the Conquest of Alexander the Great; including Egypt, Assyria, Babylonia, Media, Persia, Asia Minor, and Phœnicia. By PHILIP SMITH. Woodcuts. Post 8vo, 7s. 6d.

History of Egypt under the Pharaohs. Derived from the Monuments. With Memoir on the Exodus of the Israelites. By Dr. BRUGSCH. Maps. 2 vols. 8vo, 32s.

Nile Gleanings: the Ethnology, History, and Art of Ancient Egypt, as Revealed by Paintings and Bas-Reliefs. With Descriptions of Nubia and its Great Rock Temples to the Second Cataract. By VILLIERS STUART. With 58 Coloured and Outline Plates. Royal 8vo, 31s. 6d.

Manners and Customs of the Ancient Egyptians: their Religion, Arts, Laws, Manufactures, etc. By Sir J. GARDNER WILKINSON. Revised by SAMUEL BIRCH, LL.D. Illustrations. 3 vols. 8vo, £4 : 4s.

Popular Account of the Ancient Egyptians. By Sir J. G. WILKINSON. Illustrations. 2 vols. post 8vo, 12s.

The Five Great Monarchies of the ANCIENT EASTERN WORLD; or the History, Geography, and Antiquities of Chaldea, Assyria, Babylonia, Media, and Persia. By Canon RAWLINSON. Illustrations. 3 vols. 8vo, 42s.

Herodotus : A new English version. With notes and essays, historical and ethnographical. By Canon RAWLINSON, Sir HENRY RAWLINSON, and Sir J. G. WILKINSON. Illustrations. 4 vols. 8vo, 48s.

History of Greece, from the Earliest Period to the close of the Generation contemporary with Alexander the Great. By GEORGE GROTE. Library Edition. Portrait and Maps. 10 vols. 8vo, 120s.; or, Cabinet ed., Portrait and Plans, 12 vols. post 8vo, 6s. each.

Student's History of Greece, from the Earliest Times to the Roman Conquest, with the History of Literature and Art. By Dr. WM. SMITH. Maps and Woodcuts. Post 8vo, 7s. 6d.

Student's History of Rome, from the Earliest Times to the Establishment of the Empire. With the History of Literature and Art. By Dean LIDDELL. Woodcuts. Post 8vo, 7s. 6d.

History of the Decline and Fall of the ROMAN EMPIRE, By EDWARD GIBBON, with Notes by MILMAN and GUIZOT. Edited by Dr. WM. SMITH. Maps. 8 vols. 8vo, £3.

Student's Gibbon ; an Epitome of the History of the Decline and Fall of the Roman Empire. By EDWARD GIBBON. Woodcuts. Post 8vo, 7s. 6d.

Dictionary of Greek and Roman ANTIQUITIES. Edited by Dr. WM. SMITH. Illustrations. Royal 8vo, 28s.

Dictionary of Greek and Roman BIOGRAPHY and MYTHOLOGY. Edited by Dr. WM. SMITH. Illustrations. 3 vols. royal 8vo, 84s.

Classical Dictionary of Biography, MYTHOLOGY, and GEOGRAPHY, for the Higher Forms. By Dr. WM. SMITH. Illustrations. 8vo, 18s.

Smaller Classical Dictionary of Mythology, Biography, and Geography. Woodcuts. Crown 8vo, 7s. 6d.

Smaller Dictionary of Greek and Roman Antiquities. Abridged from the large work. By Dr. WM. SMITH. Woodcuts. Crown 8vo, 7s. 6d.

Scripture and Church History.

Student's Old Testament History: from the Creation to the Return of the Jews from Captivity. By PHILIP SMITH. Woodcuts. Post 8vo, 7s. 6d.

Student's New Testament History. With an Introduction connecting the History of the Old and New Testaments. By PHILIP SMITH. Woodcuts. Post 8vo, 7s. 6d.

History of the Jews, from the Earliest Period to Modern Times. By Dean MILMAN. 3 vols. Post 8vo, 18s.

History of the Jewish Church. By Dean STANLEY. 1st and 2d SERIES, Abraham to the Captivity. Maps. 2 vols. 8vo, 24s. 3d SERIES, Captivity to the Christian Era. Maps. 8vo, 14s.

History of Christianity, from the Birth of Christ to the Extinction of Paganism in the Roman Empire. By Dean MILMAN. 3 vols. post 8vo, 18s.

History of the Christian Church from the Apostolic Age to the Reformation, A.D. 64-1517. By Canon ROBERTSON. 8 vols. post 8vo, 6s. each.

History of Latin Christianity and of the Popes to Nicholas V. By Dean MILMAN. 9 vols. post 8vo, 54s.

Student's Manual of Ecclesi-astical History. PART I.—From the Time of the Apostles to the Full Establishment of the Holy Roman Empire and the Papal Power. PART II.—The Middle Ages and the Reformation. By PHILIP SMITH. Woodcuts. 2 vols. post 8vo, 7s. 6d. each.

History of the Gallican Church, from the Concordat at Bologna, 1516, to the Revolution. By Rev. W. H. JERVIS. Portraits. 2 vols. 8vo, 28s.

History of the Eastern Church. By Dean STANLEY. Plans. 8vo, 12s.

Student's Manual of English Church History. FIRST PERIOD—From the Planting of the Church in Britain to the Accession of Henry VIII. SECOND PERIOD—From the Time of Henry VIII. to the Silencing of Convocation in the 18th Century. By Canon PERRY. 2 vols. post 8vo, 7s. 6d. each.

History of the Church of SCOTLAND. By Dean STANLEY. 8vo, 7s. 6d.

Dictionary of Christian Anti-quities, comprising the History, Institutions, and Antiquities of the Christian Church. Edited by Dr. WM. SMITH and Archdeacon CHEETHAM. Illustrations. 2 vols. med. 8vo, £3 : 13 : 6.

Dictionary of Christian Bio-graphy, Literature, Sects, and Doctrines, from the Time of the Apostles to the Age of Charlemagne. Edited by Dr. WM. SMITH and Rev. H. WACE. Vols. I. II. and III. Medium 8vo, 31s. 6d. each.

The Jesuits, their Constitution and Teaching. An Historical Sketch. By W. C. CARTWRIGHT. 8vo, 9s.

Notes on some Passages in the Liturgical History of the Reformed English Church. By Lord SELBORNE. 8vo, 6s.

Mediæval and Modern History.

An Account of the Modern Egyptians. By E. W. LANE. Illustrations. 2 vols. crown 8vo, 12s.

History of Europe during the MIDDLE AGES. By HENRY HALLAM. Library Edition. 3 vols. 8vo, 30s.; Cabinet Edition. 3 vols. post 8vo, 12s. Student's Edition. Post 8vo, 7s. 6d.

Student's History of France. From the Earliest Times to the Establishment of the Second Empire, 1852. With Notes on the Institutions of the Country. By W. H. JERVIS. Woodcuts. Post 8vo, 7s. 6d.

Student's Hume ; a History of ENGLAND, from the Earliest Times to the Revolution of 1688. Revised and continued to the Treaty of Berlin, 1878, by J. S. BREWER. With 7 Coloured Maps and 70 Woodcuts. Post 8vo, 7s. 6d.

History of England, from the Accession of Henry VII. to the Death of George II. By HENRY HALLAM. 3 vols. 8vo, 30s.; or Cabinet Edition, 3 vols. post 8vo, 12s. Student's Edition. Post 8vo, 7s. 6d.

Literary History of Europe during the 15th, 16th, and 17th Centuries. Library Edn., 3 vols. 8vo, 36s. Cabinet Edn., 4 vols. post 8vo, 16s.

History of Charles the Bold, Duke of Burgundy. By J. FOSTER KIRK. Portraits. 3 vols. 8vo, 45s.

Historical Memorials of Canter-bury. 1. Landing of Augustine—2. Murder of Becket—3. Edward the Black Prince—4. Becket's Shrine. By Dean STANLEY. Woodcuts. Post 8vo, 7s. 6d.

History of the United Nether-LANDS, from the Death of William the Silent to the Twelve Years' Truce, 1609. By J. L. MOTLEY. Portraits. 4 vols. post 8vo, 6s. each.

Life and Death of John of BARNEVELD, Advocate of Holland. With a view of the primary causes and movements of the Thirty Years' War. By J. L. MOTLEY. Illustrations. 2 vols. post 8vo, 12s.

Student's History of Modern Europe, from the End of the Middle Ages to the Treaty of Berlin, 1878.

[In preparation.

Sir John Northcotes's Note-
book during the Long Parliament. From
the Original MS. Edited by A. H. A.
HAMILTON. Crown 8vo, 9s.

History of India—The Hindoo
and Mohammedan Periods. By the Hon.
MOUNTSTUART ELPHINSTONE. Edited
by Professor COWELL. Map. 8vo, 18s.

Historic Peerage of England,
Exhibiting the Origin, Descent, and
Present State of every Title of Peerage
which has existed since the Conquest.
By Sir HARRIS NICOLAS. 8vo, 30s.

Two Sieges of Vienna by the
TURKS. From the German. By Lord
ELLESMERE. Post 8vo, 2s.

British India from its origin to
1783. By Earl STANHOPE. Post 8vo,
3s. 6d.

History of England, from the
Reign of Queen Anne (1701) to the Peace
of Versailles (1783). By Earl STAN-
HOPE. 9 vols. post 8vo, 5s. each.

"The Forty-Five;" or, the Rebellion in Scotland in 1745. By Earl
STANHOPE. Post 8vo, 3s. 6d.

Historical Essays. By Earl
STANHOPE. Post 8vo, 3s. 6d.

French Retreat from Moscow,
and other Essays. By Earl STAN-
HOPE. Post 8vo, 7s. 6d.

Scenes from the War of Liberation in Germany. From the German.
By Sir A. GORDON. Post 8vo, 3s. 6d.

The Siege of Gibraltar,
1772-1780, with a Description of that
Garrison from the earliest periods. By
JOHN DRINKWATER. Post 8vo, 2s.

Annals of the Wars of the
18th and 19th Centuries, 1700-1815. By
Sir EDWARD CUST. Maps. 9 vols.
16mo, 5s. each.

State of Society in France
BEFORE THE REVOLUTION, 1789. By
ALEXIS DE TOCQUEVILLE. Translated
by HENRY REEVE. 8vo, 14s.

History of Europe during the
FRENCH REVOLUTION, 1789-95. From
the Secret Archives of Germany. By
Professor VON SYBEL. 4 vols. 8vo, 48s.

English Battles and Sieges of
the Peninsular War. By Sir W. NAPIER.
Portrait. Post 8vo, 9s.

The Story of the Battle of
WATERLOO. By Rev. G. R. GLEIG.
Post 8vo, 3s. 6d.

Wellington's Civil and Political
Despatches, 1819-1831. Edited by his
SON. 8 vols. 8vo, 20s. each.

Wellington's Supplementary
Despatches and Correspondence. Edited
by his SON. 15 vols. 8vo, 20s. each. An
index. 8vo, 20s.

Campaigns at Washington and
NEW ORLEANS. By Rev. G. R. GLEIG.
Post 8vo, 2s.

Sir Robert Sale's Brigade in
AFFGHANISTAN. By Rev. G. R. GLEIG.
Post 8vo, 2s.

French in Algiers ; the Soldier
of the Foreign Legion—and Prisoners
of Abd-el-Kadir. Translated by Lady
DUFF GORDON. Post 8vo, 2s.

History of the Fall of the
Jesuits in the Nineteenth Century. From
the French. Post 8vo, 2s.

English in Spain ; or, the
Story of the Civil War between Chris-
tinos and Carlists in 1834, 1840. By
Major F. DUNCAN, R.A. With plates.
8vo, 16s.

Personal Narrative of Events
in China during Lord Elgin's Second
Embassy. By H. B. LOCH. Illustrations. Post 8vo, 9s.

History of the Royal Artillery.
Compiled from the original Records.
By Major F. DUNCAN, R.A. Portraits.
2 vols. 8vo, 18s.

The Huguenots in England
& Ireland, their Settlements, Churches,
and Industries. By SAMUEL SMILES.
Crown 8vo, 7s. 6d.

Historical Memorials of Westminster Abbey, from its Foundation to
the Present Time. By Dean STANLEY.
Illustrations. 8vo, 15s.

Notices of the Historic Persons
buried in the Chapel of St. Peter, in the
Tower of London, with an Account of
the Discovery of the Remains of Queen
Anne Boleyn. By DOYNE C. BELL.
Illustrations. Crown 8vo, 14s.

Handbook to St. Paul's Cathedral. By Dean MILMAN. Illustrations.
Crown 8vo, 10s. 6d.

Annals of Winchcombe and
Sudeley. By EMMA DENT. With Plates.
4to, 42s.

English Studies. By J. S.
BREWER. CONTENTS: New Sources
of English History. Green's Short
History of the English People. The
Royal Supremacy. Hatfield House.
The Stuarts. Shakspeare. How to
Study English History. Ancient Lon-
don. Erasmus. 8vo, 14s.

BIOGRAPHY AND MEMOIRS.

Ecclesiastical and Missionary.

Dictionary of Christian Bio-graphy, Literature, Sects, and Doctrines, from the time of the Apostles to the Age of Charlemagne. Edited by Dr. WM. SMITH and Professor WACE. Vols. I. II. and III. Med. 8vo, 31s. 6d. each.

Life of St. Hugh of Avalon, Bishop of Lincoln. By Canon PERRY. Portrait. Post 8vo, 10s. 6d.

Life and Times of St. John Chrysostom. A Sketch of the Church and the Empire in the Fourth Century. By Rev. W. R. W. STEPHENS, M.A. With Portrait. 8vo, 12s.

Personal Life of Dr. Living-stone. From his unpublished Journals and Correspondence. By W. G. BLAIKIE, D.D. With Portrait and Map. 8vo, 13s.

Memoir of William Ellis, the Missionary. By his SON. Portrait. 8vo, 10s. 6d.

Memoir of Bishop Milman, Metropolitan of India. With a Selection from his Letters. By his SISTER. Map. 8vo, 12s.

Life of Bishop SUMNER, during an Episcopate of Forty Years. By Rev. G. H. SUMNER. Portrait. 8vo, 14s.

Life of Samuel Wilberforce, Bishop of Oxford and Winchester. Vol. I. By Canon ASHWELL. Vol. II. Edited by R. G. WILBERFORCE. Portraits. 8vo, 15s. each.

Life of John Wilson, D.D. (of Bombay); Fifty Years a Philanthropist and Scholar in the East. By GEORGE SMITH. Illustrations. Post 8vo, 9s.

Political and Social.

Memoir of the Public Life of Right Hon. John Charles Herries during the reigns of George III., George IV., William IV., and Victoria. By his Son, ED. HERRIES, C.B. 2 vols. 8vo, 24s.

Monographs : Personal and So-cial. By Lord HOUGHTON. Portraits. Crown 8vo, 10s. 6d.

Self-Help. With Illustrations of Conduct and Perseverance. By Dr. SMILES. Post 8vo, 6s.; or in French, 5s.

Life and Death of John of BARNEVELD, Advocate of Holland. With a View of the Primary Causes and Movements of "The Thirty Years' War." By J. L. MOTLEY. Illustrations. 2 vols. post 8vo, 12s.

Rheinsberg; Memorials of Frederick the Great and Prince Henry of Prussia. By ANDREW HAMILTON. 2 vols. crown 8vo, 21s.

Life and Correspondence of Dr. Arnold of Rugby. By Dean STANLEY. With the Author's latest Corrections, and an unpublished Poem by KEBLE. Portrait. 2 vols. cr. 8vo. 12s.

Memoir of Edward, Catherine, and Mary Stanley. By Dean STANLEY. Post 8vo, 9s.

Memoirs of Sir Fowell Buxton, with Extracts from his Correspondence. By CHARLES BUXTON. Portrait. 8vo, 16s.; or post 8vo, 5s.

King William IV.'s Corre-spondence with the late Earl GREY, 1830-1832. Edited by his SON. 2 vols. 8vo, 30s.

Life of Theodore Hook. By J. G. LOCKHART. Fcap. 8vo, 1s.

Memoir of Hon. Julian Fane. By Lord LYTTON. Portrait. Post 8vo, 5s.

Selection from the Familiar Correspondence of Sir CHARLES BELL. Portrait. Post 8vo, 12s.

Madame de Staël, a Study of her Life and Times. By Dr. A. STEVENS. With Portraits. 2 vols. Crown 8vo, 24s.

Adventures on the Road to Paris, 1813-14. From the Autobiography of HENRY STEFFENS. Post 8vo, 2s.

Sketches of Eminent Statesmen and Writers. Reprinted from the *Quarterly Review*. By A. HAYWARD, Q.C. 2 vols. 8vo, 28s. CONTENTS :—Thiers, Bismarck, Cavour, Metternich, Montalembert, Melbourne, Wellesley, Byron and Tennyson, Venice, St. Simon, Sévigné, Du Deffand, Holland House, Strawberry Hill.

Life of William Pitt. By Earl STANHOPE. Portraits. 3 vols. 8vo, 36s.

Brief Memoir of the Princess CHARLOTTE OF WALES. By Lady ROSE WEIGALL. Portrait. Crown 8vo, 8s. 6d.

Life of William Wilberforce. By his SON. Portrait. Post 8vo, 6s.

Memoirs ; By Sir Robert Peel. Edited by Earl STANHOPE and Lord CARDWELL. 2 vols. post 8vo, 15s.

Mrs. Grote ; a Sketch. By Lady EASTLAKE. Crown 8vo, 6s.

Literary and Artistic.

Dictionary of Greek & Roman BIOGRAPHY and MYTHOLOGY. Edited by Dr. WM. SMITH. 3 vols. 8vo, 84s.

Personal Life of George Grote, the Historian of Greece. Compiled from Family Documents. By Mrs. GROTE. Portrait. 8vo, 12s.

Life and Works of Albert Dürer. By MORIZ THAUSING. Edited by F. A. EATON, Sec. Royal Academy. Illustrations. 2 vols. 8vo, 42s.

Michel Angelo, Sculptor, Painter, and Architect : including Documents from the Buonarroti Archives. By C. HEATH WILSON. Plates. 8vo, 15s.

Titian : his Life and Times, with some Account of his Family from Unpublished Documents. By J. A. CROWE and G. B. CAVALCASELLE. Illustrations. 2 vols. 8vo, 21s.

The Early Life of Jonathan SWIFT. By JOHN FORSTER. 1667-1711. Portrait. 8vo, 15s.

Life of Dr. Samuel Johnson. By JAMES BOSWELL. Edited by J. W. CROKER. With Notes by Lord Stowell, Sir Walter Scott, Sir James Mackintosh, Disraeli, Markland, Lockhart, &c. Medium 8vo, 12s.

Johnson's Lives of the ENGLISH POETS. Edited by CUNNINGHAM. 3 vols. 8vo, 22s. 6d.

Life of Jonathan Swift. By HENRY CRAIK, B.A. 8vo.

Life and Letters of Lord Byron With Notices of his Life. By THOMAS MOORE. Portraits. Royal 8vo, 7s. 6d. ; or 6 vols. fcap. 8vo, 18s.

Life of Lord Byron, with an Essay on his Place in Literature. By CARL ELZE. Portrait. 8vo, 16s.

Lives of the British Poets. By THOMAS CAMPBELL. Post 8vo, 3s. 6d.

Memoir of Sir Charles Eastlake. By Lady EASTLAKE. Prefixed to his Contributions to the Literature of the Fine Arts. 2 vols. 8vo, 24s.

Popular Biographies—BUNYAN, CROMWELL, CLIVE, CONDE, DRAKE, MUNRO. See *Home and Colonial Library*, p. 30.

Life and Times of Sir Joshua Reynolds. With Notes of his Contemporaries. By C. R. LESLIE and TOM TAYLOR. Portraits. 2 vols. 8vo, 42s.

Lives of the Early Italian Painters : illustrating the Progress of Painting in Italy from Cimabue to Bassano. By Mrs. JAMESON. Illustrations. Post 8vo, 12s.

Lives of the Early Flemish Painters, and Notices of their Works. By CROWE and CAVALCASELLE. Illustrations. Post 8vo, 7s. 6d. ; or large paper, 15s.

Life of Horace. By Dean MILMAN. 8vo, 9s.

Life and Works of Sir CHARLES BARRY, R.A. By Canon BARRY, D.D. Portrait and Illustrations. 8vo, 15s.

Naval and Military.

Lives of the Warriors of the 17th Century. By Sir EDWARD CUST, D.C.L. 6 vols. crown 8vo, 50s.

Character, Actions, and Writings of Wellington. By JULES MAUREL. Fcap. 8vo, 1s. 6d.

Letters and Journals of F.-M. Sir WM. GOMM, G.C.B., Commander-in-Chief in India, Constable of the Tower, and Colonel of the Coldstream Guards, 1799-1815. By F. C. CARR GOMM. Portraits. 8vo, 12s.

Napoleon at Fontainbleau and Elba. Being a Journal of Occurrences and Notes of Conversations, &c. By Sir NEIL CAMPBELL. Portrait. 8vo, 15s.

Letters and Journals of the EARL of ELGIN, Governor-General of India. Edited by THEODORE WALROND. 8vo, 14s.

Memoirs of the Duke of Saldanha, Soldier and Statesman. With Selections from his Correspondence. By CONDE DA CARNOTA. With Portrait and Maps. 2 vols. 8vo, 32s.

Memoir of Sir John Burgoyne. By Sir FRANCIS HEAD. Post 8vo, 1s.

Autobiography of Sir John Barrow, Bart. Portrait. 8vo, 16s.

Private Diary of General Sir ROBERT WILSON : during Missions and Employments with the European Armies in 1812-1814. Map. 2 vols. 8vo, 26s.

Reminiscences of Forty Years' SERVICE IN INDIA. By Lieut.-Gen. Sir GEORGE LAWRENCE. Including the Cabul Disasters, and Captivities in Affghanistan. Crown 8vo, 10s. 6d.

Life of Belisarius. By Lord MAHON. Post 8vo, 10s. 6d.

Legal and Scientific.

Lives of the Lord Chancellors and KEEPERS of the GREAT SEAL of ENGLAND, from the Earliest Times to the death of Lord Eldon, 1838. By Lord CAMPBELL. 10 vols. post 8vo, 6s. each.

Lives of the Chief Justices of ENGLAND, from the Norman Conquest till the death of Lord Tenterden. By Lord CAMPBELL. 4 vols. cr. 8vo, 6s. each.

Life and Letters of Lord Campbell, Lord Chief-Justice, and afterwards Lord Chancellor of England. Based on his Autobiography, Journals, and Correspondence. Edited by Hon. Mrs. HARDCASTLE. With Portrait. 2 vols. 8vo, 30s.

Life of Lord Chancellor Eldon. By HORACE TWISS. Portrait. 2 vols. post 8vo, 21s.

Biographia Juridica. A Bio-graphical Dictionary of the Judges of England, from the Conquest to 1870. By EDWARD FOSS. Medium 8vo, 21s.

Lives of the Engineers. From the Earliest Times to the Death of the Stephensons. With an Account of the Steam Engine and Railway Locomotive. By SAMUEL SMILES, LL.D. 9 Portraits and 340 Woodcuts, 5 vols. crown 8vo, 7s. 6d. each.

Life, Letters, and Journals of Sir CHARLES LYELL. Edited by his Sister-in-Law, Mrs. LYELL. Portraits. 2 vols. 8vo, 30s.

Industrial Biography ; or, Iron-Workers and Tool-Makers. By SAMUEL SMILES. Post 8vo, 6s.

Life of Thomas Edward (Shoe-maker, of Banff), Scotch Naturalist. By SAMUEL SMILES. Illustrated. Crown 8vo, 10s. 6d.

Life of Robert Dick (Baker, of Thurso), Geologist and Botanist. By S. SMILES. Illustrations. Cr. 8vo, 12s.

Memoir of Sir Roderick Mur-CHISON. With Notices of his Contemporaries, and a Sketch of Palæozoic Geology in Britain. By Professor GEIKIE. Portraits. 2 vols. 8vo, 30s.

Memoir and Correspondence of Caroline Herschel, Sister of Sir William and Aunt of Sir John Herschel. Portraits. Crown 8vo, 7s. 6d.

Personal Recollections, from Early Life to Old Age. By MARY SOMERVILLE. Portrait. Crown 8vo, 12s.

Life of Erasmus Darwin. By CHARLES DARWIN. With a Study of his Scientific Works by Dr. KRAUSE. Portrait, 8vo, 7s. 6d.

GEOGRAPHY, VOYAGES, AND TRAVELS.

The East Indies, China, &c.

India in 1880. By Sir RICHARD TEMPLE, Bart. 8vo, 16s.

Student's Manual of the Geo-graphy of India. By GEORGE SMITH, LL.D. Post 8vo. [*In the Press.*

Travels of Marco Polo. A new English version. Illustrated with copious Notes. By Col. YULE, C.B. Illustrations. 2 vols. 8vo, 63s.

A Visit to High Tartary, Yar-KAND, and KASHGAR, and over the Karakorum Pass. By ROBERT SHAW. Illustrations. 8vo, 16s.

New Japan ; The Land of the Rising Sun. Its Annals during the past twenty years ; recording the remarkable progress of the Japanese in western civilisation. By SAMUEL MOSSMAN. Map. 8vo, 15s.

A Cruise in the Eastern Seas, from the Corea to the River Amur. With an Account of Russian Siberia, Japan, and Formosa. By Capt. B. W. BAX. Illustrations. Crown 8vo, 12s.

British Burma and its People : Sketches of Native Manners, Customs, and Religion. By Capt. FORBES. Crown 8vo, 10s. 6d.

The River of Golden Sand. Narrative of a Journey through China to Burmah. By Capt. WM. GILL, R.E. With a Preface by Col. YULE. With Map. 2 vols. 8vo, 30s.

The Satsuma Rebellion. An Episode of Modern Japanese History. By AUGUSTUS H. MOUNSEY. Map. Crown 8vo, 10s. 6d.

Letters from Madras. By a LADY. Post 8vo, 2s.

Journey to the Source of the River Oxus, by the Indus, Kabul, and Badakhshan. By Capt. WOOD. With the Geography of the Valley of the Oxus, by Col. YULE. Map. 8vo, 12s.

Thirteen Years' Residence at the Court of China, in the Service of the Emperor. By Father RIPA. Post 8vo, 2s.

Popular Account of the Man-ners and Customs of India. By Rev. CHAS. ACLAND. Post 8vo, 2s.

Nineveh and its Remains.
With an Account of a Visit to the Chaldean Christians of Kurdistan, and the Yezedis or Devil Worshippers, &c. By Sir H. LAYARD. Illustrations. 2 vols. 8vo, 36s.; or post 8vo, 7s. 6d.

Nineveh and Babylon ; a Narrative of a Second Expedition to the Ruins of Assyria, with Travels in Armenia. By Sir H. LAYARD. Illustrations. 8vo, 21s. ; or post 8vo, 7s. 6d.

Unbeaten Tracks in Japan.
Travels of a Lady in the Interior, including Visits to the Aborigines of Yezo and the Shrines of Nikko and Isé. By ISABELLA L. BIRD. Map and Illustrations. 2 vols. crown 8vo, 24s.

Japan ; Its History, Traditions, and Religions, with the Narrative of a Visit in 1879. By Sir E. J. REED, K.C.B. With Map and Illustrations. 2 vols. 8vo, 28s.

Africa—Egypt.

A Popular Account of Dr. Livingstone's Travels and Adventures in South Africa, 1840-56. Illustrations. Post 8vo, 7s. 6d.

A Popular Account of Dr. Livingstone's Expedition to the Zambesi, Lakes Shirwa and Nyassa, 1858-64. Illustrations. Post 8vo, 7s. 6d.

Dr. Livingstone's Last Journals in CENTRAL AFRICA, 1865-73. With a Narrative of his last moments and sufferings. By Rev. HORACE WALLER. Illustrations. 2 vols. 8vo, 15s.

Livingstonia ; Journal of Adventures in Exploring Lake Nyassa, and Establishing a Settlement there. By E. D. YOUNG, R.N. Map. Post 8vo, 7s. 6d.

Explorations in Equatorial Africa, with Accounts of the Savage Tribes, the Gorilla, &c. By P. DU CHAILLU. Illustrations. 8vo, 21s.

Journey to Ashango Land, and Further Penetration into Equatorial Africa. By P. B. DU CHAILLU. Illustrations. 8vo, 21s.

Adventures and Discoveries among the Lakes and Mountains of Eastern Africa. By Captain ELTON and H. B. COTTERILL. With Map and Illustrations. 8vo, 21s.

Wanderings South of the Atlas Mountains, in the Great Sahara. By Canon TRISTRAM. Illustrations. Post 8vo, 15s.

Six Months in Ascension. An Unscientific Account of a Scientific Expedition. By Mrs. GILL. Map. Crown 8vo, 9s.

Five Years' Adventures in the far Interior of S. Africa with the Wild Beasts of the Forests. By R. GORDON CUMMING. Woodcuts. Post 8vo, 6s.

Recollections of Fighting and Hunting in South Africa, 1834-67. By Gen. Sir JOHN BISSET, C.B. Illustrations. Crown 8vo, 14s.

Nile Gleanings : The Ethnology, History, and Art of Ancient Egypt, as revealed by Paintings and Bas-Reliefs. By H. VILLIERS STUART. With 50 coloured Illustrations. Royal 8vo, 31s.6d.

The Country of the Moors. A Journey from Tripoli in Barbary to the Holy City of Kairwan. By EDWARD RAE. Illustrations. Crown 8vo, 12s.

A Residence in Sierra Leone, described from a Journal kept on the Spot. By a LADY. Post 8vo, 3s. 6d.

British Mission to Abyssinia. With Notices of the Countries traversed from Massowah, through the Soodan, and back to Magdala. By HORMUZD RASSAM. Illustrations. 2 vols. 30s.

Sport in Abyssinia. By Earl of MAYO. Illustrations. Crown 8vo, 12s.

Abyssinia during a Three Years' Residence. By MANSFIELD PARKYNS. Woodcuts. Post 8vo, 7s. 6d.

Adventures in the Libyan Desert. By B. ST. JOHN. Post 8vo, 2s.

Travels in Egypt, Nubia, Syria, and the Holy Land. By Captains IRBY and MANGLES. Post 8vo, 2s.

The Cradle of the Blue Nile. A Visit to the Court of King John of Ethiopia. By E. A. DE COSSON. Illustrations. 2 vols. post 8vo, 21s.

An Account of the Manners and Customs of the Modern Egyptians. By EDWARD WM. LANE. Woodcuts. 2 vols. post 8vo, 12s.

Madagascar Revisited ; Describing the Persecutions endured by the Christian Converts. By Rev. W. ELLIS. Illustrations, 8vo, 16s.

Mediterranean—Greece, Turkey in Europe.

Travels in Asia Minor : With Antiquarian Researches and Discoveries, and Illustrations of Biblical Literature and Archæology. By H. VAN LENNEP. Illustrations. 2 vols. post 8vo, 24s.

Ilios ; a History of the City and Country of the Trojans, including all Recent Discoveries on the Site of Troy and the Troad in 1871-3 and 1878-9. With an Autobiography. By Dr. SCHLIEMANN. Illustrations. Imperial 8vo, 50s.

Discoveries on the Sites of Ancient Mycenæ and Tiryns. By Dr. SCHLIEMANN. With a Preface by the Right Hon. W. E. GLADSTONE, M.P. Illustrations. Medium 8vo, 50s.

Cyprus ; its Ancient Cities, Tombs, and Temples. A Narrative of Researches and Excavations during Ten Years' Residence in that Island. By 'LOUIS P. DI CESNOLA. Illustrations. Medium 8vo, 50s.

Bulgaria before the War : a Seven Years' Experience of European Turkey and its Inhabitants. By H. C. BARKLEY. Post 8vo, 10s. 6d.

Between the Danube and the Black Sea : or, Five Years in Bulgaria. By H. C. BARKLEY. Post 8vo, 10s. 6d.

Researches in the Highlands of Turkey. With Notes on the Classical Superstitions of the Modern Greek. By Rev. H. F. TOZER. Illustrations. 2 vols. crown 8vo, 24s.

Lectures on the Geography of Greece. By Rev. H. F. TOZER. Map. Post 8vo, 9s.

Twenty Years' Residence among the Bulgarians, Greeks, Albanians, Turks, and Armenians. By a Consul's Wife. 2 vols. crown 8vo, 21s.

Reminiscences of Athens and the Morea, during Travels in Greece. By Lord CARNARVON. Crown 8vo, 7s. 6d.

Asia, Syria, Holy Land.

England and Russia in the East. A Series of Papers on the Political and Geographical Condition of Central Asia. By Sir H. RAWLINSON. Map. 8vo, 12s.

The Caucasus, Persia and Tur- key in Asia. A journey to Tabreez, Kurdistan, down the Tigris and Euphrates to Nineveh and Babylon, and across the Desert to Palmyra. By Baron THIELMANN. Illustrations. 2 vols. post 8vo, 18s.

Sketches of the Manners and Customs of Persia. By Sir JOHN MALCOLM. Post 8vo, 3s. 6d.

Sinai and Palestine ; in Con- nection with their History. By Dean STANLEY. Plans. 8vo, 14s.

The Bible in the Holy Land. Extracts from the above Work. Woodcuts. Fcap. 8vo, 2s. 6d.

Journal of Researches in the Holy Land in 1838 and 1852. With Historical Illustrations. By EDWARD ROBINSON, D.D. Maps. 3 vols. 8vo, 42s.

Damascus, Palmyra, Lebanon ; with Travels among the Giant Cities of Bashan and the Hauran. By Rev. J. L. PORTER. Woodcuts. Post 8vo, 7s. 6d.

The Jordan, the Nile, Red Sea, Lake of Gennesareth, etc. The Cruise of the Rob Roy in Palestine, Egypt, and the Waters of Damascus. By JOHN MACGREGOR. Illustrations. Post 8vo, 7s. 6d.

The Land of Moab. Travels and Discoveries on the East Side of the Dead Sea and the Jordan. By Canon TRISTRAM. Illustrations. Cr. 8vo, 15s.

The Bedouins of the Euphrates Valley. By Lady ANNE BLUNT. With some account of the Arab Horses. Illustrations. 2 vols. crown 8vo, 24s.

A Pilgrimage to Nejd, the Cradle of the Arab Race, and a Visit to the Court of the Arab Emir. By Lady ANNE BLUNT. With Illustrations. 2 vols. post 8vo, 24s.

Visits to the Monasteries of the Levant. By the Hon. ROBERT CURZON (Lord de la Zouche). With Illustrations. Post 8vo, 7s. 6d.

Australia, Polynesia, &c.

Discoveries in New Guinea. A Cruise in Polynesia, and Visits to Torres Straits, etc. By Capt. MORESBY. Illustrations. 8vo, 15s.

The Gardens of the Sun ; or a Naturalist's Journal on the Mountains and in the Forests and Swamps of Borneo and the Sulu Archipelago. By F. W. BURBIDGE. With Illustrations. Crown 8vo, 14s.

A Boy's Voyage Round the World. Edited by SAMUEL SMILES. Woodcuts. Small 8vo, 6s.

Hawaiian Archipelago ; Six Months among the Palm Groves, Coral Reefs, and Volcanoes of the SANDWICH ISLANDS. By ISABELLA BIRD. Illustrations. Crown 8vo, 7s. 6d.

Ride Through the Disturbed Districts of NEW ZEALAND to Lake Taupo at the time of the Rebellion ; with notes of the South Sea Islands. By Hon. H. MEADE. Illustrations. 8vo, 12s.

Typee and Omoo ; or the Marquesas and South Sea Islanders. By H. MELVILLE. 2 vols. post 8vo, 7s.

Notes and Sketches of New South Wales. By Mrs. MEREDITH. Post 8vo, 2s.

America, West Indies, Arctic Regions.

A Lady's Life in the Rocky Mountains. By ISABELLA BIRD. Illustrations. Post 8vo, 7s. 6d.

Mexico and the Rocky Moun- tains. By GEORGE F. RUXTON. Post 8vo, 3s. 6d.

Pioneering in South Brazil.
Three Years of Forest and Prairie Life in the Province of Paraña. By T. P. BIGG WITHER. Illustrations. 2 vols. crown 8vo, 24s.

The Naturalist on the River
AMAZON, with Adventures during Eleven Years of Travel. By H. W. BATES. Illustrations. Post 8vo, 7s. 6d.

Voyage up the River Amazon
and a visit to Para. By WILLIAM H. EDWARDS. Post 8vo, 2s.

Voyage of a Naturalist round the
World. By CHAS. DARWIN. Post 8vo, 9s.

The Patagonians; a Year's
Wandering over Untrodden Ground from the Straits of Magellan to the Rio Negro. By Capt. MUSTERS. Illustrations. Post 8vo, 7s. 6d.

Voyage of the "Fox" in the
ARCTIC SEAS, and the Discovery of the Fate of Sir John Franklin and his Companions. By Sir LEOPOLD M'CLINTOCK. Illustrations. Post 8vo, 7s. 6d.

Perils of the Polar Seas. True
Stories of Arctic Discovery and Adventure. By Mrs. CHISHOLM. Illustrations. Small 8vo, 6s.

Communistic Societies of the
UNITED STATES: their Religious Creeds, Social Practices, and Present Condition. By CHARLES NORDHOFF. Illustrations. 8vo, 15s.

Europe.

The White Sea Peninsula. A
Journey to the White Sea, and the Kola Peninsula. By EDWARD RAE. With Map, 12 Etchings, and 14 Woodcuts. Crown 8vo, 15s.

The Land of the Midnight Sun.
Summer and Winter Journeys through Sweden, Norway, Lapland, and Northern Finland. With descriptions of the Inner Life of the People, their Manners, Customs, Primitive Antiquities, etc. By PAUL B. DU CHAILLU. Map and 235 Illustrations. 2 vols. 8vo, 36s.

Etchings on the Mosel: a
Series of 20 Plates, with Descriptive Letterpress. By ERNEST GEORGE. Folio, 42s.

Etchings from the Loire and
South of France. In a Series of Twenty Plates, with Descriptive Text. By ERNEST GEORGE. Folio, 42s.

Field Paths and Green Lanes.
Being Country Walks, chiefly in Surrey and Sussex. By LOUIS J. JENNINGS. Illustrations. Post 8vo, 10s. 6d.

Rambles among the Hills; or,
Walks on the Peak of Derbyshire and in the South Downs. By L. J. JENNINGS. With Illustrations. Post 8vo, 12s.

Twenty Years in the Wild
West of Ireland; or, Life in Connaught. By Mrs. HOUSTOUN. Crown 8vo, 9s.

The Ascent of the Matterhorn.
By EDWARD WHYMPER. 100 Illustrations. Medium 8vo, 10s. 6d.

Siberia in Europe; a Natural-
ist's Voyage to the Valley of the Petchora in N.E. Russia. By HENRY SEEBOHM. With Map and Illustrations. Crown 8vo, 14s.

A Month in Norway. By J. G.
HOLLWAY. Fcap. 8vo, 2s.

Letters from the Shores of the
Baltic. By a LADY. Post 8vo, 2s.

Letters from High Latitudes:
An Account of a Yacht Voyage to Iceland, Jan Mayen, and Spitzbergen. By Lord DUFFERIN. Illustrations. Crown 8vo, 7s. 6d.

The Bible in Spain; or, the
Journeys, Adventures, and Imprisonments of an Englishman in the Peninsula. By GEORGE BORROW. Post 8vo, 5s.

The Gypsies of Spain; their
Manners, Customs, Religion, and Language. By GEO. BORROW. Post 8vo, 5s.

Gatherings from Spain. By
RICHARD FORD. Post 8vo, 3s. 6d.

Bubbles from the Brunnen of
NASSAU. By Sir FRANCIS HEAD. Woodcuts. Post 8vo, 7s. 6d.

General Geography.

A History of Ancient Geo-
graphy among the Greeks and Romans, from the Earliest Ages till the Fall of the Roman Empire. By E. H. BUNBURY. 2 vols. 8vo, 42s.

Art of Travel; or, Hints on
the Shifts and Contrivances available in Wild Countries. By FRANCIS GALTON. Woodcuts. Post 8vo, 7s. 6d.

Dictionary of Greek and Roman
Geography. Edited by Dr. WM. SMITH. 2 vols. royal 8vo, 56s.

Atlas of Ancient Geography,
Biblical and Classical, compiled under the superintendence of Dr. WM. SMITH and Mr. GEORGE GROVE. Folio, £6:6s.

Student's Manual of Ancient
Geography. By Canon BEVAN, M.A. Woodcuts. Post 8vo, 7s. 6d.

Student's Manual of Modern
Geography, Mathematical, Physical, and Descriptive. By Canon BEVAN, M.A. Woodcuts. Post 8vo, 7s. 6d.

A School Manual of Modern
Geography, Physical and Political. By JOHN RICHARDSON, M.A. Post 8vo, 5s.

A Smaller Manual of Modern
Geography, Physical and Political. Post 8vo, 2s. 6d.

Journal of the Royal Geogra-
phical Society. 8vo. From 1831 to the present time.

HANDBOOKS FOR TRAVELLERS.

Foreign.

Handbook — Travel Talk ;— English, French, German, and Italian. 16mo, 3s. 6d.

Handbook—Holland and Belgium. Maps and Plans. Post 8vo, 6s.

Handbook—North Germany; the Rhine, the Black Forest, the Hartz, Thüringerwald, Saxon Switzerland, Rügen, the Giant Mountains, Taunus, Odenwald, Elass, and Lothringen. Map and Plans. Post 8vo, 10s.

Handbook—Switzerland ; The Alps of Savoy and Piedmont. Maps and Plans. In Two Parts. Post 8vo, 10s.

Handbook—South Germany; Tyrol, Bavaria, Austria, Salzburg, Styria, Hungary, and the Danube from Ulm to the Black Sea. Maps and Plans. Post 8vo, 10s.

Handbook—France. Part I. Normandy, Brittany, The French Alps, the Loire, Seine, Garonne, and Pyrenees. Maps and Plans. Post 8vo, 7s. 6d.

Handbook—France. Part II. Auvergne, the Cevennes, Burgundy, the Rhone and Saone, Provence, Nimes, Arles, Marseilles, the French Alps, Alsace, Lorraine, Champagne, etc. Maps and Plans. Post 8vo, 7s. 6d.

Handbook—Paris and its Environs. Maps and Plans. 16mo, 3s. 6d.

Handbook — Mediterranean : Its principal Islands, Cities, Seaports, Harbours, and Borderlands. With nearly 50 Maps and Plans. Post 8vo, 20s.

Handbook—Algeria and Tunis; Algiers, Constantin, Oran, the Atlas Range, etc. Maps and Plans. Post 8vo, 10s.

Handbook — Spain ; Madrid, The Castiles, Basque, Asturias, Galicia, Estremadura, Andalusia, Ronda, Granada, Murcia, Valencia, Catalonia, Aragon, Navarre, Balearic Islands. Maps and Plans. Post 8vo, 20s.

Handbook—Portugal ; Lisbon, Oporto, Cintra, etc. Map. Post 8vo, 12s.

Handbook—North Italy; Piedmont, Nice, Lombardy, Venice, Parma, Modena, and Romagna. Maps and Plans. Post 8vo, 10s.

Handbook—Central Italy; Tuscany, Florence, Lucca, Umbria, The Marches, and the Patrimony of St. Peter. Maps and Plans. Post 8vo, 10s.

The Cicerone ; or, Art Guide to Painting in Italy. By Dr. Jacob Burckhardt. Post 8vo, 6s.

Handbook—Rome and its Environs. Map and Plans. Post 8vo, 10s.

Handbook—South Italy ; Two Sicilies, Naples, Pompeii, Herculaneum, Vesuvius, Abruzzi. Maps and Plans. Post 8vo, 10s.

Handbook—Egypt ; the Nile, Egypt, Nubia, Alexandria, Cairo, The Pyramids, Thebes, Suez Canal, Peninsula of Sinai, The Oases, the Fyoom. Map and Plans. In Two Parts. Post 8vo, 15s.

Handbook — Greece ; Ionian Islands, Athens, Peloponnesus, Ægæan Sea, Albania, Thessaly, and Macedonia. Maps and Plans. Post 8vo.

Handbook—Turkey in Asia ; Constantinople, The Bosphorus, Dardanelles, Brousa, Plain of Troy, Crete, Cyprus, Smyrna, Ephesus, the Seven Churches, Coasts of the Black Sea, Armenia, Mesopotamia. Maps and Plans. Post 8vo, 15s.

Handbook—Denmark ; Sleswig-Holstein, Copenhagen, Jutland, Iceland. Maps and Plans. Post 8vo, 6s.

Handbook—Sweden ; Stockholm, Upsala, Gothenburg, the Shores of the Baltic, etc. Maps and Plans. Post 8vo.

Handbook—Norway ; Christiania, Bergen, Trondhjem, the Fjelds, Iceland. Maps and Plans. Post 8vo, 9s.

Handbook—Russia; St. Petersburg, Moscow, Poland, Finland, The Crimea, Caucasus, Siberia, and Central Asia. Maps and Plans. Post 8vo, 18s.

Handbook — Bombay. Map. Post 8vo, 15s.

Handbook — Madras. Maps and Plans. Post 8vo, 15s.

Handbook — Bengal. Map. Post 8vo, 15s.

Handbook—Holy Land; Syria, Palestine, Sinai, Edom and the Syrian Deserts, Jerusalem, Petra, Damascus, and Palmyra. Maps and Plans. Post 8vo, 20s.

Travelling Map of Palestine, *Mounted and in a Case.* 12s.

English.

Handbook—London as it is. Map and Plans. 16mo, 3s. 6d.

Handbook—Environs of London, within 20 miles round of the Metropolis. 2 vols. Post 8vo, 21s.

Handbook—England & Wales. Condensed in one Volume. Forming a Companion to Bradshaw's Railway Tables. Map. Post 8vo, 10s.

Handbook—Eastern Counties;
Chelmsford, Harwich, Colchester, Maldon, Cambridge, Ely, Newmarket, Bury, Ipswich, Woodbridge, Felixstowe, Lowestoft, Norwich, Yarmouth, Cromer. Map and Plans. Post 8vo, 12s.

Handbook — **Kent; Canter**bury, Dover, **Ramsgate, Rochester, Chatham. Map and Plans. Post 8vo,** 7s. 6d.

Handbook—**Sussex; Brighton, Eastbourne, Chichester, Hastings, Lewes, Arundel, etc. Map. Post 8vo, 6s.**

Handbook—**Surrey and Hants; Kingston, Croydon, Reigate, Guildford, Dorking, Boxhill, Winchester, Southampton, New Forest, Portsmouth, Isle of Wight. Maps and Plans. Post 8vo, 10s.**

Handbook—Berks, Bucks, **and Oxon**: Windsor, Eton, Reading, **Aylesbury**, Henley, Oxford, Blenheim, **and the Thames.** Map and Plans. Post 8vo.

Handbook—**Wilts, Dorset, and Somerset; Salisbury, Stonehenge, Chippenham, Weymouth, Sherborne, Wells, Bath, Bristol, etc. Map. Post 8vo, 10s.**

Handbook—**Devon; Exeter,** Ilfracombe, **Linton, Sidmouth, Dawlish,** Teignmouth, **Plymouth,** Devonport, Torquay. **Maps and Plans. Post 8vo,** 7s. 6d.

Handbook—**Cornwall; Launceston, Penzance, Falmouth, The Lizard, Land's End. Maps. Post 8vo, 6s.**

Handbook—Gloucester, Hereford, and Worcester; Cirencester, Cheltenham, Stroud, Tewkesbury, Leominster, Ross, Malvern, Kidderminster, Dudley, Evesham. Map. Post 8vo.

Handbook — **North Wales;** Bangor, Carnarvon, Beaumaris, **Snowdon**, Llanberis, Dolgelly, Cader **Idris**, Conway. Map. Post 8vo, **7s.**

Handbook — **South Wales;** Monmouth, Llandaff, Merthyr, **Vale of** Neath, Pembroke, Carmarthen, **Tenby**, Swansea, the Wye. Map. Post **8vo, 7s.**

Handbook—Derby, Notts, **Lei**cester, and Stafford; Matlock, Bakewell, Chatsworth, The Peak, Buxton, Hardwick, Dovedale, Ashbourn, Southwell, Mansfield, Retford, Burton, Belvoir, Melton Mowbray, Wolverhampton, Lichfield, Tamworth. Map. **Post** 8vo, 9s.

Handbook—**Shropshire & Che**shire, **Shrewsbury, Ludlow, Bridgnorth, Oswestry, Chester, Crewe, Alderley, Stockport, Birkenhead. Maps and Plans Post 8vo, 6s.**

Handbook—**Lancashire; War**rington, **Bury, Manchester, Liverpool, Burnley**, Clitheroe, Bolton, Blackburn, **Wigan**, Preston, Rochdale, Lancaster, **Southport**, Blackpool. Map. Post 8vo, 7s. 6d.

Handbook—**Northamptonshire and Rutland; Northampton, Peterborough, Towcester, Daventry, Market Harborough, Kettering, Wallingborough, Thrapston, Stamford, Uppingham, Oakham. Maps. Post 8vo, 7s. 6d.**

Handbook—**Yorkshire; Doncaster**, Hull, Selby, Beverley, Scarborough, Whitby, Harrogate, Ripon, Leeds, Wakefield, Bradford, Halifax, Huddersfield, Sheffield. Map and Plans. Post 8vo, 12s.

Handbook — **Durham and** Northumberland; Newcastle, Darlington, Bishop Auckland, Stockton, Hartlepool, Sunderland, Shields, Berwick, Tynemouth, Alnwick. Map. Post 8vo, 9s.

Handbook—**Westmorland and Cumberland; Lancaster, Furness Abbey, Ambleside, Kendal, Windermere, Coniston, Keswick, Grasmere, Ulswater, Carlisle, Cockermouth, Penrith, Appleby. Map. Post 8vo.**

Travelling Map of the Lake District, 3s. 6d.

Handbook—**Scotland; Edin**burgh, Melrose, Abbotsford, Glasgow, Dumfries, Galloway, Ayr, Stirling, **Arran**, The Clyde, Oban, Inverary, Loch Lomond, Loch Katrine and Trossachs, Caledonian Canal, Inverness, Perth, Dundee, Aberdeen, Braemar, Skye, Caithness, Ross, and Sutherland. Maps and Plans. Post 8vo, 9s.

Handbook— Ireland; Dublin, Belfast, The Giant's Causeway, Bantry, Glengariff, etc., Donegal, Galway, Wexford, Cork, Limerick, Waterford, Killarney. Maps and Plans. Post 8vo, 10s.

Handbook—Herts, Beds, Warwick. Map. Post 8vo. [*In preparation.*

Handbook — Huntingdon and Lincoln. Map. Post 8vo.
[*In preparation.*

ENGLISH CATHEDRALS.

Handbook — Southern Cathedrals. Winchester, Salisbury, Exeter, Wells, Rochester, Canterbury, Chichester, and St. Albans. Illustrations. 2 vols. Crown 8vo, 36s.

Handbook — Eastern Cathedrals. Oxford, Peterborough, Ely, Norwich, and Lincoln. Illustrations. Crown 8vo, 21s.

Handbook — Western Cathedrals. Bristol, Gloucester, Hereford, Worcester, and Lichfield. With 60 Illustrations. Crown 8vo, 16s.

Handbook — Northern Cathedrals. York, Ripon, Durham, Carlisle, Chester, and Manchester. Illustrations. 2 vols. Crown 8vo, 21s.

Handbook—Welsh Cathedrals. Llandaff, St. David's, Bangor, and St. Asaph's. Illustrations. Crown 8vo, 15s.

Handbook—St. Alban's Cathedral. Illustrations. Crown 8vo, 6s.

Handbook—St. Paul's. Illustrations. Crown 8vo, 10s. 6d.

RELIGION AND THEOLOGY.

The Speaker's Commentary on THE BIBLE. Explanatory and Critical, With a Revision of the Translation. By Bishops and Clergy of the Anglican Church. Edited by Canon COOK. Medium 8vo. Old Test.: 6 vols., 135s. New Test.: 4 vols., 94s. *See p. 2, ante.*

The New Testament : Edited, with a short Practical Commentary, by Archdeacon CHURTON and Bishop BASIL JONES. With 100 Illustrations. 2 vols. Crown 8vo, 21s.

The Student's Edition of the Speaker's Commentary on the Bible. Abridged and Edited by JOHN M. FULLER, M.A. Crown 8vo. *See p. 2.*

Dictionary of the Bible ; its Antiquities, Biography, Geography, and Natural History. By various Writers. Edited by Dr. WM. SMITH. Illustrations. 3 vols. 8vo, 105s.

Concise Bible Dictionary. For the use of Students and Families. Condensed from the above. Maps and 300 Illustrations. 8vo, 21s.

Smaller Bible Dictionary ; for Schools and Young Persons. Abridged from the above. Maps and Woodcuts. Crown 8vo, 7s. 6d.

Dictionary of Christian Antiquities ; comprising the History, Institutions, and Antiquities of the Christian Church. Edited by Dr. WM. SMITH, and Archdeacon CHEETHAM. Illustrations. 2 vols. 8vo, £3 : 13 : 6.

Church Dictionary. By Dean HOOK. 8vo, 16s.

Dictionary of Christian Biography, Literature, Sects, and Doctrines ; from the Times of the Apostles to the Age of Charlemagne. Edited by Dr. WM. SMITH and Professor WACE. Vols. I. & II. 8vo, 31s. 6d. each.

A Dictionary of Hymnology ; A Companion to existing Hymn Books. Setting forth the Origin and History of the Hymns in the most popular Hymnals, together with Biographical Notices of their Authors and Translators, and their Sources and Origins. By Rev. JOHN JULIAN. 8vo.

The Student's Manual of English Church History. By Canon PERRY. *See p. 27.*

Student's Manual of Ecclesiastical History. By PHILIP SMITH, B.A. *See p. 27.*

Student's Old Testament History. From the Creation to the return of the Jews from Captivity. By P. SMITH. Woodcuts. Post 8vo, 7s. 6d.

Student's New Testament History. With an Introduction connecting the History of the Old and New Testaments. By PHILIP SMITH. Woodcuts. Post 8vo, 7s. 6d.

History of Latin Christianity, including that of the Popes to the Pontificate of NICHOLAS V. By Dean MILMAN. 9 vols. crown 8vo, 54s.

The Gospel and its Witnesses. The Principal Facts in the Life of our Lord, and the Authority of the Evangelical Narratives. By HENRY WACE, M.A., Preacher of Lincoln's Inn, etc. Crown 8vo.

Book of Common Prayer ; with Historical Notes. By Rev. THOMAS JAMES. With Initial Letters, Vignettes, etc. 8vo, 18s.

A Book of Family Prayers : Selected from the Liturgy of the English Church. With Preface. By CHARLES E. POLLOCK. 16mo, 3s. 6d.

Signs and Wonders in the Land of HAM. With Ancient and Modern Parallels and Illustrations. By Rev. T. S. MILLINGTON. Woodcuts. 8vo, 7s. 6d.

The Talmud : Selected Extracts, chiefly Illustrating the Teaching of the Bible. With an Introduction. By Bishop BARCLAY. Illustrations. 8vo, 14s.

Notes on some Passages in the Liturgical History of the Reformed English Church. By Lord SELBORNE. 8vo, 6s.

History of the Christian Church from the Apostolic Age to the Reformation, A.D. 64-1517. By Canon ROBERTSON. 8 vols. post 8vo, 6s. each.

Undesigned Scriptural Coincidences in the Old and New Testaments; a Test of their Veracity. By Rev. J. J. BLUNT. Post 8vo, 6s.

History of the Christian Church in the First Three Centuries. By Rev. J. J. BLUNT. Post 8vo, 6s.

The Parish Priest; His Duties, Acquirements, and Obligations. By Rev. J. J. BLUNT. Post 8vo, 6s.

Biblical Researches in Palestine and the Adjacent Regions. A Journal of Travels and Researches. With Historical Illustrations. By EDWARD ROBINSON, D.D. Maps. 3 vols. 8vo, 42s.

Psalms of David; with Notes, Explanatory and Critical. By Dean JOHNSON, Canon ELLIOTT, and Canon COOK. Medium 8vo, 10s. 6d.

The Witness of the Psalms to Christ and Christianity. The Bampton Lectures for 1876. By the Bishop of DERRY. 8vo, 14s.

The Manifold Witness for Christ: being an Attempt to Exhibit the Combined Force of Various Evidences, Direct and Indirect, of Christianity. By Canon BARRY. 8vo, 12s.

University Sermons. By Rev. J. J. BLUNT. Post 8vo, 6s.

Church and the Age: a Series of Essays on the Principles and Present Position of the Anglican Church. By various Writers. 2 vols. 8vo, 26s.

The Synoptic Gospels,—The Death of Christ,—The Worth of Life,—Design in Nature, and other Essays. By Archbishop THOMSON. Cr. 8vo, 9s.

Companions for the Devout Life. Lectures delivered at St. James' Church, 1875-76. By Archb. of Dublin—Bps. of Ely and Derry—Deans of St. Paul's, Norwich, Chester, and Chichester—Canons Ashwell, Barry, and Farrar—Revs. Humphry, Carter, and Bickersteth. Post 8vo, 6s.

Classic Preachers of the English Church.
FIRST SERIES. 1877. Donne, Barrow, South, Beveridge, Wilson, Butler. With Introduction. Post 8vo, 7s. 6d.
SECOND SERIES. 1878. Bull, Horsley, Taylor, Sanderson, Tillotson, Andrewes. Post 8vo, 7s. 6d.

Masters in English Theology. Lectures delivered at King's College, London. By Canon BARRY, Dean of St. Paul's, Prof. PLUMPTRE, Canons WESTCOTT and FARRAR, and Archdeacon CHEETHAM. Post 8vo, 7s. 6d.

Essays on Cathedrals. By various Authors. Edited, with an Introduction, by Dean HOWSON. 8vo, 12s.

The Cathedral: its Necessary Place in the Life and Work of the Church. By the Bishop of TRURO. Crown 8vo, 6s.

The Outlook: a Charge delivered at his Primary Visitation, Nov. 1881. By the Bishop of ROCHESTER. Map. 8vo, 2s.

Should the Revised New Testament be Authorised? By Sir EDMUND BECKETT, Q.C. Post 8vo.

The Gallican Church. From the Concordat of Bologna, 1516, to the Revolution. With an introduction. By W. H. JERVIS. Portraits. 2 vols. 8vo, 28s.

Continuity of Scripture, as declared by the Testimony of Our Lord and of the Evangelists and Apostles. By Lord HATHERLEY. 8vo, 6s.; or cheap edition, 2s. 6d.

Bible Lands: their Modern Customs and Manners, illustrative of Scripture. By HENRY VAN LENNEP, D.D. Illustrations. 8vo, 21s.

The Shadows of a Sick Room. With Preface by Canon LIDDON. 16mo, 2s. 6d.

An Argument for the Divinity of Jesus Christ. From "Le Christianisme et les temps presents." By Abbé EM. BOUGAUD. Translated by C. L. CURRIE. Fcap. 8vo.

Manual of Family Prayer; arranged on a card. 8vo, 2s.

Treatise on the Augustinian Doctrine of Predestination. By Canon MOZLEY. Crown 8vo, 9s.

Foundations of Religion in the Mind and Heart of Man. By Sir JOHN BYLES. Post 8vo, 6s.

Hymns adapted to the Church Service. By Bishop HEBER. 16mo, 1s. 6d.

The Nicene and Apostles' Creeds. Their Literary History, with some account of "The Creed of St. Athanasius." By Canon SWAINSON. 8vo, 16s.

The Limits of Religious Thought examined. Bampton Lectures By Dean MANSEL. Post 8vo, 8s. 6d.

Christian Institutions; Essays on Ecclesiastical Subjects. By Dean STANLEY. 8vo, 12s.

Epistles of St. Paul to the Corinthians. The Greek Text; with Critical Notes and Dissertations. By Dean STANLEY. 8vo, 18s.

Lectures on the History of the EASTERN CHURCH. By Dean STANLEY. 8vo, 12s.

Lectures on the History of the JEWISH CHURCH. By Dean STANLEY. 1st and 2d SERIES, Abraham to the Captivity. Maps. 2 vols. 8vo, 24s. 3d SERIES, Captivity to the Christian Era. Maps. 8vo, 14s.

Sermons preached during the Tour of the Prince of Wales in the East. By Dean STANLEY. With Notices of the Localities visited. 8vo, 9s.

Sermons Preached in West- minster Abbey on Public Occasions. By the late Dean STANLEY. 8vo.

The Beatitudes : and other Ser- mons addressed to Children in Westminster Abbey. By the late Dean STANLEY. Fcap. 8vo.

Sermons preached in Lincoln's- Inn. By Canon COOK. 8vo, 9s.

Benedicite ; or, Song of the Three Children. Being Illustrations of the Power, Beneficence, and Design manifested by the Creator in His Works. By G. C. CHILD CHAPLIN, M.D. Post 8vo, 6s.

Sermons preached at Lincoln's- Inn. By Archbp. THOMSON. 8vo, 10s. 6d.

Life in the Light of God's Word. By Archbp. THOMSON. Post 8vo, 5s.

Life in Faith. Sermons preached at Cheltenham and Rugby. By T. W. JEX-BLAKE, D.D. Small 8vo, 3s. 6d.

A History of Christianity, from the Birth of Christ to the Abolition of Paganism in the Roman Empire. By Dean MILMAN. 3 vols. post 8vo, 18s.

History of the Jews, from the earliest period, continued to Modern Times. By Dean MILMAN. 3 vols. post 8vo, 18s.

A Smaller Scripture History of the Old and New Testaments. Edited by Dr. W. SMITH. Woodcuts. 16mo, 3s. 6d.

The Jesuits : their Constitu- tion and Teaching ; an Historical Sketch. By W. C. CARTWRIGHT. 8vo, 9s.

Rome and the Newest Fashions in Religion. By the Right Hon. W. E. GLADSTONE. Containing The Vatican Decrees—Vaticanism—Speeches of Pius IX. 8vo, 7s. 6d.

Eight Months at Rome, during the Vatican Council, with a Daily Account of the Proceedings. By POMPONIO LETO. 8vo, 12s.

Worship in the Church of ENGLAND. By A. J. B. BERESFORD-HOPE. 8vo, 9s.; *or, Popular Edition*, 8vo, 2s. 6d.

SCIENCE NATURAL HISTORY, GEOLOGY, ETC.

Science.

Connexion of the Physical Sciences. By MARY SOMERVILLE. New Edition. Revised by A. B. BUCKLEY. Plates. Post 8vo, 9s.

Molecular and Microscopic Science. By MARY SOMERVILLE. Illustrations. 2 vols. post 8vo, 21s.

Six Months in Ascension ; an Unscientific Account of a Scientific Expedition. By Mrs. GILL. Map. Crown 8vo, 9s.

The Admiralty Manual of Scientific Inquiry, prepared for the use of Officers, and Travellers in General. Map. Post 8vo, 3s. 6d.

Reports of the British Associa- TION for the Advancement of Science, from 1831 to the present time. 8vo.

Philosophy in Sport made Science in Earnest ; or, the First Principles of Natural Philosophy explained by aid of the Toys and Sports of Youth. By Dr. PARIS. Woodcuts. Post 8vo, 7s. 6d.

Metallurgy ; The Art of Ex- tracting Metals from their Ores. By JOHN PERCY, F.R.S. With Illustrations. 8vo.
FUEL, WOOD, PEAT, COAL, &c. 30s.
LEAD, and Part of SILVER. 30s.
SILVER and GOLD, 30s.

The Manufacture of Russian Sheet-iron. By JOHN PERCY, 8vo, 2s. 6d.

A Manual of Naval Architec- ture for the Use of Officers of the Royal Navy, Mercantile Marine, Yachtsmen, Shipbuilders, and others. By W. H. WHITE. Illustrations. 8vo, 24s.

Ironclad Ships; their Qualities, Performances, and Cost, with Chapters on Turret Ships, Rams, &c. By Sir E. J. REED, C.B. Illustrations. 8vo, 12s.

Natural Philosophy ; an Intro- duction to the study of Statics, Dynamics, Hydrostatics, Light, Heat, and Sound : with numerous Examples. By SAMUEL NEWTH. Small 8vo, 3s. 6d.

The Freedom of Science in the Modern State. By Rudolf Virchow. Fcp. 8vo, 2s.

Mathematical Examples. A Graduated Series of Elementary Examples in Arithmetic, Algebra, Logarithms, Trigonometry, and Mechanics. By Samuel Newth. Small 8vo, 8s. 6d.

Elements of Mechanics, including Hydrostatics, with numerous Examples. By Samuel Newth. Small 8vo, 8s. 6d.

Patterns for Turning; to be cut on the Lathe *without* the use of *any* Ornamental Chuck. By W. H. Elphinstone. Illustrations. Small 4to, 15s.

Natural History and Medicine.

Siberia in Europe. A Naturalist's Visit to the Valley of the Petchora in North-East Russia. With Notices of Birds and their Migrations. By Henry Seebohm. Map and Illustrations. Crown 8vo, 14s.

Life of a Scotch Naturalist (Thomas Edward). By S. Smiles. Illustrations. Crown 8vo, 10s. 6d.

The Cat; an Introduction to the Study of Backboned Animals, especially Mammals. By St. George Mivart. With 200 Illustrations. 8vo, 30s.

Lessons from Nature; as manifested in Mind and Matter. By St. George Mivart, F.R.S. 8vo, 16s.

The Origin of Species, by Means of Natural Selection; or the Preservation of Favoured Races in the Struggle for Life. By Charles Darwin. Post 8vo, 7s. 6d.

Voyage of a Naturalist; a Journal of Researches into the Natural History and Geology of the Countries visited during a Voyage round the World. By Charles Darwin. Illustrations. Post 8vo, 9s.

Variation of Animals and Plants under Domestication. By C. Darwin. Illustrations. 2 vols. cr. 8vo, 18s.

The Various Contrivances by which Orchids are Fertilised by Insects. By Charles Darwin. Woodcuts. Post 8vo, 9s.

The Effects of Cross and Self Fertilisation in the Vegetable Kingdom. By Charles Darwin. Crown 8vo, 12s.

Expression of the Emotions in Man and Animals. By Charles Darwin. Illustrations. Crown 8vo, 12s.

Descent of Man and Selection in Relation to Sex. By Charles Darwin. Illustrations. Crown 8vo, 9s.

Insectivorous Plants. By Charles Darwin. Post 8vo, 14s.

The Movements and Habits of Climbing Plants. By Chas. Darwin. Post 8vo, 6s.

The Different Forms of Flowers on Plants of the same Species. By Charles Darwin. Woodcuts. Crown 8vo, 10s. 6d.

The Power of Movement in Plants. By Charles Darwin, assisted by Francis Darwin. Woodcuts. Crown 8vo, 15s.

The Formation of Vegetable Mould through the Action of Worms. With Observations on their Habits. By Charles Darwin. Woodcuts. Post 8vo, 9s.

Facts and Arguments for Darwin. By Fritz Müller. Illustrations. Post 8vo, 5s.

Geographical Handbook of all the known Ferns, with Tables to show their Distribution. By K. M. Lyell. Post 8vo, 7s. 6d.

The Gardens of the Sun; or, a Naturalist's Journal on the Mountains and in the Forests and Swamps of Borneo and the Sulu Archipelago. By F. W. Burbidge. With Illustrations. Crown 8vo, 14s.

Harvest of the Sea. An Account of the British Food Fishes. With Sketches of Fisheries and Fisher-Folk. By James G. Bertram. Illustrations. Post 8vo, 9s.

Household Surgery; or, Hints for Emergencies. By John F. South. With new Preface and Additions. Woodcuts. Fcap. 8vo, 3s. 6d.

Kirkes' Handbook of Physiology. By W. Morrant Baker. 420 Woodcuts. Post 8vo, 14s.

Gleanings in Natural History. By Edward Jesse. Woodcuts. Fcap. 3s. 6d.

Geography and Geology.

Student's Elements of Geology. By Sir CHARLES LYELL. Woodcuts. Post 8vo, 9s.

Principles of Geology; or, the Modern Changes of the Earth and its Inhabitants, as Illustrative of Geology. By Sir CHARLES LYELL. Woodcuts. 2 vols. 8vo, 32s.

Physical Geography. By MARY SOMERVILLE. New Edition, Revised by Rev. J. RICHARDSON. Portrait. Post 8vo, 9s.

Physical Geography of the Holy Land. By EDWARD ROBINSON, Post 8vo, 10s. 6d.

Siluria ; a History of the Oldest FOSSILIFEROUS ROCKS and their Foundations ; with a Brief Sketch of the Distribution of Gold over the Earth. By Sir RODERICK MURCHISON. Illustrations. 2 vols. 8vo, 18s.

Records of the Rocks; or, Notes on the Geology, Natural History, and Antiquities of North and South Wales, Devon, &c. By Rev. W. S. SYMONDS. Illustrations. Crown 8vo, 12s.

Life of a Scotch Geologist and Botanist (ROBERT DICK). By S. SMILES. Illustrations. Crown 8vo, 12s.

Scepticism in Geology, and the Reasons for it. An assemblage of Facts from Nature opposed to the Theory of "Causes now in Action," and refuting it. By VERIFIER. Post 8vo, 6s.

FINE ARTS, ARCHITECTURE, & ANTIQUITIES.

The National Memorial to the PRINCE CONSORT at KENSINGTON. A Descriptive and Illustrated Account, consisting of Coloured Views and Engravings of the Monument and its Decorations, its Groups, Statues, Mosaics, Architecture, and Metalwork. With descriptive text by DOYNE C. BELL. Folio, £12 : 12s.

A Handbook to the Albert Memorial. Fcap. 8vo, 1s. ; or with Illustrations, 2s. 6d.

Mediæval and Modern Pottery and PORCELAIN. By JOSEPH MARRYAT. Illustrations. Medium 8vo, 42s.

Old English Plate : Ecclesiastical, Decorative, and Domestic ; its Makers and Marks. With Illustrations and Improved Tables of the Date Letters used in England, Scotland, and Ireland. By WILFRED J. CRIPPS. 70s. Illustrations. Medium 8vo, 16s.

Old French Plate : Furnishing Tables of the Paris Date Letters, and Facsimiles of other marks. By W. J. CRIPPS. With Illustrations. 8vo, 8s. 6d.

Cyprus ; its Ancient Cities, Tombs, and Temples. A Narrative of Researches and Excavations during Ten Years' Residence in that Island. By LOUIS P. DI CESNOLA. 400 Illustrations. Medium 8vo, 50s.

A History of Greek Sculpture, from the Earliest Times down to the age of Pheidias. By A. S. MURRAY. With Illustrations. Royal 8vo, 21s.

Ancient Mycenæ ; Discoveries and Researches on the Sites of Mycenæ and Tiryns. By Dr. SCHLIEMANN. With Preface by the Right Hon. W. E. GLADSTONE. 500 Illustrations. Medium 8vo, 50s.

Ilios ; a Complete History of the City and Country of the Trojans, including all Recent Discoveries and Researches made on the Site of Troy and the Troad in 1871-3 and 1878-9. With an Autobiography of the Author. By Dr. SCHLIEMANN. With nearly 2000 Illustrations. Imperial 8vo, 50s.

Nile Gleanings : the Ethnology, History, and Art of Ancient Egypt, as Revealed by Paintings and Bas-Reliefs. With Descriptions of Nubia and its Great Rock Temples to the Second Cataract. By VILLIERS STUART. With 50 Coloured Plates. Royal 8vo, 31s. 6d.

The Cities and Cemeteries of Etruria. By GEORGE DENNIS. 200 Illustrations. 2 vols. medium 8vo, 42s.

History of Painting in North Italy, 14th to 16th Century. Venice, Padua, Vicenza, Verona, Ferrara, Milan, Friuli, Breschia. By CROWE and CAVALCASELLE. Illustrations. 2 vols. 8vo, 42s.

Titian : his Life and Times. By CROWE and CAVALCASELLE. Illustrations. 2 vols. 8vo, 21s.

Handbook to the Italian Schools of Painting ; Based on the work of Kugler. Revised by Lady EASTLAKE. 140 Illustrations. 2 vols. crown 8vo, 30s.

Handbook to the German, Dutch, and Flemish Schools of Painting. Based on the work of Kugler. Revised by J. A. CROWE. 60 Illustrations. 2 vols. post 8vo, 24s.

Lives of the Italian Painters ; and the Progress of Painting in Italy. Cimabue to Bassano. By Mrs. JAMESON. Illustrations. Post 8vo, 12s.

Lives of the Early Flemish Painters, with Notices of their Works. By CROWE and CAVALCASELLE. Illustrations. Post 8vo, 7s. 6d. ; or large paper, 8vo, 15s.

Albert Dürer ; a History of his Life and Works. By MORIZ THAUSING, Vienna. Edited by F. A. EATON, Secretary of the Royal Academy. With Portrait and Illustrations. 2 vols. Med. 8vo, 42s.

The Cicerone ; or, Art Guide to Painting in Italy. By Dr. BURCKHARDT. Post 8vo, 6s.

History of Architecture in all Countries, from the Earliest Times to the Present Day. By JAMES FERGUSSON. With 1600 Illustrations. 4 vols. Medium 8vo.
I. & II. Ancient and Mediæval, 63s.
III. Indian and Eastern, 42s.
IV. Modern, 31s. 6d.

Rude Stone Monuments in all Countries : their Age and Uses. By JAMES FERGUSSON. Illustrations. Medium 8vo, 24s.

The Temples of the Jews and other Buildings in the Haram Area at Jerusalem. By JAMES FERGUSSON. Illustrations. 4to, 42s.

Leaves from My Sketch-Book, By E. W. COOKE, R.A. 50 Plates. With Descriptive Text. 2 vols. Small folio, 31s. 6d. each. 1st SERIES, Paris, Arles, Monaco, Nuremberg, Switzerland, Rome, Egypt, etc. 2d SERIES, Venice, Naples, Pompeii, Poestum, the Nile, etc.

The Holy Sepulchre and the Temple at Jerusalem. By JAS. FERGUSSON. Woodcuts. 8vo, 7s. 6d.

Life of Michel Angelo, Sculptor, Painter, and Architect, including unedited Documents in the Buonarroti Archives, by CHARLES HEATH WILSON. With Index and Illustrations. 8vo, 15s.

A Descriptive Catalogue of the Etched Work of Rembrandt ; with Life and Introductions. By CHAS. H. MIDDLETON. Plates. Medium 8vo, 31s. 6d.

The Rise and Development of Mediæval Architecture. By Sir G. GILBERT SCOTT. 450 Illustrations. 2 vols. Medium 8vo, 42s.

Secular and Domestic Architecture. By Sir G. SCOTT, R.A. 8vo, 9s.

The Gothic Architecture of ITALY. By G. E. STREET, R.A. Illustrations. Royal 8vo, 26s.

The Gothic Architecture of SPAIN. By G. E. STREET, R.A. Illustrations. Royal 8vo, 30s.

The Rise of Styles in Architecture. By G. E. STREET, R.A. Illustrations. 8vo.

Notes on the Churches of Kent. By Sir STEPHEN GLYNNE. With a Preface by W. H. GLADSTONE. Illustrations. 8vo, 12s.

Handbooks to English Cathedrals. See p. 14.

Purity in Musical Art. By A. F. J. THIBAUT. With Memoir by W. H. GLADSTONE. Post 8vo, 7s. 6d.

Handbook for Young Painters. By C. R. LESLIE. Illustrations. Post 8vo, 7s. 6d.

Life and Times of Sir Joshua Reynolds, with notices of his Contemporaries. By C. R. LESLIE and TOM TAYLOR. Portraits. 2 vols. 8vo, 42s.

Lectures on Architecture. Delivered before the Royal Academy. By EDWARD M. BARRY, R.A. Edited with Memoir by Canon BARRY. Portrait and Illustrations. 8vo, 16s.

Contributions to the Literature of THE FINE ARTS. By Sir C. LOCK EASTLAKE, R.A. With a Memoir by Lady EASTLAKE. 2 vols. 8vo, 24s.

School Architecture. Practical
Information on the Planning, Designing,
Building, and Furnishing of School-
houses, etc. By E. R. ROBSON. Illustrations. Medium 8vo, 18s.

The Choice of a Dwelling ; a
Practical Handbook of useful information
on all points connected with a House.
Plans. Post 8vo, 7s. 6d.

Life of Sir Charles Barry, R.A.,
Architect. By Canon BARRY. Illustrations. Medium 8vo, 15s.

London — Past and Present :
alphabetically arranged. By PETER
CUNNINGHAM. A new and revised edition. 3 vols. 8vo.   [*In the Press.*

PHILOSOPHY, LAW, AND POLITICS.

The Eastern Question. By
Viscount STRATFORD DE REDCLIFFE,
Being a Selection from his Recent
Writings. With a Preface by Dean
STANLEY. Post 8vo, 9s.

Letters on the Politics of
Switzerland, pending the outbreak of
the Civil War in 1847. By GEORGE
GROTE. 8vo, 6s.

Constitutional Progress. A
Series of Lectures. By MONTAGUE
BURROWS. Post 8vo, 5s.

Constitution and Practice of
Courts-Martial. By Capt. SIMMONS.
8vo, 15s.

Administration of Justice under
Military and Martial Law, as applicable to the Army, Navy, Marine, and
Auxiliary Forces. By C. M. CLODE.
8vo, 12s.

Student's Blackstone. A Systematic Abridgment of the entire Com-
mentaries. By R. MALCOLM KERR.
Post 8vo, 7s. 6d.

Communistic Societies of the
United States. With Accounts of the
Shakers and other Societies ; their
Creeds, Social Practices, Industries, etc.
By C. NORDHOFF. Illustrations. 8vo, 15s.

The English Constitution ; its
Rise, Growth, and Present State. By
DAVID ROWLAND. Post 8vo, 10s. 6d.

Laws of Nature the Foundation
of Morals. By DAVID ROWLAND. Post
8vo, 6s.

A Handbook to the Political
Questions of the day, with the Argu-
ments on Either Side. By SYDNEY C.
BUXTON. 8vo, 6s.

A Manual of Moral Philo-
sophy. With Quotations and Refer-
ences. By WILLIAM FLEMING. Post
8vo, 7s. 6d.

Gleanings of Past Years, 1843-
78. By the Right Hon. W. E. GLAD-
STONE, M.P. Small 8vo, 2s. 6d. each.
I. The Throne, Prince Consort, Cabinet,
and Constitution. II. Personal and
Literary. III. Historical and Speculative. IV. Foreign. V. and VI. Ecclesiastical. VII. Miscellaneous.

Speeches and Addresses, Political and Literary. Delivered in the
House of Lords, in Canada, and elsewhere. By the Right Hon. the EARL OF
DUFFERIN. 8vo.

Philosophy of the Moral Feel-
ings. By JOHN ABERCROMBIE. Fcap.
8vo, 2s. 6d.

The Intellectual Powers, and
the Investigation of Truth. By JOHN
ABERCROMBIE. Fcap. 8vo, 3s. 6d.

Hortensius ; an Historical
Essay on the Office and Duties of an
Advocate. By WILLIAM FORSYTH. Illus-
trations. 8vo, 7s. 6d.

Lectures on General Jurispru-
dence ; or, the Philosophy of Positive
Law. By JOHN AUSTIN. Edited by
ROBERT CAMPBELL. 2 vols. 8vo, 32s.

Student's Edition of Austin's
Lectures on Jurisprudence. Compiled
from the larger work. By ROBERT
CAMPBELL. Post 8vo, 12s.

An Analysis of Austin's Jurisprudence for the Use of Students. By
GORDON CAMPBELL, M.A. Post 8vo,
6s.

England and Russia in the East.
A Series of Papers on the Political and
Geographical Condition of Central Asia.
By Sir H. RAWLINSON. Map. 8vo,
12s.

Ancient Law : its Connection
with the Early History of Society, and
its Relation to Modern Ideas. By Sir
HENRY S. MAINE. 8vo, 12s.

Village Communities in the East and West. By Sir HENRY S. MAINE. 8vo, 12s.

The Early History of Institutions. By Sir HENRY MAINE. 8vo, 12s.

Local Taxation of Great Britain and Ireland. By R. H. I. PALGRAVE. 8vo, 5s.

Plato and other Companions of Socrates. By GEORGE GROTE. 3 vols. 8vo, 45s.

Artistotle. By GEORGE GROTE. Second Edition. With Additions. 8vo, 18s.

Minor Works of George Grote. With Critical Remarks on his Intellectual Character, Writings, and Speeches. By ALEX. BAIN. Portrait. 8vo, 14s.

The Bengal Famine. How it will be Met, and how to Prevent Future Famines. By Sir BARTLE FRERE. Maps. Crown 8vo, 5s.

India in 1880. By Sir R. TEMPLE. 8vo, 16s.

Men and Events of my Time in India. By Sir RICHARD TEMPLE, Bart. 8vo.

Results of Indian Missions. By Sir BARTLE FRERE. Small 8vo, 2s. 6d.

Eastern Africa viewed as a Field for Mission Labour. By Sir BARTLE FRERE. Crown 8vo, 5s.

The Lex Salica; The Ten Texts, With the Glosses and the Lex Emendata. Synoptically Edited by J. H. HESSELS. With Notes on the Frankish Words in the Lex Salica by Professor KERN. 4to, 42s.

Researches into the Early History of Mankind, and the Development of Civilisation. By E. B. TYLOR. 8vo, 12s.

Primitive Culture : Researches into the Development of Mythology, Philosophy, Religion, Art, and Custom. By E. B. TYLOR. 2 vols. 8vo, 24s.

Ricardo's Political Works. With a Biographical Sketch. By J. R. M'CULLOCH. 8vo, 16s.

The Moral Philosophy of Aristotle. Consisting of a Translation of the Nicomachean Ethics, and of the Paraphrase attributed to Andronicus of Rhodes; with Introductory Analysis of each Book. By the late WALTER M. HATCH, M.A. 8vo, 18s.

History of British Commerce, and of the Economic Progress of the Nation, 1763-1878. By LEONE LEVI. 8vo, 18s.

Ideas of the Day on Policy. By CHARLES BUXTON. 8vo, 6s.

Judgments of the Privy Council, with an Historical Account of the Appellate Jurisdiction in the Church of England. By G. C. BRODRICK and W. H FREMANTLE. 8vo, 10s. 6d.

A Little Light on the Cretan Question. By A. F. YULE. Post 8vo. 2s. 6d.

History of the English Poor Laws. By Sir G. NICHOLLS. 2 vols. 8vo.

Consolation in Travel; or, the Last Days of a Philosopher. By Sir HUMPHRY DAVY. Woodcuts. Fcap. 8vo, 3s. 6d.

GENERAL LITERATURE AND PHILOLOGY.

The Quarterly Review. 8vo, 6s.

Prince Albert's Speeches and Addresses on Public Occasions; with an outline of his Character. Portrait. Fcap. 8vo, 1s.

The Modern Ducange. A New Mediæval Latin-English Dictionary, occupying the ground of Ducange, but Edited in accordance with the Modern Science of Philology. By E. A. DAYMAN, B.D., Prebendary of Sarum, formerly Fellow and Tutor of Exeter College, Oxford, and J. H. HESSELS. Small 4to.

The Talmud and other Literary Remains of EMANUEL DEUTSCH. With a Memoir. 8vo, 12s.

Letters, Lectures, and Reviews, including the Phrontisterion, or Oxford in the 19th Century. By Dean MANSEL. 8vo, 12s.

The Novels and Novelists of the 18th Century; in Illustration of the Manners and Morals of the Age. By WM. FORSYTH. Post 8vo, 10s. 6d.

Principles of Greek Etymology. By Professor CURTIUS. Translated by A. S. WILKINS, M.A., and E. B. ENGLAND, M.A. 2 vols. 8vo, 15s. each.

The Greek Verb. Its Structure and Development. By Professor CURTIUS. Translated by A. S. WILKINS and E. B. ENGLAND. 8vo, 18s.

Miscellanies. By Earl STANHOPE. 2 vols. post 8vo, 13s.

Historical Essays. By Earl STANHOPE. Post 8vo, 3s. 6d.

French Retreat from Moscow, and other Essays. By the late Earl STANHOPE. Post 8vo, 7s. 6d.

The Papers of a Critic. Selected from the Writings of the late C. W. DILKE. 2 vols. 8vo, 24s.

Gleanings of Past Years. I. The Throne, Prince Consort, Cabinet, and Constitution. II. Personal and Literary. III. Historical and Speculative. IV. Foreign. V. and VI. Ecclesiastical. VII. Miscellaneous. By the Right Hon. W. E. GLADSTONE, M.P. Small 8vo. 2s. 6d. each.

Lavengro : the Scholar—the Gipsy—and the Priest. By GEORGE BORROW. Post 8vo, 5s.

The Romany Rye : a Sequel to 'Lavengro.' By GEORGE BORROW. Post 8vo, 5s.

Wild Wales : its People, Language, and Scenery. By GEORGE BORROW. Post 8vo, 5s.

Romano Lavo-Lil ; Word-Book of the Romany, or English Gypsy Language ; with an Account of certain Gypsyries. By GEORGE BORROW. Post 8vo, 10s. 6d.

Field Paths and Green Lanes : Country Walks, chiefly in Surrey and Sussex. By L. J. JENNINGS. Woodcuts. Post 8vo, 10s. 6d.

Rambles among the Hills ; or Walks in the Peak of Derbyshire and in the South Downs. By L. J. JENNINGS. Illustrations. Post 8vo, 12s.

Old Deccan Days : Hindoo Fairy Legends current in Southern India. Collected by MARY FRERE. With Introduction by Sir BARTLE FRERE. Illustrations. Post 8vo, 7s. 6d.

Livonian Tales. By a LADY. Post 8vo, 2s.

The Amber-Witch : a Trial for Witchcraft. Translated by Lady DUFF GORDON. Post 8vo, 2s.

The Handwriting of Junius. Professionally investigated by C. CHABOT. Edited by the Hon. EDWARD TWISLETON. With Facsimiles. 4to, 63s.

The Literary History of Europe. By HENRY HALLAM. Library edition, 3 vols. 8vo, 36s. ; or Cabinet edition, 4 vols. post 8vo, 16s.

English Studies : Essays by the late Rev. J. S. BREWER. 8vo, 14s.

Stokers and Pokers, or the London and North-Western Railway. By Sir F. HEAD. Post 8vo, 2s.

Specimens of the Table-Talk of SAMUEL TAYLOR COLERIDGE. Portrait. Fcap. 8vo, 3s. 6d.

The Remains in Prose and Verse of Arthur Hallam. With Memoir. Portrait. Fcap. 8vo, 3s. 6d.

Self-Help. With Illustrations of Conduct and Perseverance. By Dr. SMILES. Small 8vo, 6s.

Character. A Book of Noble Characteristics. By Dr. SMILES. Small 8vo, 6s.

Thrift. A Book of Domestic Counsel. By Dr. SMILES. Post 8vo, 6s.

Duty, with Illustrations of Courage, Patience, and Endurance. By Dr. S. SMILES. Post 8vo, 6s.

Mottoes for Monuments ; or, Epitaphs selected for General Study and Application. By Mrs. PALLISER. Illustrations. Crown 8vo, 7s. 6d.

Words of Human Wisdom. Collected and Arranged by E. S. With Preface by Canon LIDDON. Fcap. 8vo, 3s. 6d.

Æsop's Fables. A new Version. With Historical Preface. By Rev. THOMAS JAMES. Woodcuts, by TENNIEL. Post 8vo, 2s. 6d.

Letters from the Baltic. By a LADY. Post 8vo, 2s.

Literary Essays from the 'Times.' By SAMUEL PHILLIPS. Portrait. 2 vols. fcap. 8vo, 7s.

Rejected Addresses. By JAMES and HORACE SMITH. Woodcuts. Post 8vo, 3s. 6d. ; or fcap. 8vo, 1s.

Lispings from Low Latitudes ; or, the Journal of the Hon. Impulsia Gushington. Edited by Lord DUFFERIN. Plates. 4to, 21s.

An English Grammar. Methodical, Analytical, and Historical. With a Treatise on the Orthography, Prosody, Inflections, and Syntax of the English Tongue. By Professor MAETZNER. 3 vols. 8vo, 36s.

POETRY, THE DRAMA, ETC.

The Prose and Poetical Works of Lord Byron. With Notes by SCOTT, JEFFREY, WILSON, GIFFORD, CRABBE, HEBER, LOCKHART, etc., and Notices of his Life. By THOMAS MOORE. Illustrations. 2 vols. royal 8vo, 15s.

Poetical Works of Lord Byron. Library Edition. Portrait. 6 vols. 8vo, 45s.

Poetical Works of Lord Byron. Cabinet Edition. Plates. 10 vols. fcap. 8vo, 30s.

Poetical Works of Lord Byron. Pocket Edition. 8 vols. bound and in a case. 18mo, 21s.

Poetical Works of Lord Byron. Popular Edition. Plates. Royal 8vo, 7s. 6d.

Poetical Works of Lord Byron. Pearl Edition. Post 8vo, 2s. 6d.

Childe Harold. By Lord Byron. 80 Engravings. Crown 8vo, 12s.

Childe Harold. By Lord Byron. 2s. 6d., 1s., and 6d. each.

Tales and Poems. By Lord Byron. 24mo, 2s. 6d.

Miscellanies. By Lord Byron. 2 vols. 24mo, 5s.

Dramas. By Lord Byron. 2 vols. 24mo, 5s.

Don Juan and Beppo. By Lord Byron. 2 vols. 24mo, 5s.

Beauties of Byron. Prose and Verse. Portrait. Fcap. 8vo, 3s. 6d.

Oliver Goldsmith's Works, edited by PETER CUNNINGHAM. Vignettes. 4 vols. 8vo, 30s.

Agamemnon. Translated from Æschylus. By the Earl of CARNARVON. Small 8vo, 6s.

Argo, or, the Quest of the Golden Fleece, a Metrical Tale in ten books. By the Earl of CRAWFORD and BALCARRES. 8vo, 10s. 6d.

Vie de Seint Auban: a Poem in Norman-French, ascribed to Matthew Paris. Edited, with Notes, by ROBERT ATKINSON. Small 4to, 10s. 6d.

The Vaux-de-Vire of Maistre Jean le Houx, Advocate of Vire. Translated by J. P. MUIRHEAD. Illustrations. 8vo, 21s.

Life and Poetical Works of Rev. George Crabbe. Plates, royal 8vo, 7s.

Life and Works of Alexander Pope. Edited by Rev. W. ELWIN and W. J. COURTHOPE. Portraits, vols. 1, 2, 3, 6, 7, 8. 8vo, 10s. 6d. each.

Iliad of Homer. Translated into English blank verse. By the Earl of DERBY. Portrait. 2 vols. post 8vo, 10s.

The Odyssey of Homer. Rendered into English Verse. VOL. I.: Books I.—XII. VOL. II.: Books XIII.—XXIV. By General SCHOMBERG, C.B. 8vo, 12s. each.

Poetical Works of Bishop Heber. Portrait. Fcap. 8vo, 3s. 6d.

Hymns adapted to the Church Service. By Bishop HEBER. 16mo, 1s. 6d.

The Sonnet; its Origin, Structure, and Place in Poetry. With Translations from Dante and Petrarch. By CHARLES TOMLINSON. Post 8vo, 9s.

The Fall of Jerusalem. By Dean MILMAN. Fcap. 8vo, 1s.

Horace. By Dean MILMAN. Illustrated with 100 Woodcuts. Post 8vo, 7s. 6d.

Ancient Spanish Ballads. Historical and Romantic. Translated by J. G. LOCKHART. Woodcuts. Crown 8vo, 5s.

Remains in Prose and Verse of Arthur Hallam. With Memoir. Portrait. Fcap. 8vo, 3s. 6d.

Rejected Addresses. By JAMES and HORACE SMITH. With Biographical Notices. Portraits. Post 8vo, 3s. 6d. ; or fcap. 8vo, 1s.

An Essay on English Poetry. With short lives of the British Poets. By THOMAS CAMPBELL. Post 8vo, 3s. 6d.

Poems and Fragments of Catullus. Translated in the Metres of the Original. By ROBINSON ELLIS. 16mo, 5s.

Poetical Works of Lord Houghton. New Edition. 2 vols. fcap. 8vo, 12s.

Gongora's Poetical Works. With an Historical Essay on the Age of Philip III. and IV. of Spain. By Archdeacon CHURTON. Portrait. 2 vols. small 8vo, 12s.

Poetical Remains of the late Archdeacon Churton. Post 8vo, 2s. 6d.

NAVAL AND MILITARY WORKS.

Army List. (Published by Authority.) With an Alphabetical Index. Monthly. 16mo, 2s.

The Official Army List. With an Index. 8vo, 15s. Published Quarterly.

Navy List. (Published by Authority.) Quarterly, 16mo, 3s. Monthly, 1s. 6d.

Nautical Almanack. (Published by Authority.) 8vo, 2s. 6d.

Hart's Army List. (Published Quarterly and Annually.) 8vo.

Admiralty Publications, issued by direction of the Lords Commissioners of the Admiralty.

Admiralty Manual of Scientific Enquiry, for the use of Travellers. Edited by Sir J. HERSCHEL and ROBERT MAIN. Woodcuts. Post 8vo, 3s. 6d.

A Dictionary of Naval and Military Technical Terms. English-French, French-English. By Colonel BURN. Crown 8vo, 15s.

Our Ironclad Ships : their Qualities, Performances, and Cost, including Chapters on Turret Ships, Ironclad Rams, etc. By E. J. REED, C.B. Illustrations. 8vo, 12s.

Manual of Naval Architecture for Officers of the Royal Navy, Mercantile Marine, Yachtsmen, Shipowners, and Shipbuilders. By W. H. WHITE. With 130 Woodcuts. 8vo, 24s.

Modern Warfare as Influenced by Modern Artillery. By Col. P. L. MACDOUGALL. Plans. Post 8vo, 12s.

Naval Gunnery ; for the Use of Officers and the Training of Seaman Gunners. By Sir HOWARD DOUGLAS. 8vo, 21s.

The Royal Engineer and the Royal Establishments at Woolwich and Chatham. By Sir FRANCIS B. HEAD. Illustrations. 8vo, 12s.

The Principles and Practice of Modern Artillery, including Artillery Material, Gunnery, and Organisation and Use of Artillery in Warfare. By Lieut.-Col. C. H. OWEN. Illustrations. 8vo, 15s.

The Administration of Justice under Military and Martial Law, as applicable to the Army, Navy, Marine, and Auxiliary Forces. By C. M. CLODE. 8vo, 12s.

History of the Administration and Government of the British Army from the Revolution of 1688. By C. M. CLODE. 2 vols. 8vo, 21s. each.

Constitution and Practice of Courts-Martial, with a Summary of the Law of Evidence, and some Notice of the Criminal Law of England with reference to the Trial of Civil Offences. By Capt. T. F. SIMMONS, R.A. 8vo, 15s.

History of the Royal Artillery. Compiled from the Original Records. By Major FRANCIS DUNCAN, R.A. 2 vols. 8vo, 18s.

The English in Spain. The True Story of the War of the Succession in 1834-1840. Compiled from the Reports of the British Commissioners with Queen Isabella's Armies. By Major FRANCIS DUNCAN, R.A. Illustrations. 8vo, 16s.

Wellington's Supplementary Despatches and Correspondence. Edited by his SON. 15 vols. 8vo, 20s. each. An Index. 8vo, 20s.

Wellington's Civil and Political Correspondence, 1819-1831. 8 vols. 8vo, 20s. each.

The Light Cavalry Brigade in the Crimea : Extracts from Letters and Journals during the Crimean War. By General Lord GEORGE PAGET. With Map. Crown 8vo, 10s. 6d.

Lives of the Warriors of the Seventeenth Century. By Gen. Sir EDWARD CUST. 6 vols. post 8vo. 1st Series.—THE THIRTY YEARS' WAR, 1600-48. 2 vols. 16s. 2d Series.—THE CIVIL WARS OF FRANCE AND ENGLAND. 1611-75. 2 vols. 16s. 3d Series.—COMMANDERS OF FLEETS AND ARMIES, 1648-1704. 2 vols. 18s.

Annals of the Wars of the 18th and 19th Centuries, 1700-1815. Compiled from the most Authentic Histories of the Period. By Gen. Sir E. CUST. Maps. 9 vols. fcap. 8vo, 5s. each.

Deeds of Naval Daring ; or, Anecdotes of the British Navy. By EDWARD GIFFARD. Fcap. 8vo, 3s. 6d.

RURAL AND DOMESTIC ECONOMY, ETC.

A Popular Account of the Introduction of Peruvian Bark from South America into British India and Ceylon, and of the Progress of its Cultivation. By CLEMENTS R. MARKHAM. With Maps and Woodcuts. Post 8vo, 14s.

Plain Instructions in Gardening; with a Calendar of Operations and Directions for every Month. By Mrs. LOUDON. Woodcuts. Fcap. 8vo, 3s. 6d.

A Geographical Handbook of FERNS. By K. M. LYELL. Post 8vo, 7s. 6d.

Alpine Flowers for English GARDENS. How they may be grown in all parts of the British Islands. By W. ROBINSON. Illustrations. Crown 8vo, 7s. 6d.

The Illustrated Wild Garden; or, Our Groves and Gardens made Beautiful by the Naturalisation of Hardy Exotic Plants. By W. ROBINSON. With 90 Woodcuts. 8vo, 10s. 6d.

Sub-Tropical Garden; or, Beauty of Form in the Flower Garden, with Illustrations of all the finer Plants used for this purpose. By W. ROBINSON. Illustrations. Small 8vo, 5s.

Modern Domestic Cookery, Founded on Principles of Economy and Practice, and adapted for private families. By a LADY. Fcap. 8vo, 5s.

Thrift: a Book of Domestic Counsel. By SAMUEL SMILES. Small 8vo, 6s.

Duty: With Illustrations of Courage, Patience, and Endurance. By SAMUEL SMILES. Small 8vo, 6s.

Royal Agricultural Journal (published half-yearly). 8vo.

Bees and Flowers. By Rev. THOMAS JAMES. Fcap. 8vo, 1s. each.

Music and Dress. By a LADY. Fcap. 8vo, 1s.

Choice of a Dwelling; a Practical Handbook of Useful Information on all Points connected with Hiring, Buying, or Building a House. Plans. Post 8vo, 7s. 6d.

Household Surgery; or Hints for Emergencies. By JOHN F. SOUTH. Woodcuts. Fcap. 8vo, 3s. 6d.

FIELD SPORTS.

Dog-breaking; the most Expeditious, Certain, and Easy Method. By General HUTCHINSON. Woodcuts. 8vo, 7s. 6d.

My Boyhood a Story of Country Life and Sport for Boys. By H. C. BARKLEY, Civil Engineer. With Illustrations. Post 8vo, 6s.

Wild Sports and Natural History of the Highlands. By CHARLES ST. JOHN. New and Beautifully Illustrated Edition. Crown 8vo. 15s.: or cheap ed., post 8vo, 3s. 6d.

The Chase—The Turf—and the ROAD. By NIMROD. Illustrations. Crown 8vo, 5s.; or coloured plates, 7s. 6d.

Salmonia; or Days of Fly-Fishing. By Sir HUMPHRY DAVY. Woodcuts. Fcap. 8vo, 3s. 6d.

Horse-Shoeing; as it is, and as it should be. By WILLIAM DOUGLAS. Plates. Post 8vo, 7s. 6d.

Five Years' Adventures in the far Interior of South Africa with the Wild Beasts and Wild Tribes of the Forests. By R. GORDON CUMMING. Woodcuts. Post 8vo, 6s.

Sport and War. Recollections of Fighting and Hunting in South Africa, from 1834-67, with an Account of the Duke of Edinburgh's Visit. By General Sir JOHN BISSET, C.B. Illustrations. Crown 8vo, 14s.

Western Barbary, its Wild Tribes and Savage Animals. By Sir JOHN DRUMMOND HAY. Post 8vo, 2s.

Sport in Abyssinia. By Earl of MAYO. Illustrations. Crown 8vo, 12s.

EDUCATIONAL WORKS.

DR. WM. SMITH'S DICTIONARIES.

A Dictionary of the Bible ; Its Antiquities, Biography, Geography, and Natural History. Illustrations. 3 vols. 8vo, 105s.

A Concise Bible Dictionary. For the use of Students and Families. Condensed from the above. With Maps and 300 Illustrations. 8vo, 21s.

A Smaller Bible Dictionary. For Schools and Young Persons. Abridged from the above. With Maps and Woodcuts. Crown 8vo, 7s. 6d.

A Dictionary of Christian An-tiquities. The History, Institutions, and Antiquities of the Christian Church. With Illustrations. 2 vols. medium 8vo, £3 : 13 : 6.

A Dictionary of Christian Bio-graphy, Literature, Sects, and Doctrines. From the Time of the Apostles to the Age of Charlemagne. Vols. I. II. and III. Medium 8vo, 31s. 6d. each.

A Dictionary of Greek and Roman Antiquities. Comprising the Laws, Institutions, Domestic Usages, Painting, Sculpture, Music, the Drama, etc. With 500 Illustrations. Medium 8vo, 28s.

A Dictionary of Greek and Roman Biography and Mythology, containing a History of the Ancient World, Civil, Literary, and Ecclesiastical, from the earliest times to the capture of Constantinople by the Turks. With 564 Illustrations. 3 vols. medium 8vo, 84s.

A Dictionary of Greek and Roman Geography, showing the Researches of modern Scholars and Travellers, including an account of the Political History of both Countries and Cities, as well as of their Geography. With 530 Illustrations. 2 vols. medium 8vo, 56s.

A Classical Dictionary of Mythology, Biography, and Geography. With 750 Woodcuts. 8vo, 18s.

A Smaller Classical Dictionary. Abridged from the above. With 200 Woodcuts. Crown 8vo, 7s. 6d.

A Smaller Dictionary of Greek and Roman Antiquities. Abridged from the larger work. With 200 Woodcuts. Crown 8vo, 7s. 6d.

A Latin - English Dictionary. Based on the works of Forcellini and Freund. With Tables of the Roman Calendar, Measures, Weights, and Monies. Medium 8vo, 21s.

A Smaller Latin-English Dic-tionary. With Dictionary of Proper Names, and Tables of Roman Calendar, etc. Abridged from the above. Square 12mo, 7s. 6d.

An English-Latin Dictionary, Copious and Critical. Medium 8vo, 21s.

A Smaller English-Latin Dic-tionary. Abridged from the above. Square 12mo, 7s. 6d.

DR. WM. SMITH'S SMALLER HISTORIES.

A Smaller Scripture History of the Old and New Testaments. Woodcuts. 16mo, 3s. 6d.

A Smaller Ancient History of the East, from the Earliest Times to the Conquest of Alexander the Great. With 70 Woodcuts. 16mo, 3s. 6d.

A Smaller History of Greece, from the Earliest Times to the Roman Conquest. With Coloured Maps and 74 Woodcuts. 16mo, 3s. 6d.

A Smaller History of Rome, from the Earliest Times to the Establishment of the Empire. With Coloured Map and Woodcuts. 16mo, 3s. 6d.

A Smaller Classical Mythology. With Translations from the Ancient Poets, and Questions on the Work. With 90 Woodcuts. 16mo, 3s. 6d.

A Smaller Manual of Ancient Geography. 36 Woodcuts. 16mo, 3s. 6d.

A Smaller History of England, from the Earliest Times to the year 1868. With Coloured Maps and 68 Woodcuts. 16mo, 3s. 6d.

A Smaller History of English Literature ; giving a Sketch of the Lives of our chief Writers. 16mo, 3s. 6d.

Short Specimens of English Literature. Selected from the chief Authors, and arranged chronologically. 16mo, 3s. 6d.

MURRAY'S STUDENT'S MANUALS.

A Series of Historical Class Books for advanced Scholars. Forming a complete chain of History from the earliest ages to modern times.

Student's Old Testament His-tory, from the Creation to the Return of the Jews from Captivity. With an Introduction by PHILIP SMITH. Maps and Woodcuts. Post 8vo, 7s. 6d.

Student's New Testament History. With an Introduction connecting the History of the Old and New Testaments. By PHILIP SMITH. Maps and Woodcuts. Post 8vo, 7s. 6d.

Student's Manual of Ecclesiastical History of the Christian Church, PART I.—From the Times of the Apostles to the full Establishment of the Holy Roman Empire and the Papal Power. PART II.—The Middle Ages and the Reformation. By PHILIP SMITH. Woodcuts. 2 vols. Post 8vo, 7s. 6d. each.

Student's Manual of English Church History. FIRST PERIOD—From the Planting of the Church in Britain to the Accession of Henry VIII. SECOND PERIOD—From the Time of Henry VIII. to the Silencing of Convocation in the 18th Century. By Canon PERRY, M.A. 2 vols. Post 8vo, 7s. 6d. each.

Student's Ancient History of the East. Egypt, Assyria, Babylonia, Media, Persia, Phœnicia, &c. By PHILIP SMITH. Post 8vo, 7s. 6d.

Student's History of Greece, from the Earliest Times to the Roman Conquest; with the History of Literature and Art. By Dr. WM. SMITH. Woodcuts. Post 8vo, 7s. 6d.

Student's History of Rome, from the Earliest Times to the Establishment of the Empire; with the History of Literature and Art. By Dean LIDDELL. Woodcuts. Post 8vo, 7s. 6d.

Student's History of the Decline and Fall of the Roman Empire. By EDWARD GIBBON. Woodcuts. Post 8vo, 7s. 6d.

Student's History of Modern Europe. From the End of the Middle Ages to the Treaty of Berlin, 1878. Post 8vo. [*In Preparation.*]

Student's History of England from the Accession of Henry VII. to the Death of George II. By HENRY HALLAM. Post 8vo, 7s. 6d.

Student's Hume: a History of England from the Invasion of JULIUS CÆSAR to the Revolution in 1688. New edition. Continued to the Treaty of Berlin, 1878. By J. S. BREWER. With 7 Coloured Maps and Woodcuts. Post 8vo, 7s. 6d.

Student's History of Europe during the MIDDLE AGES. By HENRY HALLAM. Post 8vo, 7s. 6d.

Student's History of France, from the Earliest Times to the Establishment of the Second Empire, 1852. By Rev. W H. JERVIS. Woodcuts. Post 8vo, 7s. 6d.

Student's Manual of Ancient Geography. By Canon BEVAN. Woodcuts. Post 8vo, 7s. 6d.

Student's Manual of Modern Geography, Mathematical, Physical, and Descriptive. By Canon BEVAN. Woodcuts. Post 8vo, 7s. 6d.

Student's Manual of the Geography of India. By Dr. GEORGE SMITH. Post 8vo.

Student's Manual of the English Language. By GEORGE P. MARSH. Post 8vo, 7s. 6d.

Student's Manual of English Literature. By T. B. SHAW. Post 8vo, 7s. 6d.

Student's Specimens of English Literature. By T. B. SHAW. Post 8vo, 7s. 6d.

Student's Manual of Moral Philosophy. By WILLIAM FLEMING. Post 8vo, 7s. 6d.

The Student's Manual of the Evidences of Christianity. By HENRY WACE, M.A. Post 8vo.

The Student's History of the Roman Empire, from the Establishment of the Empire to the Accession of Commodus, A.D. 180. Post 8vo.

*** This Work will take up the History at the point at which Dean Liddell leaves off, and carry it down to the period at which Gibbon begins.

MARKHAM'S HISTORIES.

A History of England, from the First Invasion by the Romans to 1878. With Conversations at the end of each Chapter. By Mrs. MARKHAM. With 100 Woodcuts. 12mo, 3s. 6d.

A History of France, from the Conquest by the Gauls to 1878. With Conversations at the end of each Chapter. By Mrs. MARKHAM. Woodcuts. 12mo, 3s. 6d.

A History of Germany, from the Invasion of the Kingdom by the Romans under Marius to 1880. On the Plan of Mrs. MARKHAM. With 50 Woodcuts. 12mo, 3s. 6d.

Little Arthur's History of England. By Lady CALLCOTT. Continued down to the year 1878. With 36 Woodcuts. 16mo, 1s. 6d.

DR. WM. SMITH'S EDUCATIONAL WORKS.

ENGLISH COURSE.

A Primary History of Britain for Elementary Schools. Edited by Dr. WM. SMITH. 12mo, 2s. 6d.

A School Manual of English Grammar, with Copious Exercises. By Dr. WM. SMITH and T. D. HALL. Post 8vo, 3s. 6d.

A Primary English Grammar for Elementary Schools. With 134 Exercises and Questions. By T. D. HALL. 16mo, 1s.

A Manual of English Composition. With Copious Illustrations and Practical Exercises. By T. D. HALL. 12mo, 3s. 6d.

A School Manual of Modern Geography, Physical and Political. By JOHN RICHARDSON. Post 8vo, 5s.

A Smaller Manual of Modern Geography, for Schools and Young Persons. 16mo, 2s. 6d.

LATIN COURSE.

The Young Beginner's First Latin Book: Containing the Rudiments of Grammar, Easy Grammatical Questions and Exercises, with Vocabularies. Being Introductory to Principia Latina, Part I. 12mo, 2s.

The Young Beginner's Second Latin Book: Containing an Easy Latin Reading Book, with an Analysis of the Sentences, Notes, and a Dictionary. Being Introductory to Principia Latina, Part II. 12mo, 2s.

Principia Latina, Part I. A First Latin Course, comprehending Grammar, Delectus, and Exercise Book, with Vocabularies. With Accidence adapted to the Ordinary Grammars, as well as the Public School Latin Primer. 12mo, 3s. 6d.

Appendix to Principia Latina. Part I.: Additional Exercises, with Examination Papers. 12mo, 2s. 6d.

Principia Latina, Part II. A Latin Reading Book, an Introduction to Ancient Mythology, Geography, Roman Antiquities, and History. With Notes and Dictionary. 12mo, 3s. 6d.

Principia Latina, Part III. A Latin Poetry Book, containing Easy Hexameters and Pentameters, Eclogæ Ovidianæ, Latin Prosody, First Latin Verse Book. 12mo, 3s. 6d.

Principia Latina, Part IV. Latin Prose Composition, containing the Rules of Syntax, with copious Examples, and Exercises. 12mo, 3s. 6d.

Principia Latina, Part V. Short Tales and Anecdotes from Ancient History, for Translation into Latin Prose. 12mo, 3s.

A Latin-English Vocabulary: arranged according to subjects and etymology; with a Latin-English Dictionary to Phædrus, Cornelius Nepos, and Cæsar's "Gallic War." 12mo, 3s. 6d.

The Student's Latin Grammar. Post 8vo, 6s.

A Smaller Latin Grammar. Abridged from the above. 12mo, 3s. 6d.

Tacitus. Germania, Agricola, and First Book of the Annals. English Notes. 12mo, 3s. 6d.

GREEK COURSE.

Initia Græca, Part I. A First Greek Course: comprehending Grammar, Delectus, and Exercise-book. With Vocabularies. 12mo, 3s. 6d.

Appendix to Initia Græca, Part I.—Additional Exercises, with Examination Papers and Easy Reading Lessons, with the Sentences analysed, serving as an Introduction to Part II. 12mo, 2s. 6d.

Initia Græca, Part II. A Greek Reading Book, containing Short Tales, Anecdotes, Fables, Mythology, and Grecian History. Arranged in a systematic progression, with Lexicon. 12mo, 3s. 6d.

Initia Græca. Part III. Greek Prose Composition: containing a Systematic Course of Exercises on the Syntax, with the Principal Rules of Syntax, and an English-Greek Vocabulary to the Exercises. 12mo, 3s. 6d.

The Student's Greek Grammar. By Professor CURTIUS. Post 8vo, 6s.

A Smaller Greek Grammar. Abridged from the above. 12mo, 3s. 6d.

Greek Accidence. Extracted from the above work. 12mo, 2s. 6d.

Elucidations of Curtius's Greek Grammar. Translated by EVELYN ABBOTT. Post 8vo, 7s. 6d.

Plato. The Apology of So- crates, the Crito, and Part of the Phædo; with Notes in English from Stallbaum, and Schleiermacher's Introductions. 12mo, 3s. 6d.

FRENCH, GERMAN, AND ITALIAN COURSE.

French Principia, Part I. A First French Course, containing Grammar, Delectus, and Exercises, with Vocabularies and materials for French Conversation. 12mo, 3s. 6d.

Appendix to French Principia. Part I. Being Additional Exercises and Examination Papers. 12mo, 2s. 6d.

French Principia, Part II. A Reading Book, with Notes, and a Dictionary. 12mo, 4s. 6d.

Student's French Grammar: Practical and Historical. By C. HERON-WALL. With Introduction by M. Littré. Post 8vo, 7s. 6d.

A Smaller Grammar of the French Language. Abridged from the above. 12mo, 3s. 6d.

German Principia, Part I. A First German Course, containing Grammar, Delectus, Exercises, and Vocabulary. 12mo, 3s. 6d.

German Principia. Part II. A Reading Book, with Notes and a Dictionary. 12mo, 3s. 6d.

Practical German Grammar. With an Historical development of the Language. Post 8vo, 3s. 6d.

The Italian Principia, Part I. A First Course, containing a Grammar, Delectus, Exercise Book, with Vocabularies, and Materials for Italian Conversation. By Signor RICCI. 12mo, 3s. 6d.

Italian Principia, Part II. A Reading-Book, containing Fables, Anecdotes, History, and Passages from the best Italian Authors, with Grammatical Questions, Notes, and a Copious Etymological Dictionary. 12mo, 3s. 6d.

SCHOOL AND PRIZE BOOKS.

A Child's First Latin Book, comprising a full Praxis of Nouns, Adjectives, and Pronouns, with Active Verbs. By T. D. HALL. 16mo, 2s.

King Edward VI.'s Latin Accidence. 12mo, 2s. 6d.

King Edward VI.'s Latin Grammar. 12mo, 3s. 6d.

Oxenham's English Notes for Latin Elegiacs. Designed for early proficients in the art of Latin Versification. 12mo, 3s. 6d.

Hutton's Principia Græca : an Introduction to the study of Greek, comprehending Grammar, Delectus, and Exercise Book, with Vocabularies. 12mo, 3s. 6d.

Buttmann's Lexilogus; a Critical Examination of the Meaning and Etymology of Passages in Greek Writers. 8vo, 12s.

Matthiæ's Greek Grammar. Revised by CROOKE. Post 8vo, 4s.

Horace. With 100 Vignettes. Post 8vo, 7s. 6d.

Practical Hebrew Grammar; with an Appendix, containing the Hebrew Text of Genesis I. VI. and Psalms I. VI. Grammatical Analysis and Vocabulary. By Rev. STANLEY LEATHES. Post 8vo, 7s. 6d.

First Book of Natural Philosophy: an Introduction to the Study of Statics, Dynamics, Hydrostatics, Light, Heat, and Sound. By Prof. NEWTH. Sm. 8vo, 3s. 6d.

Elements of Mechanics, including Hydrostatics. By Prof. NEWTH. Sm. 8vo, 8s. 6d.

Mathematical Examples. A Graduated Series of Elementary Examples in Arithmetic, Algebra, Logarithms, Trigonometry, and Mechanics. By Professor NEWTH. Small 8vo, 8s. 6d.

Progressive Geography. By J. W. CROKER. 18mo, 1s. 6d.

Æsop's Fables, chiefly from Original Sources, by Rev. THOS. JAMES. With 100 Woodcuts. Post 8vo, 2s. 6d.

Gleanings in Natural History. By EDWARD JESSE. Fcap. 8vo, 3s. 6d.

Philosophy in Sport made Science in Earnest; or Natural Philosophy inculcated by the Toys and Sports of Youth. By Dr. PARIS. Woodcuts. Fcap. 8vo, 7s. 6d.

Puss in Boots. By OTTO SPECKTER. Illustrations. 16mo, 1s. 6d.

The Charmed Roe. By OTTO SPECKTER. Illustrations. 16mo, 5s.

Hymns in Prose for Children. by Mrs. BARBAULD. Illustrations. Fcap. 8vo, 3s. 6d.

A Boy's Voyage Round the World. By SAMUEL SMILES. Illustrations. Small 8vo, 6s.

The Home & Colonial Library.

Class A—BIOGRAPHY, HISTORY, &c.

1. DRINKWATER's Gibraltar.   2s.
2. The Amber Witch.   2s.
3. SOUTHEY's Cromwell and Bunyan.   2s.
4. BARROW's Sir Francis Drake.   2s.
5. British Army at Washington.   2s.
6. French in Algiers.   2s.
7. Fall of the Jesuits.   2s.
8. Livonian Tales.   2s.
9. Condé. By Lord MAHON. 3s. 6d.
10. Sale's Brigade in Affghanistan. 2s.
11. Sieges of Vienna.   2s.
12. MILMAN's Wayside Cross.   2s.
13. Liberation War in Germany. 3s. 6d.
14. GLEIG's Battle of Waterloo. 3s. 6d.
15. STEFFENS' Adventures.   2s.
16. CAMPBELL's British Poets. 3s. 6d.
17. Essays. By Lord MAHON. 3s. 6d.
18. GLEIG's Life of Lord Clive. 3s. 6d.
19. Stokers and Pokers.   By Sir FRANCIS HEAD.   2s.
20. GLEIG's Life of Munro.   3s. 6d.

Class B—VOYAGES and TRAVEL.

1. BORROW's Bible in Spain. 3s. 6d.
2. BORROW's Gipsies of Spain. 3s. 6d.
3. 4. HEBER's Indian Journals.   7s.
5. Holy Land. IRBY & MANGLES. 2s.
6. HAY's Western Barbary.   2s.
7. Letters from the Baltic.   2s.
8. MEREDITH's New S. Wales. 2s.
9. LEWIS' West Indies.   2s.
10. MALCOLM's Persia.   3s. 6d.
11. Father Ripa at Pekin.   2s.
12, 13. MELVILLE's Marquesas   7s.
14. ABBOT's Missionary in Canada. 2s.
15. Letters from Madras.   2s.
16. St. JOHN's Highland Sports. 3s. 6d.
17. The Pampas.   Sir F. HEAD.   2s.
18. FORD's Spanish Gatherings. 3s. 6d.
19. EDWARDS' River Amazon.   2s.
20. ACLAND's India.   2s.
21. RUXTON's Rocky Mountains. 3s 6d
22. CARNARVON's Portugal.   3s. 6d.
23. HAYGARTH's Bush Life.   2s.
24. ST. JOHN's Libyan Desert.   2s.
25. Letters from Sierra Leone. 3s. 6d

DR. WM. SMITH'S ANCIENT ATLAS.

AN ATLAS OF ANCIENT GEOGRAPHY, BIBLICAL AND CLASSICAL. Intended to illustrate the 'Dictionary of the Bible,' and the 'Dictionaries of Classical Antiquity.' Compiled under the superintendence of WM. SMITH, D.C.L., and GEORGE GROVE, LL.D.   Folio, half-bound, £6 : 6s.

1. Geographical Systems of the Ancients.
2. The World as known to the Ancients.
3. Empires of the Babylonians, Lydians, Medes, and Persians.
4. Empire of Alexander the Great.
5. 6. Kingdoms of the Successors of Alexander the Great.
7. The Roman Empire in its greatest extent.
8. The Roman Empire after its division into the Eastern and Western Empires.
9. Greek and Phœnician Colonies.
10. Britannia.
11. Hispania.
12. Gallia.
13. Germania, Rhætia, Noricum.
14. Pæonia, Thracia, Mœsia, Illyria, Dacia.
15. Italy, Sardinia, and Corsica.
16. Italia Superior.
17. Italia Inferior.
18. Plan of Rome.
19. Environs of Rome.
20. Greece after the Doric Migration.
21. Greece during the Persian Wars.
22. Greece during the Peloponnesian War.
23. Greece during the Achæan League.
24. Northern Greece.
25. Central Greece—Athens.
26. Peloponnesus.—With Plan of Sparta.
27. Shores and Islands of the Ægean Sea.
28. Historical Maps of Asia Minor.
29. Asia Minor.
30. Arabia.
31. India.
32. Northern Part of Africa.
33. Ægypt and Æthiopia.
34. Historical Maps of the Holy Land.
35, 36. The Holy Land.   North and South.
37. Jerusalem, Ancient and Modern.
38. Environs of Jerusalem.
39. Sinai.
40. Asia, to illustrate the Old Testament.
41. Map, to illustrate the New Testament.
42, 43. Plans of Babylon, Nineveh, Troy, Alexandria, and Byzantium.

INDEX.